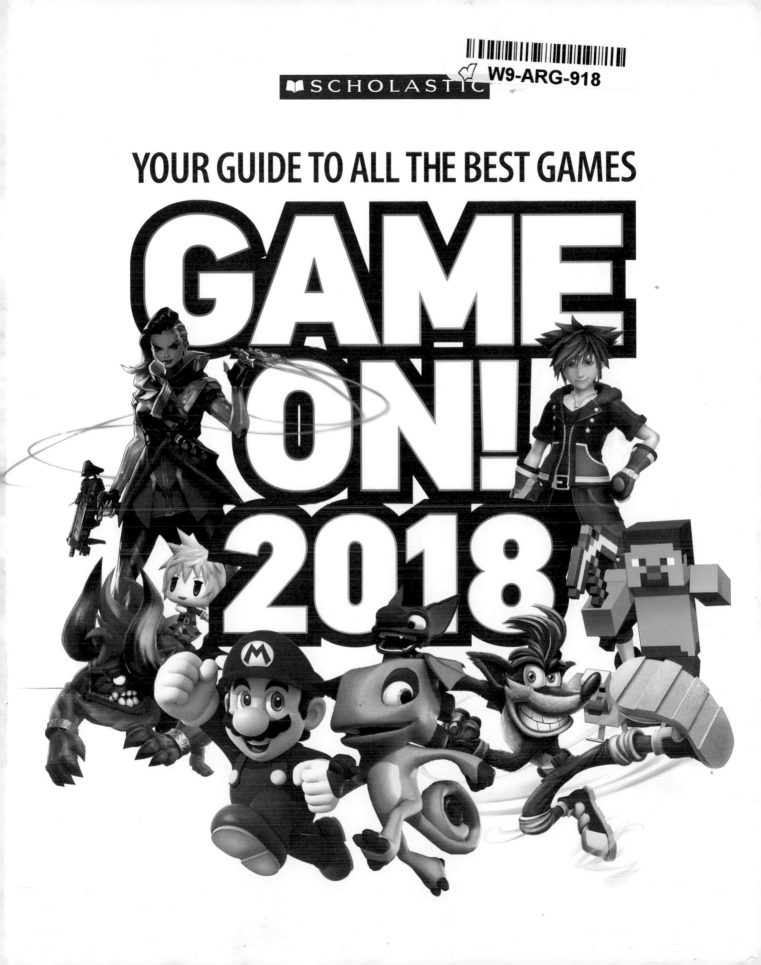

W9-ARG-918

YOUR GUIDE TO ALL THE BEST GAMES

GAME ON! 2018

EDITOR IN CHIEF
Jon White

EDITOR
Luke Albigés

CONTRIBUTORS
Stephen Ashby, Ryan King, Drew Sleep, Nick Thorpe,
Paul Walker-Emig, Mitch Wallace, Josh West

LEAD DESIGNER
Adam Markiewicz

DESIGNERS
Andy Downes, Ali Innes, Will Shum

PRODUCTION
Sarah Bankes, Sanne de Boer, Carrie Mok, Jen Neal

COVER IMAGES
The Legend of Zelda: Breath Of The Wild © 2017 Nintendo Co. Ltd. All rights reserved.
Mario Party: Star Rush © 2017 Nintendo Co. Ltd. All rights reserved.
Overwatch © 2016 Blizzard Entertainment, Inc. All rights reserved.
Crash Bandicoot © 2017 Activision Publishing, Inc. All rights reserved.
Street Fighter V © CAPCOM, U.S.A., Inc. 2015 All rights reserved.
Minecraft © 2017 Microsoft Inc. All rights reserved.
Splatoon 2 © 2017 Nintendo Co. Ltd. All rights reserved.
Yooka-Laylee. Developed by Playtonic Games. © 2017. Published by Team17. Team17
are trademarks or registered trademarks of Team17 Digital Limited. All other
trademarks, copyrights and logos are property of their respective owners.
Skylanders Academy ©2016 Activision Publishing, Inc., SKYLANDERS, SKYLANDERS
IMAGINATORS, CRASH, CRASH BANDICOOT, SKYLANDERS SUPERCHARGERS,
SKYLANDERS TRAP TEAM, SKYLANDERS SPYRO'S ADVENTURE, SKYLANDERS GIANTS,
SKYLANDERS SWAP FORCE, SWAP FORCE, LIGHTCORE, PORTAL OF POWER and
ACTIVISION are trademarks of Activision Publishing, Inc. All rights reserved.

ISBN 978-1-338-18993-3
10 9 8 7 6 5 4 3 2 1   17 18 19 20 21
Printed in the U.S.A. 40
First printing, September 2017

Scholastic is constantly working to lessen the environmental impact of our
manufacturing processes. To view our industry-leading paper procurement policy,
visit www.scholastic.com/paperpolicy.

All statistics, facts, and other information in this book are accurate
at the time of going to press.

The publisher does not have any control over and does not assume any responsibility
for author or third party websites or their content, including the websites of any
brands, gamers, and social media personalities included in this book.

THE LEGEND OF ZELDA: BREATH OF THE WILD

It's the biggest *Zelda* game ever! Explore the huge world of Hyrule as the legendary hero Link however you choose, and restore peace to the land!

STAYING SAFE AND HAVING FUN

Games can be amazing, but it's important that you know how to stay safe when playing online. These ten simple tips will help you to have fun while playing—follow these and you can have a great time online, while your parents can rest easy in the knowledge that you know how to stay safe.

1 Discuss and agree to rules with your parents regarding how long you can stay online, what websites you can visit on the Internet, and what apps and games you can use.

2 Remember to take frequent breaks during gaming sessions.

3 Never give out personal information such as passwords, your real name, phone number, or anything about your parents.

4 Never agree to meet in person with someone you've met online.

5 Tell your parents or a teacher if you come across anything online that makes you feel uncomfortable, upset, or scared.

6 Whenever you're online, be nice to other people and players. Never say or do anything that might hurt someone else's feelings or make them feel unhappy.

7 Pay attention to age ratings on games. They exist for a reason—to help protect you from any content that's not right for you, not to stop you from having fun!

8 Don't download or install software or apps to any device, or fill out any forms on the Internet, without checking first with the person who owns the device you're using.

9 If you play mobile games outside, be aware of your surroundings at all times, and don't play alone— always have a friend or family member with you.

10 When using streaming services, always check with an adult before changing to a different video or game.

CONTENTS

TURN TO **PAGE 26** FOR OUR EXCLUSIVE **CAPTAIN SPARKLEZ** INTERVIEW!

⭐ FEATURES

🎮 GAME SERIES

⏱ SPLIT SECOND

📷 CAPTURE THIS!

▶ CHANNEL OVERVIEW

TOP 10

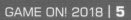

24–29

188–189

52–53

70–73

44–45

124–125

54–55

102–103

WHAT A YEAR!

Gaming just keeps getting better! Three new consoles, hundreds of incredible games, and even more great stuff on the horizon—there's never been a more exciting time to be a gamer!

On PS4, we saw stunning new experiences like *Horizon: Zero Dawn* and fresh takes on classics such as *Crash Bandicoot* and *WipEout*. Not to be outdone, Microsoft unleashed what it called "Project Scorpio," the most powerful console on the planet, with its own wave of hot new games. Meanwhile, Nintendo threw out the rulebook to create its cool console/handheld hybrid, Switch—now you can play *Mario*, *Zelda*, *Splatoon*, and tons of other awesome Nintendo games wherever you are, and they all look better than ever!

Join us as we look back at an amazing year for gaming, and look forward to what the next year might have in store . . .

92–93

56–59

76–77

122–123

50–51

NINTENDO SWITCH

50 GREATEST MOMENTS IN GAMING

TAKING A JOURNEY IN THE TRAIL

50

The Trail is essentially a game about walking. It sounds boring, but you'll soon be too involved to even care about anything like that. In your quest to walk to Eden Falls, you make clothes, find food, hunt rabbits, chop wood, and trade with other online players. And there's so much more to discover once you venture beyond Eden Falls!

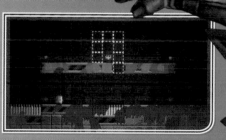

STRETCHING YOUR BRAIN IN TELEPAINT

49

In tiny, metallic rooms full of traps, you create portals to safely guide a waddling can of paint to the exit. Seems simple, right? But as the chaos builds and the puzzles get tougher, you'll have to think fast to unscramble the mess of spike pits and keys between you and the exit point.

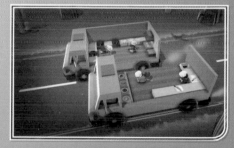

COOKING BAD FOOD IN OVERCOOKED

48

"Too many cooks spoil the broth," as the old saying goes. *Overcooked* is the proof. Have three friends play this manic cooking game alongside you, and watch helplessly while the anarchy unfolds. You'll be scrambling and pushing past each other in a tiny kitchen to get orders out on time.

ABZÛ TAKING US TO THE BOTTOM OF THE OCEAN

47

Many great games show us worlds we'd never normally experience for ourselves. *Abzû* takes us to the beautiful, tranquil world under the sea. You can swim with the fish, poke through seaweed, explore aquatic ruins, and discover curious mysteries in this serene, enthralling game.

THE RETURN OF CRASH BANDICOOT

46 The mischievous PlayStation mascot made a dramatic return to gaming, appearing as a guest character in *Skylanders Imaginators*. Crash Bandicoot shows no signs of rustiness, hunting down old nemesis Dr. Neo Cortex, while munching on wumpa fruit, and bouncing on fragile crates. It's so much fun, you'll wonder why he ever left!

GANG BEASTS GOING WILD

45 If you like your gaming without too many rules, you'll love *Gang Beasts*. You pick up your opponents, and throw them to their doom to win. Fighting desperately for survival against other players is a much harder task than it first seems, though, because your own character is so wobbly.

TAKING TO THE SKIES IN WORMS W.M.D

44 *Worms* is known as one of the most fiercely competitive multiplayer games ever made. *Worms W.M.D* cranks up the multiplayer tension, as you can now build your own weapons and even continue the fight in a tank or helicopter. You choose from a hilarious arsenal of weapons to whittle down the other team's health.

CONQUERING THE WORLD IN CIVILIZATION VI

43 There are more paths to victory in gaming than through brute force. *Civilization VI* gives budding leaders different ways to triumph and take over the imaginary game world. You can build power through your military, emerge on top in a global space race, or just win over the people through diplomatic leadership. You can play at your own pace in this turn-based strategy game—it's the flexibility to become a leader in your own style that makes *Civilization VI* such a fun game to play.

SLIPPING PAST THE DEFENSE IN MADDEN NFL 17

42 There are few feelings better than slipping past the defensive line in *Madden*, and leaving them eating the grass as you sprint downfield for a touchdown. *Madden NFL 17* gives you even more ways to break free of the opposition, making you feel like the real MVP at the end of the game. You can even hurdle over them, for added style points.

"THIS BIZARRE PIECE OF TECHNOLOGY FIRES OUT A DISCO BALL"

MAKING ENEMIES DANCE WITH THE GROOVITRON IN RATCHET & CLANK

41 One of the unusual sci-fi weapons you can get your hands on in *Ratchet & Clank* is the Groovitron. This bizarre piece of technology fires out a disco ball, whipping up nearby robots into an uncontrollable dancing frenzy until they overheat and explode. Disco inferno!

DID YOU KNOW?

The latest *Ratchet & Clank* game is a remastered version of the first title in the series, and was released alongside the duo's first animated movie.

SHUTTING DOWN THE OPPOSITION IN PES 2017

40 Outplaying your friends in games is always satisfying, but what about outthinking them too? *PES 2017* lets you create strategies before kick-off, then activate them during the game. Take a 1-0 lead, then throw all your players behind the ball in a defensive strategy. You'll soon hear the frustrated, angry cries of your opponents as they desperately try to score.

WITNESSING THE BIGGEST DC COMICS FIGHT NIGHT EVER

39 Even if you're a DC Comics giga-fan, *Injustice 2* has something new for you. Gorilla Grodd versus Atrocitus? Deadshot versus Supergirl? Blue Beetle versus, well, anybody? Seeing some of the lesser-known characters suit up for battle is a real treat for any DC fan.

STAR WARS BATTLEFRONT GOING ROGUE

38 With its *Battle of Jakku* and *Rogue One* DLC packs, *Star Wars Battlefront* allows fans to relive some of the most exciting moments from the last two *Star Wars* movies. It's great to see the game keeping up with the movies, and with a new *Battlefront* adventure on the horizon, things are only getting better for *Star Wars* fans.

STARDEW VALLEY SURPRISES ALL OF US

37 Eric Barone created cutesy farming simulator *Stardew Valley* because it was the game he wanted to play. As it turns out, it wasn't just Eric who wanted to play it—*Stardew Valley* has now sold more than a million copies worldwide. Maybe that will inspire you to take a crack at creating your own cool game in the future!

NAMING YOUR OWN PLANETS IN NO MAN'S SKY

36 Whenever you find a planet first in *No Man's Sky*, you get to name it. And with more than 18 quintillion in the game, you're bound to find plenty. The slow exploration might not be to every player's taste, but few games let you leave your mark on the universe in such a personal way.

SONIC MANIA PLEASING OLD FANS AND NEW

35 The old gang are back together as Sonic, Tails, and Knuckles team up once again for 2-D platforming fun. The trio reunite for a supersonic dash through new zones and reimagined classics. *Sonic Mania* goes right back to the blue hedgehog's roots, and its mix of jumping for rings, bouncing on bad guys, and racing through loop-the-loops is as much fun today as it ever was.

DID YOU KNOW?

You need to work together with your crew in *Sea of Thieves*. The person at the wheel can't see the map, so you'll need to tell them where to go!

PLAYING CRAZY MINI-GAMES IN 1-2-SWITCH

33 The latest mini-game collection from Nintendo aims to show off what the Switch console can do. Whether you're playing digital table tennis or milking a cow, you'll need to use the Switch's JoyCon motion controllers to beat your friends in each ridiculous challenge.

DISCOVERING ALIEN RUINS IN ELITE DANGEROUS

32 Other players aren't the only thing to look out for in *Elite Dangerous*. No matter what kind of space pilot you choose to be, you'll need to be on the lookout for aliens, too. Some players have discovered mysterious extra-terrestrial ruins, and even encountered huge, strange creatures. What other secrets are hidden in *Elite Dangerous*?

JOINING A BAND OF PIRATES IN SEA OF THIEVES

34 *Sea of Thieves* lets you live out your swashbuckling dreams, as you and a gang of friends can sail the seven seas together. Whether it's manning the cannons, fixing the sails, bailing out water, or one of the many other tasks on board, everyone has a role to play. You can explore mysterious caves to find hidden treasure, fight off skeletons who guard valuable loot, and even work together to defeat teams of other players in epic ship battles on the open sea.

DEUS EX GO TURNING ACTION INTO A BOARD GAME

31 Just like *Hitman GO* and *Lara Croft GO*, *Deus Ex GO* throws out the action of the series that it's based on to focus on strategy. The lush, sci-fi visuals of *Deus Ex GO* look great on tablets and phones, but it's the board-game-style gameplay, testing your brain rather than your reactions, that is truly special.

MAKING SOMEONE KNOCK THEMSELVES OUT IN STREET FIGHTER V

30

The only thing better than beating someone at a fighting game is making them defeat themselves. Downloadable *Street Fighter V* character Urien makes this possible. His trademark special move, Aegis Reflector, bounces projectiles away. With the right timing, you can reflect someone's fireball back at them to knock them out with their own attack!

SHU COMBINING THE BEST OF BOTH WORLDS

29

Shu combines 3-D and 2-D in a glorious visual cocktail of intriguing worlds and detailed characters. You take control of Shu, who meets other villagers during the journey through each amazing level. As the group travels, Shu must use each villager's unique abilities to progress, opening new paths in the quest to save this incredible world.

ROCKET LEAGUE GOING UNDERWATER

28

Not happy with world domination through its monstrous sales on PC, PS4, and Xbox One, *Rocket League* has now gone underwater to dominate the ocean, too. *AquaDome* is a DLC that places the action among the seaweed, sharks, and jellyfish of the deep, blue sea. Better still, *AquaDome* is a free download for all *Rocket League* players.

MARIO ON MOBILE

27

It was a huge moment in gaming, as Nintendo finally unleashed Mario on mobile with *Super Mario Run*. It's the first time a *Mario* game can be played with one hand, as you guide the plump plumber past Piranha Plants, over jumps, and into coins.

EXPLORING A WASTELAND WITH A ROBOT DOG IN RECORE

26 Dogs are a human's best friend, and in *ReCore*, you'll be grateful for Mack, the canine companion by your side—even if he is made of wires and metal rather than fur. While you explore the futuristic world as Joule, Mack can sniff out electrical gizmos and even shoot lasers if you run into enemies.

ORI AND THE BLIND FOREST GETS EVEN BETTER

24 With its gorgeous, hand-painted art style and skillful platforming, *Ori and the Blind Forest* won enough awards to fill a forest upon its release. Longtime fans of the game and newcomers all celebrated when *Ori* returned with a *Definitive Edition*, bringing new difficulty modes, abilities, environments, and story modes with it.

PAPER MARIO BRIGHTENS EVERYONE'S DAY WITH A SPLASH OF COLOR

25 At last, a game that combines two of our favorite things: Mario and making a mess. The color has been sucked out of Prism Island in *Paper Mario*, leaving you to splish, splash, and splosh paint all over the world to bring it back to life.

PIKACHU BECOMING A WRESTLER

23 The Pokémon-focused fighting game, *Pokkén Tournament*, takes Pokémon battling to new levels. But the real standout is Pikachu Libre—in this game, the famous Pokémon does its best wrestler impersonation. Masked Pikachu even has a Stone Cold Stunner move!

THE EXPERT SAYS ...
PHIL DUNCAN
Designer, *Overcooked*

It might be a little corny, but I think my favorite gaming moment of the year was when we had just finished working on *Overcooked*. After months of fixing bugs, we'd finally passed all the various console tests, and found ourselves with the first afternoon off we'd had in about 18 months. Oli (cofounder of Ghost Town Games) had his PlayStation 4 at my house, so we both treated ourselves to a copy of *No Man's Sky*. When we sat down to play, and we first experienced that feeling when you take off from a planet and launch into outer space—after having spent months working so hard on our game—it felt so perfect and such a fitting way to celebrate.

DID YOU KNOW?

The famous role-playing game *World of Warcraft* had a whopping 12 million subscribers playing at its peak, back in October 2010.

LEGION BRINGING US ALL BACK TO WORLD OF WARCRAFT

22 Some 11 years after its original release, *World of Warcraft* proved it still has plenty of life left. The Legion expansion brought a new level cap and playing area called Broken Isles, but best of all, it had the powerful new Demon Hunter class. This lets you fight fire with fire by using demon magic against fiends.

MINECRAFT: STORY MODE OFFERING A NEW ADVENTURE

21 We were only promised five episodes of the fantastic *Minecraft: Story Mode*. Fortunately, developer Telltale followed up with three additional episodes, which continued the adventures of Jesse and his gang. In each episode you must make decisions and solve puzzles to progress through the story.

BACKWARDS COMPATIBILITY BRINGS BACK A CULT CLASSIC

19 Xbox One's backwards compatibility means you can play hundreds of Xbox 360 games on it, too. The list keeps growing too, from big-name games like *Sonic & SEGA All-Stars Racing* and *Lost Odyssey*, to niche titles like *Puzzle Quest: Galactrix* and *Guwange*. It's the return of cult classic *Skate 3*, though, that's been the highlight so far.

SUPER MARIO MAKER ON THE MOVE

20 Budding game designers could put their unique twist on *Mario* levels with *Super Mario Maker* on Wii U. The subsequent 3DS release of *Super Mario Maker* makes this even better, since it doesn't matter where you are when inspiration strikes—you can work on it right away using the 3DS's touch screen and stylus.

TEKKEN 7 BRINGING TIGERS AND CYBORG NINJAS TOGETHER

18 *Tekken 7* is a world of cyborg ninjas, rogue military experiments, and an android with chainsaws for arms. One fighter can summon pet tigers for battle. Even *Street Fighter* boss Akuma shows up. It's the most eccentric cast of characters ever, and the only place you'll see a cyborg ninja fight a dancing kickboxer.

PLAYING WITH THE FASTEST CARS IN FORZA HORIZON 3

17 *Forza Horizon 3*'s garage is stuffed with a whole host of exotic cars for you to play with. But power your way into the game's VIP Membership and you can choose cars that reach incredible speeds, such as the Ford Falcon GT and the Koenigsegg Regera. You can almost feel the pad rumble with their engine power.

UNLEASHING YOUR CREATIVITY WITH LEGO WORLDS

16 LEGO is putting its own twist on world-building games with LEGO *Worlds*. The game gives you a huge world to explore, and you can build anything you want within it. But destroying stuff is also lots of fun, with structures exploding into showers of bricks and studs as you carve through them with drills, or blow chunks out of them with your pet dragon's fireballs.

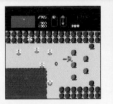
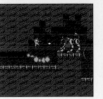

NES CLASSIC MINI DELIVERING SOME RETRO DELIGHTS

15 Nintendo released a miniature version of its classic console, NES, which even has a replica controller modeled on the 1983 original. With 30 games, like *Super Mario Bros.* and *Donkey Kong*, built into the system, you can play some of the best games ever made at the touch of a button.

USING POKÉMON'S MOST POWERFUL MOVES EVER

14 *Pokémon Sun* and *Pokémon Moon* take their battles to dramatic new heights with Z-Moves. These new moves are so powerful, you can use them only once during battle. From Pikachu's Catastropika to Snorlax's Pulverizing Pancake, these Z-Moves are every bit as powerful as they sound.

THE LAST GUARDIAN SHOWING THAT SOME THINGS REALLY ARE WORTH THE WAIT

13 It's here. Two words that *The Last Guardian* fans thought they would never get to say. This intriguing tale about a boy and a mythical creature struggling to escape a fortress together took nine years of development before it finally hit the shelves. It has been worth the wait. The story tugs at your heartstrings in a way that only games can, as you learn to live with and love the mythical creature by your side. Part mystery, part adventure, part puzzler, it's how *The Last Guardian* puts these elements together that makes the game really shine.

FIGHTING TACTICALLY AND PHYSICALLY WITH ARMS

12 Nintendo has created a new kind of boxing game with *Arms*. Unlike previous games, like *Wii Sports*, which had players just swinging wildly to punch, *Arms* makes you think tactically. Your cartoon character's arms are on giant springs, and twisting your wrist can curve their paths. Blocking and grabbing help to mix things up, ensuring every battle is unique.

LEAGUE OF LEGENDS PROVING IT WILL NEVER RUN OUT OF IDEAS

11 With more than 130 playable champions in *League of Legends*, you would think Riot Games might run out of ideas. Yet it continues to keep the game fresh with an onslaught of new playable characters. There's Taliyah and her earth-shattering powers, Ivern who commands nature to aid him in battle, Kled who fights on his cowardly steed, Skaarl, plus many more.

EXPLORING A NEW WORLD WITH MARIO

10 Fans have been waiting for a long time for a new 3-D game with Mario as the solo star, but that wait is finally over. *Super Mario Odyssey* takes the hero to a new world, with cool areas to explore—including a realistic city complete with skyscrapers and taxis. And he can explore it all using his new hat, which will help Mario navigate tough areas by acting like a platform!

COMPLETING THE JOURNEY IN FIFA 17

9 Although known for intense multiplayer battles, *FIFA 17* braved something different with *The Journey*. This single-player story saw you play as Alex Hunter, a soccer player whose performance on the field and decisions off it shape his career as he attempts to join an English Premier League club.

MORE AMAZING WORLDS COLLIDE IN LEGO DIMENSIONS

8 LEGO *Dimensions* is the game that never stops growing. We already had Batman, Homer Simpson, and the Ghostbusters to play around with, among others. Now, we've also got characters and levels from *Fantastic Beasts, Sonic the Hedgehog, Gremlins, A-Team, Harry Potter, Adventure Time, Knight Rider, E.T.* and more, and they keep coming!

DID YOU KNOW?

Final Fantasy XV isn't done yet—2017 marks the franchise's 30th anniversary, and Square Enix has big plans for *XV* and the future of the series!

FINAL FANTASY XV PUSHES GRAPHICS TO A NEW LEVEL

7 The summon attacks in *Final Fantasy XV* are jaw-dropping, and these huge gods can help you win tough battles. From colossal giants made of rock, to angry thunder monsters, each summon will blow you away as you watch them use their devastating attacks. The scale and detail make this a visual treat that has to be seen to be believed.

THE LEGEND OF ZELDA: BREATH OF THE WILD LETS YOU DO ANYTHING

6 You can surf your shield. You can hunt down rare ingredients and cook up delicious meals. You can glide through the sky. You can summon ice towers. You can chop down trees. You can climb the tallest cliffs and watch the Sun set. You can do anything you want in *Breath of the Wild*, and that's what makes the adventure so fun.

PS4 PRO AND XBOX SCORPIO MAKE GAMING EVEN PRETTIER

5 With 4K televisions becoming more common, Sony and Microsoft released new versions of their consoles to take advantage of the ultra-detailed display. You don't have to have one of these devices to play the coolest games, but the games will look better than ever with them!

SHUTTING PLAYERS DOWN IN OVERWATCH

4 New character Sombra can wreak havoc in *Overwatch*, thanks to her ability to hack into other players and switch their abilities off. It opens all sorts of mischievous possibilities: disabling Reinhardt's shields, stopping Mei from creating ice walls, even disabling Pharah's flight ability so she tumbles back down to Earth!

VR GIVES US A NEW WAY TO PLAY

3 The future is here, as VR places you right into the heart of your favorite games. Weird, wireframe, sci-fi shooter *Rez Infinite* on PS4 is the highlight so far, as the world distorts and twists around you with each successful attack. Playing in VR is a unique experience, and you and your friends will be amazed as you pass the headset around.

POKÉMON GO TAKING OVER THE WORLD

2 It broke records; it made the news; it became a global phenomenon. *Pokémon GO* has been downloaded more than 500 million times, as a global army of fans took to the streets to catch Pokémon hiding in the real world. After a massively popular release for the game, new features, such as PvP battling, have kept it feeling fresh. There's still nothing out there quite like it, partly thanks to the way the augmented reality (or AR) part of the game makes it seem like the Pokémon are right in front of you!

SWITCH TRANSFORMS GAMING

1 Nintendo does it again. The Japanese company has earned a reputation for being brave and innovative with its consoles, as seen with Wii's motion controls and Wii U's second screen. Now Switch will combine the best of home console and portable handheld device. You can remove the Switch "tablet" from its dock at home and slide the controllers into the side of the unit so you can play it on the go. It means you can transition from playing *Breath of the Wild* at home to playing it outdoors in seconds. You can even remove the controllers and set up the screen on a small table somewhere, so you can play multiplayer while outside. It's a slick idea, and Switch proves that—once again —Nintendo is happy to be a little different to stand out from the crowd and deliver something fresh to its fans.

THE EXPERT SAYS …
KEVIN CARTHEW
Creative Director, Team17

My favorite recent gaming moment is experiencing *Thumper* in VR for the first time. As soon as you don the headset, *Thumper* starts to work its magic on you. The shiny, metal rail stretches out into infinity, the inverted pyramid looming in the distance spins slowly, and the ominous title music seeps into your ears. It's a genuinely otherworldly experience, and is—to me—a perfect example of art, design, code, and audio coming together to present something that feels larger than the sum of its parts. It works exactly the same way when playing it on a TV screen compared to playing with a headset, but in VR it takes on a new life and becomes something else. It's a great example of what VR can add to games.

NINTENDO SWITCH

SPLIT SECOND

OVERCOOKED

No other game will make you sweat like *Overcooked* does. It's just a game about cooking, so why does it cause so much panic? Well, the chefs have to work in crazy conditions and get meals out on time without getting in each other's way. It's multiplayer madness at its best, and no game will make you laugh (or cry) as much as this one. And that's before the later levels take you to pirate ships, the Arctic, and even space, where it's even harder to cook and get orders out without something going wrong!

1 The first two levels give you a gentle introduction to the world of *Overcooked*, but it's the third stage where things really start to heat up. You're not even preparing meals in a kitchen anymore. The action has shifted to the deck of a pirate ship!

2 Now to cook meals for the crew, starting with soup. The main obstacle is a barrier down the middle of the kitchen on the deck. This forces cooperation from all players to quickly get the ingredients over to the prep station.

Press Ⓧ to open Account Picker

Press Ⓨ to open Controller Split Settings

Level 1-3

015

Score : 90

Press Ⓐ to Join

Press Ⓐ to Join

✓ 40
✓ 80
☆ 100

Press Ⓐ to Join

3 But things are never straightforward in *Overcooked*. Just as you establish a kitchen routine, the ship starts to tilt, sending everything sliding across the floor! If you're not prepared, this can cut you off from the ingredients and the equipment. Think fast!

03:29

0

03:1

4 What happens if you leave food on the stove for too long? It catches fire, leaving you scrambling for the fire extinguisher. You must be quick—the longer the fire burns, the more it spreads, and the less time you have left to prepare food . . .

▶ CAPTAINSPARKLEZ

YOUTUBE'S BRIGHTEST STAR

CLAIM TO FAME

With 166 million YouTube views, Revenge is the most popular *Minecraft* video ever made.

If you love *Minecraft*, you should check out CaptainSparklez. He was one of the earliest *Minecraft* superstars on YouTube thanks to his Revenge music video, made in the game. He still specializes in *Minecraft* now, too. There's almost nothing about the block-building game that he hasn't made videos about, and every one is either entertaining or informative, or both! A lot of YouTubers will scream and shout for your attention, but CaptainSparklez knows he doesn't need to do that. He just draws you in with his natural charisma and easygoing gameplay.

CaptainSparklez now likes to include other kinds of video on his channel too—covering *Trials Fusion*, *Pokémon GO*, and even his real-life adventures—but even so, *Minecraft* will always be the game closest to his heart.

▮▮▮ STATS

▶ **Year started** 2010

NUMBER OF SUBS
10 million

NUMBER OF VIDEOS
3,500

TOTAL VIEW COUNT
2.6 billion

MOST WATCHED VIDEO
"Revenge: A *Minecraft* Original Music Video"
166 million views

EXPECT TO SEE/HEAR
- ▶ *Minecraft* animations and parodies
- ▶ Chilled-out vibe
- ▶ Let's Play videos with his friends

SIMILAR CHANNELS

SkyDoesMinecraft
Minecraft meets comedy

No prizes for guessing what game SkyDoesMinecraft covers (clue: it's not *Terraria*). Although Sky also covers *Minecraft* mini-games and mods, he goes for a more comedic angle. If you're looking for *Minecraft* videos that will make you laugh, this channel is the one to watch!

StacyPlays
Minecraft fun and games

StacyPlays is another YouTuber who specializes in *Minecraft,* and she likes videos about the fun games and mods that other people have made for Mojang's game. Like CaptainSparklez, she often gets her friends involved with her videos, too.

Crainer
The hype man

In contrast to the relaxed style of CaptainSparklez, Crainer operates at 100 miles per hour, constantly excited and hyped about what's happening on the screen. See if you have the energy to keep up with him as he blasts his way through all kinds of *Minecraft* adventures!

HIS BIGGEST GAMES

Minecraft
Parodies, mods, and songs

Like many YouTubers, CaptainSparklez started out making Let's Play videos of regular *Minecraft* gameplay. Since then, he's branched out into playing mods, *Minecraft* songs, and other unusual takes on the world's most-loved game.

Trials Fusion
The difficult racer

CaptainSparklez has met his match with the *Trials* series, games about racing through controller-crushingly difficult obstacle courses in the fastest possible times. He loves multiplayer *Trials* showdowns with his friends, but they don't always go as well as he would like . . .

Pokémon GO
CaptainSparklez on the move

Pokémon GO is a great opportunity to see videos of CaptainSparklez out and about, as he searches the parks of Los Angeles in order to hunt Pokémon. As well as watching the game, it's fun to see his reaction in his videos when he encounters and attempts to catch something rare!

MEET CAPTAIN SPARKLEZ

AN EXCLUSIVE ONE-ON-ONE WITH THE YOUTUBE SUPERSTAR!

At what age did you start gaming?

I got a Game Boy Color when I was around five years old and that was the first time I had something I could play games on. I remember going over to friends' houses and playing Nintendo 64, but it was really with the Game Boy that I started playing pretty frequently.

Do you remember what the first game you played was?

The first game I have a good memory of playing was *Sonic Adventure*. I think I first played that on the in-store console demo setup for Dreamcast. Then I really enjoyed playing it once I did get a Dreamcast. It took a little while to convince my mom that I should be able to get one of those machines!

How did you get started with your current channel?

I was a senior in high school and played lots of video games throughout high school. I would look on YouTube for videos that would give advice and strategy. From there, it led me into seeing videos that other people were doing at the time, where they would just record a multiplayer game they did well in and then talk over it and say what they did in order to do well and give advice on that. I was fairly decent at multiplayer so I thought "maybe this would be cool." I had talked to another person who had just recently got a capture device so I figured I'd ask for one for my birthday which was right around that time. So my mom, all the way from when I was seven years old and having to really convince her to get me one of the game consoles, was kind enough to get me the recording device so I

You'll often see CaptainSparklez playing with or against other famous YouTubers, including SSundee and Crainer.

could spend even *more* time on gaming! Whenever I got a good game, I would take it into iMovie and talk over it. In retrospect, looking back at the early videos—and most YouTubers probably say this—they were absolutely terrible! Fortunately, I was able to work on that over the years and for some reason people watched, and that's where it started!

So where exactly does *Minecraft* come into all this?

It was actually a friend of mine, another YouTuber named SeaNanners—back in the summer of 2010, he was like, "I found this game that I love, there are chickens and pigs…" I swear this was actually the pitch. "There are chickens and pigs and you can do things with blocks!"

***Minecraft* is the focus of CaptainSparklez's channel, but he plays other games, too!**

I thought, "That sounds . . . odd, but sure, I'll give it a try!" That ended up being *Minecraft*, and I posted a video of it not really expecting anything major to come out of it, but everyone was all over it! So I started down that road, and it ended up here through just continuing to do new things with the game. It's still with me today.

Out of all of your videos, which one is your favorite?

Oh gosh, that's difficult. Probably the most recent music video of mine. It's called "Dragonhearted" and it was a *long* time in production due to some speed bumps along the way. But I think the finished product turned out very, very nicely, so I'm very happy with it.

Which of your videos would you recommend people who are new to your channel watch first?

You know, probably the same one! Even though it's not necessarily a

representation of most of the content that I post, it tends to be something that all ages of people can appreciate, whereas usually, the stuff I'm posting on a day-to-day basis appeals to a specific audience. If I have a relative ask what I do, it's not necessarily their thing and they'll be like, "What is this? I don't get it!" Otherwise, I have animations that go up on a weekly basis and tend to have a wider appeal.

What is the coolest thing that has been added to Minecraft?

Let's see . . . the most memorable thing was the addition of the piston block. That had been a mod beforehand and I made some videos on it, like "this would be really cool if it were actually in the game." Lo and behold, it was actually added. I don't know if that's the most dramatic improvement that's ever been made in an update but it's certainly a memorable thing.

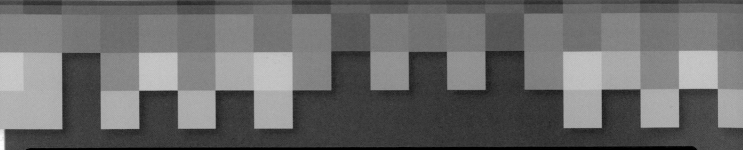

What was it like appearing as yourself in *Minecraft: Story Mode*?

That was super fun! I was a bit hesitant just because I didn't know if I'd be able to hold up as a voice actor. I didn't want to be the odd man out, to have everyone say the voice acting is pretty good except that one guy—he ruined the whole thing! Even when I was watching the trailer for it, I was like "Oh man, I really hope the whole thing turns out well, I'm kinda nervous!" And then as I was playing through it, everyone did a really good job and I didn't feel detached from the game or have the atmosphere broken due to the voice acting. It turned out way better

It's not all gaming videos—you'll also see Jordan doing vlogs, funny challenges, and reaction videos.

than I expected. Hopefully in the future I'll have another opportunity to do a voiceover on something. It was an honor to be invited, out of all the *Minecraft* YouTubers that are out there, so hopefully it's something I'll get to do again!

How do you come up with the ideas for your *Minecraft* songs?

We had a storyline that we were following up until the "Dragonhearted" video, which concluded that storyline. So that's actually a good question, because I don't know yet where the idea for the next one is going to come from. I'm just gonna have to think of something! Whatever the next video is, it's gonna be a song that I have produced because I'm also trying to get into music myself. I've released a few songs on my other channel but I've not yet incorporated one of those into one of the music videos on the CaptainSparklez channel. So that's the next goal. Usually when it comes to music videos, you have the song and

Most animations use *Minecraft*-style graphics, but others use stop-motion versions of the Tube Heroes toys.

the lyrics done and you model the video after that, so I'll probably take the same approach.

What has been your most memorable moment in gaming on camera so far?

That's tough! That's like going through seven years of memories all at once! It's probably posting my first ever music video and just being in my college dorm not expecting much out of it and then it ending up doing pretty well.

Over 100 million total views could certainly be considered "doing pretty well" . . .

Sure, I suppose so. I do remember that when I passed that threshold, I was pretty stoked!

Any plans for when you hit your next subscriber milestone?

I do not have anything planned! I've been really bad at timing things with milestones. It can be kind of difficult to predict—you don't want to make something, then wait on posting it until you hit the milestone but also, if you *do* hit the milestone then it's hard to put something really awesome together in a timely fashion. Maybe we'll put together an animation or something of the sort around the time.

Who would you say are the other YouTubers that you admire?

People that have been able to stick around and do well on the gaming scene over the course of many, many years. I have a lot of respect for those guys—it's tough to maintain things in such a constantly changing environment. As far as other channels I actually enjoy . . . it's funny, despite doing so much stuff on YouTube, I don't have too much time to watch other YouTube videos because I'm so focused on my own. But there is one channel. It's called TeamFourStar and they do a series where they do satirized versions of *Dragon Ball Z*. It's great because I grew up watching *Dragon Ball Z* and I loved it—it's one of my favorite shows and I love being able to relive it in a joking, entertaining fashion. Whenever I see a new episode of that, I'm all over it immediately!

What has been your favorite video game released in the last few years, and why?

I've said this in videos before so it's not like a huge shock, but I'm the world's worst video game channel! I don't have too much time to play

It's really cool to see Jordan's setup from the other side of the camera for a change. Everything from the chair to the audio kit is top-end gear—no wonder his channel is so good!

video games outside of when I'm recording because there are so many things I want to do. The problem is that when I sit down to play a video game for fun, I realize that I could be working on music or another video idea, and that becomes problematic. I would say the game I've played the most for fun since I started on YouTube is *Dota 2*. I haven't had too much time lately to play it but I do really enjoy it.

Finally, is there anything in particular that you would like to say to your millions of fans?

Thank you for watching my videos and enabling me to do what I do! I hope I'll be able to continue this as long as I possibly can while there are still people watching, and I'm going to try to keep on making cool content to the best of my ability. So thanks!

DID YOU KNOW?

The seven most popular CaptainSparklez videos are all *Minecraft* music videos, with over 500 million views total. It's easy to see what his fans like!

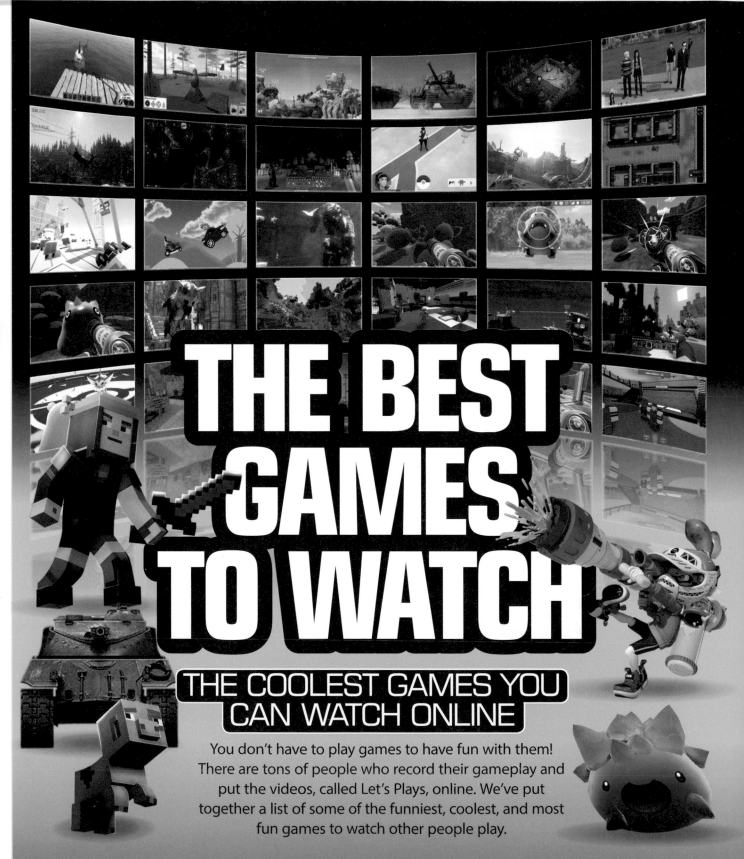

THE BEST GAMES TO WATCH

THE COOLEST GAMES YOU CAN WATCH ONLINE

You don't have to play games to have fun with them! There are tons of people who record their gameplay and put the videos, called Let's Plays, online. We've put together a list of some of the funniest, coolest, and most fun games to watch other people play.

THE LAST GUARDIAN (PS4)

Even though *The Last Guardian* is a slow-burner, and might not have the immediate thrills of other games on this list, it's been a huge hit with YouTubers. Why? Because of Trico. Watching this unpredictable creature in action is mesmerising, because it reacts to everything the player does in surprising ways. Most YouTubers also end up developing an emotional connection with *The Last Guardian*, so it's the perfect antidote to some of the messier, more frantic games on this list.

RAFT (PC)

Watching YouTubers trying to fight off a hungry shark in *Raft* is much more fun than it sounds. They will desperately hook floating wood, weeds, and other objects to build their raft and survive . . . but there's a shark roaming the ocean, too, which eats huge chunks of the raft unless the player can drive it away. The panicked reactions are always funny!

"MOST YOUTUBERS ALSO END UP DEVELOPING AN EMOTIONAL CONNECTION WITH THE LAST GUARDIAN."

CLUSTERTRUCK (PC)

In *ClusterTruck,* running along the top of moving trucks and jumping between them is totally normal. But when the trucks start to collide, things can get pretty crazy! The game is really fast-paced, making it an exciting and unpredictable game to watch others play.

SLIME RANCHER (PC, Xbox One)

Watching YouTubers try and stay on top of their slime farm is great fun. They need to capture slimes, look after them, and feed them if they want to build a successful farm. The slimes will soon start fighting each other, though, so keeping them all happy is vital to success!

MINECRAFT (PC, PS4, Xbox One)

Did you know that YouTube is one of the main reasons that *Minecraft* became a worldwide hit? The game became a favorite for gaming YouTubers when it first launched. Then, because the original release didn't have any instructions, other players turned to these videos to learn what the game was about, and how to play it! Now, *Minecraft*-playing YouTubers focus more on "mods" that change the way the game is played. If you want to try a new kind of *Minecraft* adventure, checking out some of the big YouTube names is a great place to start.

DID YOU KNOW?

Goat Simulator started as a joke! The developer let their team create any new idea they wanted, and one was about a goat that just destroyed stuff.

110 X1

GOAT SIMULATOR
(PC, PS4, Xbox One)

Who knew that goats could be so funny? This is a game series that cranks the craziness up to 11, so you can see a goat climbing construction cranes, strutting its stuff on the dance floor, and even flying through space. Fun oozes out of every pore in *Goat Simulator*, making it a great game to watch as well as play.

TRIALS FUSION
(PC, PS4, Xbox One)

Trials is a series of motorbike obstacle courses that need to be completed in the fastest possible time. It's the hilarious noises every *Trials* player makes that makes the game great to watch, as the bike *just* about crawls over each obstacle without the rider tumbling off.

THE ESCAPISTS
(PC, Xbox One, PS4)

There are more ways to break out of *The Escapists'* jails than you can imagine. You just need to be clever, resourceful, and patient. That's why it's so much fun watching what other YouTubers come up with . . . and sometimes their dumb escape attempts are even funnier to watch than the smart ones!

POKÉMON GO
(iOS, Android)

Pokémon GO takes players from their bedroom to the great outdoors, to hunt down the elusive Pokémon. That's what makes *Pokémon GO* so interesting to watch. It takes your favorite YouTubers outside, so you'll get to learn more about what happens when they leave their gaming chairs . . . and share their excitement about new Pokémon.

TERRARIA
(PC, PS4, Xbox One)

Although you can build and create in *Terraria*, most fans tune in to watch YouTubers explore its dangerous world. The deeper you go in *Terraria*, the stranger the monsters become . . . and there are always odd secrets to be unearthed. Whether you're a *Terraria* newbie or veteran, there's something strangely compelling about watching what others have found—both good and bad!

THE SIMS 4
(PC)

The Sims 4 is a game where you can raise a family, build a home, have a regular job, and enjoy an ordinary life. But no one really plays it that way. Many YouTubers like to use the game as a way to make new characters and tell stories. You'll soon get caught up in them, and want to see what happens to each Sim next.

DON'T STARVE
(PC, PS4, Xbox One)

Don't Starve checks all the boxes a game needs for essential YouTube viewing. It has lots of secrets to discover, different playing styles to study, and a desperate scramble for survival that puts the YouTuber under immense pressure. You'll learn a lot and you'll laugh a lot, and that's exactly what you want when you watch someone playing a game on YouTube.

THE EXPERT SAYS ...
CAPTAINSPARKLEZ
YouTube sensation

With *Minecraft*, there are so many different ways to play the game. You have the base vanilla game—try to survive, kill monsters, work your way to the End, and defeat the dragon. That's one way to play, but then you also have Creative, and people build adventure maps that you're able to download as a save file and try out. You can go on multiplayer servers and play games with your friends on there. You can install mods and totally rework how the game runs. Because of all that, there's an unlimited amount of things to do, and I think that it's really because of the community that *Minecraft* has had such a long shelf life. And hopefully it'll continue that way long into the future as well!

WORLD OF TANKS
(PC, PS4, Xbox One)

This tactical tank battler is perfect for YouTube viewing, because games only take a few minutes. Each team rumbles onto the battlefield, blasts away at their opponents, and when the dust clears, the last tank standing is the winner. The fast games combined with a steady stream of new tanks being unlocked is what makes it such compelling viewing.

WORMS W.M.D
(PC, PS4, Xbox One)

Worms W.M.D is a tactical showdown, with a huge variety of comedy weapons to choose from. You can analyze how the experts use some of the stranger weapons in *Worms W.M.D* and maybe pick up a few ideas to use when you play it yourself. But it's more likely you'll enjoy watching YouTubers crumble and wail with frustration, as their team succumbs to a dramatic comeback win, or make a stupid mistake and lose the game.

ROBLOX (PC, Xbox One)

YouTubers have been drawn to *Roblox* because of the huge variety of games it offers, while viewers love watching to find out the best new games to try themselves! There are so many free games to play, from natural disaster simulators to hide-and-seek titles, that there is always something new, fun, and weird for YouTubers to try.

POKÉMON SUN AND MOON
GOTTA CATCH 'EM ALL!

Greetings from Alola, the latest region where new Pokémon have been discovered! This tropical paradise, based loosely on the Hawaiian islands, plays host to the series' most radical shake-up in its 20-year history. There are no Gyms to challenge or Badges to earn any more—that old system has been replaced with the Island Trials, an entirely new set of unique tasks and challenges to prove your worth as a Trainer.

As well as cool new Pokémon, *Sun* and *Moon* introduce new variants of existing creatures. Their looks are altered due to Alola's varied climate—Sandshrew and Vulpix get frosty new forms, while Exeggutor grows super-tall in the tropical Sun! With four huge islands to explore, there's a lot to do even after you've beaten all the Island Trials. This latest adventure will test even the strongest would-be *Pokémon* masters!

STATS

802 different Pokémon to catch

29 powerful Z-Moves to use

Ride on **7 kinds** of Pokémon

Fill your Pokédex by scanning **up to 10 QR codes per day**

41 new Abilities to spice up battles

TOP 5 NEW POKÉMON

Newcomers that deserve a space on your team

DID YOU KNOW?

By scanning enough QR codes, you are able to perform an Island Scan—an awesome process that reveals the location of a rare Pokémon not native to Alola.

Primarina

1 All three of the fully evolved forms of the Alola starters are great, but we think Primarina *just* edges ahead. It's the most powerful attacker of the bunch, and Water/Fairy is an excellent combination—it can attack with both crashing waves and powerful songs.

Mimikyu

2 This Ghost type just wants to be loved, so it has made itself a crude Pikachu disguise! Considering its small size, Mimikyu is surprisingly dangerous—there are chilling stories about what happened to people who saw the ghost that lives inside the costume. Probably best not to look . . .

Wishiwashi

3 This little fish might look pathetic, but it's actually one of the strongest Pokémon in the game! Its power comes from its Ability, Schooling—while Wishiwashi is healthy, it can call lots of friends to form a giant version of itself. When weakened, though, its allies flee.

Vikavolt

4 What do you get when you combine a beetle, a spaceship, and a railgun? Vikavolt, that's what! Like its previous form Charjabug, it's able to build up and store vast amounts of electrical power, which it blasts at its foes. It's also quite slow, but Vikavolt makes up for it with raw power.

Kommo-o

5 This mighty dragon attacks by clanging its metallic scales to create a deafening din. It isn't normally seen in the wild, but it has been known to appear to protect any Jangmo-o in trouble. Only the best Trainers can even hope to find this majestic beast, let alone tame it!

TIME LINE

1996 Gen1: Red/Blue/Yellow
The first games released for Game Boy, featuring 151 obtainable Pokémon.

2002 Gen3: Ruby/Sapphire/Emerald
Game Boy Advance enabled better visuals and mechanics. Pokémon count grew to 386.

2010 Gen5: Black/White/Black 2/White 2
The only generation to see direct sequels, *Black* and *White* are among the best games in the whole series.

2016 Gen7: Sun/Moon
Pokémon count reaches 802. *Sun* and *Moon* are the biggest and best *Pokémon* games yet!

1999 Gen2: Gold/Silver/Crystal
The sequels added 100 new Pokémon, and let players return to the Kanto region.

2006 Gen4: Diamond/Pearl/Platinum
Another generational leap, this time adding 3-D visuals as well as more than 100 new Pokémon.

2013 Gen6: X/Y/Omega Ruby/Alpha Sapphire
The power of 3DS allowed for full 3-D graphics and movement, now with more than 720 Pokémon in total.

MEET THE SUPERFAN

TEAM ROCKET wants to fight!

HP

TINA GUO

Who?
A world-famous cellist, Tina Guo's amazing skills can be heard on the soundtracks to movies such as *Iron Man 2*, *Rango*, and *X-Men: First Class*, television shows, video games (*Journey*'s beautiful score was Grammy-nominated), and more. Most recently, she performed the theme for the *Wonder Woman* movie.

Why?
Guo's latest album, *Game On!* (great title, right?), features incredible instrumental versions of music from many of her favorite games. In the first music video, for the track *Pokémon*, Guo dresses up in Ash's iconic gear and goes out searching for Pokémon, but ends up in an incredible musical battle against a nasty Team Rocket agent—who she also plays!

DID YOU KNOW?

When wild Pokémon call for help, each assistant will have better stats and a higher chance of being shiny. Keep that chain going!

A TOURIST'S GUIDE TO ALOLA

What sights will you see as you hunt down the regional variations of the new dancing bird Pokémon, Oricorio?

Poni Island
This will be the last island you visit, and it's nowhere near as developed as the others. Expect to find plenty of rare and powerful Pokémon roaming the cliffs, craters, and canyons while you're here.
Oricorio: Sensu Style (Ghost/Flying)

ALSO CHECK OUT . . .

Paws ot Fury

Yo-kai Watch
This cool series is absolutely massive in Japan. It's not just a ghost-catching RPG, either—there are comics, television shows, movies, toys, and even more.

Melemele Island

This is the very first island you visit, and the most "traditional" of the four. Melemele is home to a lot of cool Pokémon that are new to *Sun* and *Moon*, making it a great place to begin your adventure!

Oricorio: Pom-Pom Style (Electric/Flying)

Akala Island

This is your second stop, and where things really start to heat up—literally! Many Fire Pokémon can be found at the island's central volcano, but there are lush jungles and underground lakes as well.

Oricorio: Pa'u Style (Psychic/Flying)

Aether Paradise

A research facility dedicated to the preservation and safety of Pokémon. Use of Poké Balls is prohibited throughout the complex, so don't expect to catch any of the rare Pokémon you might see here!

Oricorio: N/A

Ula'ula Island

This is where you'll find the second-tallest mountain in the Alola region (note the frozen peak—brrrr!), as well as an entire town that has been overrun by Team Skull. The island has a really cool, Asian vibe.

Oricorio: Baile Style (Fire/Flying)

THE EXPERT SAYS...
JOE MERRICK
Webmaster of popular *Pokémon* site serebii.net

The fan community is by far my favorite thing about the *Pokémon* phenomenon. It's one of the friendliest communities around. People go out of their way to help others to find Pokémon, with battle strategies or just in general. *Pokémon*, by design, has mandated to get people together to battle and trade, and it has continued to do that. There are people alive today because their parents met due to *Pokémon*, and that is utterly phenomenal to me.

World of Final Fantasy

All of the best *Final Fantasy* monsters appear here as Mirages, which can be added to your party and stacked into towers to make them even more powerful than ever!

Ni No Kuni

This is a collaboration between legendary animation house Studio Ghibli and *Dragon Quest* developer, Level-5. It features loads of weird and wonderful creatures to train, just like you do in *Pokémon* games!

LEGO WORLDS
LEGO COMES TO LIFE

You can create a house, then a town, then a city, and then an entire world. And you can do it all with a friend! In LEGO *Worlds*, you can create anything, as long as you have the bricks—and the skill—to do it. And then, if you want, you can smash it all to bits. The beauty of LEGO *Worlds* is you can do whatever you want—it's a giant, blocky playground for you to mess around in. The interface makes it really easy to create new structures, too, so building is fast and fun.

You can even play LEGO *Worlds* like a regular game if you'd prefer, battling bad guys like dark wizards, skeletons, and flying dragons. And, of course, you can bring in a friend to help you in the split-screen multiplayer mode as well. It's all the fun of LEGO without the need to clean up all those bricks afterwards. What's not to like about that?

DID YOU KNOW?
You can build everything brick-by-brick if you like, but LEGO *Worlds* also offers tools that let you make gigantic creations in just a few minutes.

STATS

2 player split-screen

5,300,000 YouTube views for Stampy's LEGO *Worlds* video

61 Achievements to unlock

19th LEGO game by Traveller's Tales

OVER 8,000 "Very Positive" reviews on Steam

TOP 5 FUN THINGS TO DO

Building stuff

1 Just like with the actual toy, it's the simple things that fuel the fun in LEGO *Worlds*. Whether you're building a small house with flowers and a white-picket fence or a towering structure, nothing matches the thrill of standing back proudly reflecting on your creation.

Destroying stuff

2 Almost as fun as building structures is knocking them down. You could plow through them with a vehicle or even shoot them from the back of a fire-breathing dragon!

Creating your own hero

3 Intrepid jungle explorer. Hairy caveman with dinosaur bone through his hair. Cavewoman with a giant club. Indiana Jones lookalike. Astronaut. No matter who you want to create, you can do it here.

Skydiving

4 LEGO *Worlds* isn't a game that takes place just on the ground. You can use jetpacks to fly around your creations, ride on the backs of dragons, and even soar among the clouds in a plane you made yourself before skydiving back down to Earth.

Leading enemies into traps

5 Don't just beat enemies in fistfights. Build pits of doom and lead them on a merry chase towards the pit, as they scramble to take a bite out of your health bar. Leap over and watch as they all tumble in. See what other traps you can come up with!

ALSO CHECK OUT . . .

Minecraft
Minecraft used to be compared to LEGO, but now it's the other way around with LEGO *Worlds*! If you like building with blocks, *Minecraft* is perfect.

Terraria
It's the same concept of building (and destroying!), although the gameplay here is in a 2-D world rather than a 3-D LEGO universe.

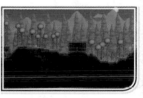

LEGO City Undercover
Instead of building up a LEGO world, you're playing an undercover cop in one. As Chase McCain, you need to hunt criminals throughout LEGO City.

TIPS & TRICKS

Animals are different
Each kind of creature in the game will react to your actions in their own unique way. Learn the differences in animal behavior to become a master of critters.

Stay away from dark wizards
Unless you're confident enough that you can win in battle, it's best to avoid dark wizards altogether. They're powerful foes!

Keep vehicles away from water
If you don't want to lose vehicles, avoid water. A car is no good to you on the bottom of the ocean!

Switch to first-person
If you need help exploring tight spaces, switch to first-person view so you can get a clearer view of what's in front of you.

Don't be scared of lava
You can "bounce" off lava a few times before it kills you. Use this to cross narrow areas if you have enough health.

▶ DanTDM

MASTER OF MINECRAFT!

CLAIM TO FAME

Dan is so famous that there's an entire line of toys based on him and his other popular *Minecraft* characters!

Minecraft remains one of the most popular games in the world, and DanTDM is the biggest name in the business. TheDiamondMinecart is among the most successful gaming channels on YouTube. New videos typically rack up over a million views just on the first day.

He started out exclusively covering *Minecraft*, but Dan now covers a broader range of games. He tackles each with the same sense of fun, and is always engaging and entertaining. Still, fans of Dan's *Minecraft* content are never left waiting for too long, as new videos still go up on his channel regularly.

A huge star and a gaming legend, DanTDM adds awesome new videos every day. Check out his channel and you might find a new game to try!

▥ STATS

▶ **Year started** 2012

NUMBER OF SUBS
13 million

NUMBER OF VIDEOS
2,200

TOTAL VIEW COUNT
8.5 billion

MOST-WATCHED VIDEO
"How I met Dr. Trayaurus | *Minecraft*"
34 million views

EXPECT TO SEE/HEAR
- ▶ Dan shouting "WHAT?!"
- ▶ New hair colors every few months
- ▶ *Minecraft* pushed to its limits!

SIMILAR CHANNELS

ThnxCya
Family friendly fun

If it's more *Minecraft* videos you're looking for, this guy has you covered! He's always upbeat and very friendly, plus he sometimes produces songs about *Minecraft*. They are really good, and he does other regular video content, too!

Thinknoodles
A huge variety of awesome games!

Skylanders, Minecraft, Pokémon GO, Super Mario Maker, Roblox . . . you name it, Thinknoodles probably plays it! Together with his dog, Kopi, he goes on all kinds of adventures in loads of different games. He makes videos dedicated to answering his fans' questions as well.

Sqaishey Quack
Loveable *Minecraft* duck!

Minecraft is the main focus of Sqaishey's great videos. Her *Feather Adventures* series runs for more than 200 episodes! You'll also find her playing all kinds of other cool games, such as *Rayman Legends* and *Terraria*, and sometimes even hanging out with her friend, Stampy.

HIS BIGGEST GAMES

Minecraft
Over 1,000 epic videos

The vast majority of Dan's videos are *Minecraft*-related. These span everything from mod showcases and reviews to extreme survival mode runs. Watch him explore strange worlds, meet a cast of crazy characters, and discover the very best that *Minecraft* has to offer.

Roblox
Anything can happen!

There are so many unique games within *Roblox* that you never know what you'll see. It's a popular game with YouTubers and streamers for this very reason. There are new experiences popping up every day, and videos like these can be a great way to find out about them before you play.

Tomodachi Life
TDM goes handheld

Dan doesn't always play on PC, you know. He's made videos about mobile games like *Pokémon GO*, too, as well as a really cool series about *Tomodachi Life*. This Nintendo life simulator throws up all kinds of unexpected situations—what will Dan and friends stumble upon next?

TOP 10
BEST-LOOKING GAMES

Journey

1 It was already heralded as one of the best-looking games ever made for PS3. Now, remastered for PS4, *Journey* somehow looks even better. As the adventure guides you through wide-open deserts and beguiling crypts, the real masterstroke is how there are no enemies to fight. You get to drink in the gorgeous scenery at your leisure, and try to figure out the mysteries of this beautiful game for yourself.

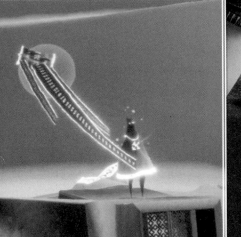

Horizon Zero Dawn

2 One of the reasons that *Horizon Zero Dawn* is so good is that the world you explore feels so alive. Dinosaur-like machines wander through fields as you creep through long grass. The developers studied all kinds of animals, from kangaroos to giraffes, to get their movements right, so they look incredibly realistic.

SIMPLE BUT BEAUTIFUL
Six games that don't need amazing graphics to impress

Thomas Was Alone
Thomas Was Alone is a game about blocks. You play as a block, you will meet other blocks, and you move through equally simple blocky levels.

The Trail
Who knew a game about walking could be so pretty? The blocky shading and pastel colors make *The Trail* look a lot more like a vacation destination than a video game.

Monument Valley
Each puzzle in *Monument Valley* looks like a painting that you could hang on your wall, with intricate detail and bright colors bringing each screen to life.

The Room Three
The Room is little more than a series of locked boxes that you need to crack into. Even with that simple concept, the detail on the boxes is great and the atmosphere is surprisingly creepy.

The Deer God
Even though this pixel adventure has simplistic graphics, it still has room for moments of magic. Watch the glow of the moon casting shadows through the forest, for example.

Fez
In *Fez*, you can rotate the entire level, a trick that's essential to completing some of the puzzles. Watching the towering pixel structures spinning around is strangely enchanting.

Resogun

3 Although this was a PlayStation 4 launch title, it's still one of the best-looking games around. Using "voxel-based" graphics, everything in *Resogun* shatters into tiny cubes when shot. It isn't long before the stage floor is coated in a blanket of these little blocks—there are a lot of explosions, after all!

Final Fantasy XV

4 *Final Fantasy XV* blows you away on every level. It's a game that knows how to go small, with cute animations of characters joking around during mission downtime. But it can also go big, with the earth-shattering attacks of each summon dwarfing the action. Whatever it is, you know it'll look incredible.

Super Time Force

5 When you die in this game you can rewind time to start again, but your previous life will play alongside you, retracing its steps. If you keep rewinding, the screen fills with chaos, and the anarchy is truly incredible.

Transistor

6 *Transistor* is packed with visual creativity in its glorious, futuristic setting. Every corner of its sci-fi world was crafted with love, from the soft lighting that casts shadows over you, to the handcrafted detail of each brick, stick, and stone. You'll quickly fall in love with this stylish world.

THE EXPERT SAYS ...
HEYCHRISSA
Popular YouTuber and streamer

The one that sticks out the most to me is *Abzû*, from the art director of *Journey* and *Flower*. It became one of my all-time favorite indie games and quite possibly the most beautiful game I've ever played. *Abzû* is an underwater adventure focused around swimming and exploration. You're able to interact and discover hundreds of species, and explore chapters set in different ecosystems including vibrant coral reefs and deep caverns. The game is bursting with color and detail, and the soundtrack is beautifully done, setting a tone that is both calming and filled with mystery. The stress-free gameplay and freedom of movement means it can be enjoyed by players of all ages.

Abzû

7 *Abzû* is a game full of gorgeous images. The deep blue ocean at the start of the game, as you take your first tentative dive underwater. The sunlight piercing through the dense seaweed. The schools of fish being chased away by predators. Everything in *Abzû* is picturesque, leaving you swimming through its world like an underwater tourist.

Beyond Eyes

8 In *Beyond Eyes*, you play as a blind girl called Rae looking for her missing cat. When you start, the world is white and without detail. But as Rae approaches objects and can hear or touch them, she fills in the blanks—colorful paint strokes splash the white canvas of her world with life and detail.

Rez Infinite

9 Less can be more. *Rez Infinite* creates its visual rollercoaster using little more than wireframe graphics and neon colors, but it's still like an explosion in a candy factory. Watching as levels break apart and re-form in the mind blowing VR setting really has to be seen to be believed.

Forza Horizon 3

10 *Forza Horizon 3* is stunning to look at, especially when you park and take in the scenery. Whether it's the long grass gently blowing in the breeze, sunlight bouncing off your hood, or rolling mountains that stretch out for miles, there's beauty everywhere. You can even use an in-game photography mode to snap any particularly lush scenes.

YOOKA-LAYLEE
THE GREAT GAMING COMEBACK

DID YOU KNOW?

Yooka-Laylee's music is by Grant Kirkhope, the award-winning composer who created the music for *Viva Piñata* and *Star Fox Adventures*.

Yooka-Laylee is bringing a long-forgotten genre back to life: the collect-'em-up. The term was coined for platforming games where the emphasis is on discovering hidden collectibles, tucked away in areas that only adventurous and determined gamers can reach. The creators of *Yooka-Laylee* have worked on some of the best collect-'em-up games of all time, including *Banjo-Kazooie* and *Donkey Kong Country*, so it has everything that makes for a fantastic game: a large open world, unforgettable characters, dramatic boss battles, secret paths, and side objectives. The bright, colorful levels are littered with things to discover—you'll find yourself going back to each one over and over, trying to find the last few items that you missed.

STATS

$2,530,000 pledged on Kickstarter

1st game by Playtonic Games

2 player co-op

4 player competitive multiplayer

8 different mini-games

TOP 5 REASONS YOOKA-LAYLEE ROCKS

Collectibles

1 *Yooka-Laylee* is bursting with secret collectibles for you to discover, each level stuffed with hidden goodies and tantalizing secrets. Are you smart enough to explore every hidden area and find them all? This is one game that will truly test all of your skills. You'll need to leap, dive, and swim to 100% complete the game.

Humor

2 From lame puns to bathroom jokes, there is plenty to laugh at in *Yooka-Laylee*. Each character you meet is hilariously weird, and they're sure to make you smile. Plus, you're never too far from another joke, making light of the bizarre situations you'll find yourself in. You'll be laughing constantly!

GOSH! I SEEM TO HAVE GOTTEN MYSELF INTO A POT OF BOTHER...

Platforming

3 It's the foundation on which *Yooka-Laylee* is built. You won't spend long on the ground, as you must scurry up ancient ruins and leap between floating platforms. You'll need a steady hand and perfect timing to survive *Yooka-Laylee*'s toughest platforming tests, but beat them and you'll feel like a gaming pro.

Puzzles

4 *Yooka-Laylee* isn't the toughest game, but there are some puzzles that will test you. From collectibles that are dangling just out of reach, to tile puzzles where one wrong step can be disastrous, *Yooka-Laylee* knows when to change the pace and give you a new challenge to beat.

THANKS FOR CLEARING THE WINDOWS UP TOP, WHAT-NOT!

Dungeons

5 Not all of the action in *Yooka-Laylee* takes place outdoors. You'll often end up inside some sort of dungeon, cave, or tomb. In these confined areas, you'll find a specific test of your skills. You might have to take part in a target challenge, for example, or cross a deadly pit.

ALSO CHECK OUT . . .

Banjo-Kazooie
The graphics are dated, but the classic bear-and-bird platforming has aged beautifully. It's available thanks to the Xbox One's backward compatibility.

Super Mario 3D World
Super Mario 3D World packs tons of platforming into small, dense arenas, full of enemies to defeat and secrets to discover.

Crash Bandicoot N. Sane Trilogy
Three of the greatest platforming games of all time, spruced up with shiny PS4 graphics, while the classic retro gameplay has been left intact.

TIPS & TRICKS

Spin to win
Learn the range of Yooka's spin attack. Attacking enemies from the farthest possible range keeps you safe.

Roll to get around
When you unlock Yooka and Laylee's roll move, use it to get around, as it's quicker than walking—and more fun!

Get up high
The best way to start figuring out where the secrets might be hidden on a level is to head up to the highest point, and scout from there.

Don't rush
Yooka-Laylee is full of challenging jumps, tricky traps, and hidden paths that you'll miss if you rush. Take your time and you'll find more stuff!

Return to previous levels
Don't worry about collecting all the secrets on your first run through a level. You can always come back with new skills.

CAPTURE THIS!

SPLATOON

Show off your style!

As you paint your way to victory in this awesome multiplayer game, you will unlock a bunch of cool new weapons and gear. Suit up in the kit you like the most and you can snap a picture of your Inkling in its battle-ready best, then wear your new gear in a multiplayer match and show off your hot new look to your friends!

▶ STAMPYLONGHEAD

FUN TIMES GUARANTEED

With Stampy, you're guaranteed *Minecraft* adventures, silly voices, gaming with friends, and a fun time. Stampy—real name Joseph Garrett—started out wanting to become a games journalist.

However, his success with *Minecraft* "Let's Play" videos meant he switched to making YouTube videos full-time instead. And he hasn't slowed down since. In fact, Stampy still uploads a *Minecraft* video every single day! With his own character, Mr. Stampy Cat, his adventures have taken him around *Minecraft* in a hot air balloon, traveling back in time, and saving zombie villagers. But whatever he's up to, you just need to hear his trademark laugh to know that you're in for a good time.

STATS

▶ **Year started** 2011

NUMBER OF SUBS
8.1 million

NUMBER OF VIDEOS
2,500

TOTAL VIEW COUNT
5.6 billion

MOST WATCHED VIDEO
"Minecraft Xbox—Sinking Feeling [124]"
52 million views

EXPECT TO SEE/HEAR
- ▶ New *Minecraft* videos every day
- ▶ His trademark laugh
- ▶ Stampy staying upbeat whatever happens

SIMILAR CHANNELS

CLAIM TO FAME

Mr. Stampy Cat is such a famous *Minecraft* personality, he's even one of the characters in *Minecraft: Story Mode*, voiced by Stampy himself!

iBallisticSquid
Stampy's friend

iBallisticSquid has starred alongside Stampy in many of his *Minecraft* videos, and they have even done TV interviews together. His channel is the same sort of *Minecraft* fun Stampy specializes in, although iBallisticSquid does play a wider range of games.

LittleLizardGaming
Minecraft **mod specialists**

LittleLizard loves playing *Minecraft* and trying out the weirdest new mods people have made. LittleLizard is part of The Little Club, and plays *Minecraft* with other characters like Little Kelly, Tiny Turtle, Donut the Dog, and Max the Monkey. Loads of new friends!

AmyLee33
Minecraft **storytellers**

AmyLee uses *Minecraft* as a way to tell stories. Her imagination and endless creativity can barely be contained on YouTube. From *Land of Love* to *Mermaid Mondays*, she's already got several different *Minecraft* series to choose from.

HIS BIGGEST GAMES

Minecraft
Stampy's favorite

On May 19, 2012, Stampy uploaded a video called "Welcome To Stampy's Lovely World." That launched Stampy's popular *Lovely World* series, as he embarked on adventures in *Minecraft*'s unpredictable world as Mr. Stampy Cat.

King's Quest
The grand adventure

One of Stampy's most-loved games is *King's Quest*, an epic tale spread over five episodes about a knight in training. From surviving fiery encounters to winning battles against fellow knights, Stampy seems to enjoy *King's Quest* even more than we enjoy his videos—and that's quite a lot!

"WITH HIS OWN CHARACTER, MR. STAMPY CAT, HIS ADVENTURES HAVE TAKEN HIM ALL AROUND MINECRAFT IN A HOT AIR BALLOON!"

The Last Guardian
The emotional game

If you want to hear Stampy getting emotional about a game, check out his playthrough of *The Last Guardian*. From the first awkward moments with Trico to the dramatic conclusion, Stampy gets taken on an emotional roller coaster ride as he befriends the gigantic creature.

SWITCH IT UP!

The best thing about Switch is just how versatile it is. You can use it like a regular handheld gaming device simply by clicking the Joy-Con controllers onto the sides of the screen. You can use the Switch's kick stand to prop it up anywhere, removing the controllers to use either individually (one in each hand) or in a controller grip. You can slot Switch into its docking unit connecting it to a TV, to go from portable play to home gaming in a matter of seconds. Play how you want, when you want—that's the beauty of Switch.

NINTENDO SWITCH
GAMING TRANSFORMS!

Best For . . .
- Console gaming on the go
- Cool new ways to play
- Updates of your favorites

Nintendo often focuses on invention and innovation, rather than power, which is why its consoles are often so unique. Switch combines handheld systems and home gaming into one unit, meaning you'll be able to play wherever you are. The two Joy-Con controllers have an incredible amount of tech packed into their tiny frames. "HD Rumble" lets you feel things like never before, an IR pointer offers additional motion-control options, and NFC support means you can use amiibo. Plus, with a great battery life and comfortable design, they're good for longer gaming sessions.

Launch title *1-2-Switch* showcases all of this tech with a host of crazy mini-games that tell you to look your competitor in the eye, not watch the screen. It's more about interacting directly with other players in fun and silly ways. With this console, Nintendo has laid down a challenge to developers to think up new kinds of games!

KEY FEATURES

Multiple Modes

With its various configurations, Switch can allow for all kinds of unique gaming experiences. From throwing motion-controlled punches in *Arms* to enjoying split-screen multiplayer on a portable screen with one Joy-Con each, developers are free to create whatever kind of games they like. And best of all, they're all really fun!

Shakin' All Over

Rumble and feedback are hardly uncommon in gaming controllers, but the Switch Joy-Cons take this to the next level with what has been called "HD Rumble" by Nintendo. This allows the controllers to accurately simulate things like ice cubes rattling in a glass, or balls rolling around in a box. It's really impressive.

NFC Connectivity

If you've got a healthy collection of amiibo figures already, the good news is that all your existing friends will continue to work with Switch. There's an NFC reader/writer—the device used to interface with and save data to amiibo figures—inside the right Joy-Con, so expect to see more uses for amiibo, and an increasing number of them, too!

TOP 4 STAR GAMES

The Legend of Zelda: Breath of the Wild

1 This epic launch title is the one game everyone wanted when Switch first launched, and it still sits among the system's best games to date. It's Link's biggest adventure, with the sprawling world of Hyrule brought to life beautifully by the enhanced power of Switch.

Super Mario Odyssey

2 The latest 3-D *Mario* platformer takes the franchise in a bold new direction. It has a realistic world called New Donk City—based loosely on New York City—from which Mario can zoom off to all kinds of weird and wonderful locations to do his thing. Oh, and his hat is alive now, too . . .

Splatoon 2

3 After the first *Splatoon* game performed so well and built up such a strong fan base, a sequel was always going to be on the cards. Exclusive to Switch, this refined and improved version of the ink-based shooter plays a lot like its predecessor, only with all kinds of new weapons, abilities, and modes to try out. Get out there and get messy!

Arms

4 *Arms* isn't just a great game—it's a great workout, too! The game uses motion controls to let players throw punches with each character's extendable limbs, but you can't just flail around like crazy. There's a level of subtlety and depth to the one-on-one fights that means you'll need to think fast. Precision and strategy are key, which is rare in motion-controlled games like this.

Best for . . .
- Console VR
- Japanese RPGs
- Fighting games

SONY PLAYSTATION 4
ARE YOU READY TO GO PRO?

The PlayStation 4 was already a powerful console, but by adding the PS4 Pro to the family, Sony went all out for players who want the best tech. Today, there are two PS4 models available. The high-end Pro is somewhat larger and more powerful than the regular model, but it's also more expensive. The standard PS4 was redesigned in 2016 to be smaller and less angular than the launch model. Plus, it still runs all the same great games as its big brother, so you won't miss out no matter which one you have! Better yet, if you have a PlayStation Vita as well, you can use the two devices together—PS4 games can be streamed to the handheld either locally or across wireless networks, giving you console games in the palm of your hand. With a superb library of games, a selection of music and video apps, and some interesting tech backing it up (such as virtual reality, streaming, and motion control), PS4 is a pretty epic all-rounder.

KEY FEATURES

4K gaming

The enhanced PS4 Pro is capable of outputting visuals up to four times the resolution of a standard HD display. If you have access to an Ultra HD 4K TV, your PS4 games will look better than ever, although the extra power that enables this can also make games look better on older televisions, too.

PlayStation VR

Sony's VR headset is the cheapest of all the high-end options, but offers slightly less power than the HTC Vive and Oculus Rift. Still, the sense of immersion is amazing (you feel like you're really in the games), although those who suffer from motion sickness might not get along so well with VR.

PlayStation Now

While the PS4 can't usually play last generation games, Sony's PS Now service lets you play a wide variety of popular PS3 games. The service streams the game from Sony's own servers, so you'll need a fast Internet connection to use it. It's still really impressive, though, and more games are being added all the time.

TOP 4 STAR GAMES

Horizon: Zero Dawn

1 What's even cooler than dinosaurs? Robot dinosaurs, of course! These giant mechanical monsters have taken over the land, and it's up to Aloy, a master huntress, to get the robosaurs under control, and take back the planet. It's another visually stunning game that shows off the power of the PS4, especially the Pro.

Uncharted 4: A Thief's End

2 Sony's flagship franchise bows out in style—this final chapter of Nathan Drake's globe-hopping adventure is the best yet. It's absolutely incredible to look at even on a regular PS4, but it's even crisper and more detailed on a PS4 Pro. The views are incredible—as you can see!

Ratchet & Clank

3 While many modern games continue to chase realism, this gorgeous and often chaotic cartoon shooter feels almost like a playable animated movie in places. The range of crazy weapons is sure to bring a smile to your face and, again, enhancements to the PS4 Pro version make it one of the best-looking games we've ever seen.

RIGS: Mechanized Combat League

4 Among the greatest showcases for PlayStation VR, *RIGS* is a simple arena combat game. In it, you control a giant mech, and compete in different sport-inspired games. The feeling of actually being a mech pilot is awesome, although the action is so intense that you should take a break after each match!

PURE POWER

Not to be outdone by Sony's PS4 Pro, Microsoft has released two enhanced versions of its latest console. The first of these, the Xbox One S, offers a sleek new design, additional storage, HDR support, and 4K output, with a small amount of additional power over the launch machine. But the latest Xbox, originally codenamed "Scorpio," is the most powerful console in the world. It's almost five times as powerful as the original Xbox One, which means your games will look better than ever on normal TVs and in 4K!

XBOX ONE
MICROSOFT POWERS UP!

Best For . . .
- All-in-one media hub
- 4K Blu-ray playback
- Backward compatibility

The Xbox 360 was one of the most successful consoles ever, so Microsoft was under a lot of pressure when creating its successor. Fortunately, the tech giant managed to deliver and, thanks to several great hardware revisions, the Xbox is now in a better place than ever. Just like PlayStation 4, Xbox One comes in two main models—the slimline Xbox One S as an entry-level option, and a new, more powerful model for those looking for true 4K gaming.

Whichever you go for, you'll find the Xbox One to be just as good as an all-in-one media device or a console. That's why it's called Xbox One—Microsoft sees it as the one device you need under your TV, and that's not far from the truth. It's the only console that offers 4K video playback via Blu-ray, and it also has all of the apps and services you'd expect to see on a modern platform—from Netflix to catch-up TV services—to ensure that you'll never be bored again!

KEY FEATURES

Backward Compatibility

Microsoft is constantly adding support for old Xbox 360 games on Xbox One, with over 20 percent of the previous generation console's library now playable on the new Xbox. All you do is put in your old disc and the game will automatically be downloaded and installed to your Xbox One, ready to play. Easy!

Smartglass

Download a free app on your smartphone or tablet and you can control your console with a few taps. This second-screen experience lets you browse Xbox Live messages, download new games, and even take control of your media with your smart device. Just log in with your Gamertag and you're ready to go!

Hands-Free Control

With the Kinect sensor attached, you don't even need a controller to navigate through all of the Xbox One's great features. You can do everything from turning on your console to recording gameplay, from swapping between games and apps to joining parties, just by talking to your console. How cool is that?

TOP 4 STAR GAMES

Forza Horizon 3

1 Racing games don't get much better than this! Set in and around a cool music festival in Australia, this stunning game lets you speed around in some of the world's most powerful cars. There are all kinds of different events to participate in and challenges to complete, so what are you waiting for? Get out on the open road and burn some rubber!

Halo 5: Guardians

2 The legendary FPS saga continues, with a completely reworked multiplayer mode offering more intense competitive play than ever before. Meet a cast of new characters in the campaign, get creative in the awesome Forge mode, team up with friends in Firefight, or take them on in competitive online matches . . .

Ori and the Blind Forest

3 This gorgeous platform adventure is one of the most beautiful games we've ever seen, and it plays amazingly too! Guide the lovable Ori around a 2-D fantasy landscape, acquiring awesome new abilities that let you explore further and fight harder. With amazing design and story, it's an adventure you'll never forget.

EA Access

4 Why have one game when you can have tons? EA Access is a subscription service that offers open access to the EA Vault, containing over 30 full games that you can play as much as you like. These include some really big names, such as *Plants vs. Zombies: Garden Warfare 2*, *Madden*, *FIFA*, and *Need for Speed*. And more games are being added to the Vault all the time!

THE LEGEND OF ZELDA: BREATH OF THE WILD

TAKE MY BREATH AWAY

DID YOU KNOW?

Monolith Soft, the famous *Xenoblade Chronicles* developer, helped Nintendo to develop *Breath of the Wild*.

The latest *Legend of Zelda* game is the standout title for the flagship series, and Nintendo has gone bigger than ever before. After waking from a 100-year slumber to see his homeland of Hyrule in ruins, Link embarks on a quest to defeat the evil Phantom Ganon in *Breath of the Wild's* huge open world. And he has new tools at his disposal to help him do it, including a magical tablet that enables him to create bombs, build blocks of ice, and even freeze objects in time. The most exciting thing about the game is that you can go anywhere, and do anything in the huge land of Hyrule. If you want to follow the main story and try to save the world from the Ganon, you can—but if you'd rather talk to people, ride horses, and explore the mountains, you can do that, too. The choice is yours!

STATS

4 years in development

19th *Legend of Zelda* game

There are **16 regions** of Hyrule to explore in the game

2,400,000 fans on Facebook

10,000,000 YouTube views for E3 trailer

TOP 5 BREATH OF THE WILD MOMENTS

Fighting Guardians

1 There are tons of incredible boss battles that we won't spoil for you here, but your first fight against a Guardian is truly special. These robot sentries won't think twice about blasting you with their laser eye. How do you defeat them? Keep moving and aim your arrows at that laser eye . . .

Knocking enemies into each other

2 Nintendo worked hard to make *Breath of the Wild* feel realistic. Hit a tree with an ax and it'll fall. Take a flame to grass to start a fire. Our favorite is striking an enemy back to hit another—they'll tumble over like bowling pins.

Causing an explosion

3 Explosions in *Breath of the Wild* create huge clouds of red and yellow flames that reach for the sky. But they're not just pretty to look at; explosions scare nearby bad guys, which is a perfect way to start an ambush on a bunch of Moblin enemies.

Meeting new characters

4 Hyrule is filled with awesome new characters to find, and some of them will even help you on your adventure. Speak to everyone you meet—some NPCs will ask for your help, and by completing their tasks you can earn big rewards!

Teaming up with Wolf Link

5 If you have a Wolf Link amiibo, you can scan it in the game to unlock Wolf Link, a companion who joins Link on his adventure. He stays by his human master's side, helping Link in combat and digging up food whenever he catches its scent.

TIME LINE

1986 The Legend of Zelda
This is where it all began. The mix of adventure and RPG made it one of the most influential games ever made.

1998 Ocarina of Time
Released for Nintendo 64, this time-traveling adventure is considered one of the greatest games of all time.

2000 Majora's Mask
With its unusual color scheme and melancholic storyline, this is the darkest outing in the series.

2002 The Wind Waker
Though it divided fans, a recent HD re-release has seen this bright and beautiful *Zelda* become a classic.

2006 Twilight Princess
Link can take the form of a wolf in this *Zelda* outing, which received rave reviews from critics and fans.

2011 Skyward Sword
A streamlined *Zelda*, this entry in the series had a heavy emphasis on the Wii motion controls.

MEET THE SUPERFAN

IKHANA

Who?

Ikhana, also known as Anne Martha Harnes, has one of the most impressive *Zelda* collections in the world. Her "Kingdom" includes thousands of figures, posters, toys, and games from *Zelda*'s 30 year lifespan.

How?

Ikhana started collecting in 2008, buying her first Link stuffed toy on eBay. She mainly collects what she describes as "stuff," rather than copies of the games themselves. This includes promotional materials and limited edition items. Her two rarest pieces are a Zoraxe guitar replica—from her favorite game in the series *Majora's Mask*—and a prototype *Twilight Princess* GameCube controller. She thinks the controller is one of just two in the world!

IN DEPTH ZELDA TRADEMARKS

Fierce combat

As you progress through the game, you'll run into tougher enemies who will fight harder. If you dodge their attacks at the right time, though, you can use a special "Flurry Rush" attack to do a ton of damage!

Large distant castles

Zelda is about scale, and staring out across the distant land often means a towering structure staring right back at you. And once you see it, you'll probably want to explore it .

ALSO CHECK OUT

Okami

An epic adventure inspired by Japanese folklore, *Okami* follows a goddess who takes the form of a white wolf. The gameplay is very similar to *Zelda*, with some fantastic twists.

Venturing where you shouldn't venture

Can I go here? That's a question that drives your exploration in *Zelda*, as you poke and prod the world around you to see where you can reach.

Jump X   Let go B

DID YOU KNOW?

Link is left-handed in previous games, but for *Breath of the Wild*, he's right-handed. Nintendo made the change to match the controls.

Solving Puzzles

These mazelike dungeons are dotted throughout *Breath of the Wild*. As you solve the puzzles within them, they may reward you with new items, which will help you reach a different area or beat a boss.

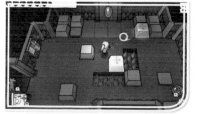

Ittle Dew 2

Heavily inspired by the older *Zelda* titles, this is as close as you can get to playing the *Zelda* classics on your Xbox One or PS4. Set on an island filled with puzzles, the comparisons are easily drawn.

The Trail: A Frontier Journey

It might take place along a linear path but *The Trail* inspires a similar sense of awe, as you gawp at the beautiful world around you. The soft color scheme has a *Breath of the Wild* vibe.

▶ JeromeASF

THE MINECRAFT SPARKPLUG

JeromeASF's YouTube mission statement is that he tries to have as much fun as possible, and that's exactly what he does in his unpredictable *Minecraft* videos. JeromeASF dives headfirst into all kinds of *Minecraft* mods and emerges with a huge smile on his face—he's tackled zombie survival maps, *Pokémon* tributes, upside-down dimensions, and even adventures in space.

Jerome can typically be seen playing online, so he doesn't have to try and fill any silence with forced chatter. It's like dropping in on a bunch of friends playing through *Minecraft*, and it's all held together by Jerome's lively, upbeat nature. Energetic and always happy, Jerome's sparky personality will motivate you to boot up *Minecraft* and try some of the mods in your own game.

 **STATS**

▶ **Year started** 2011

NUMBER OF SUBS
4.4 million

NUMBER OF VIDEOS
4,500

TOTAL VIEW COUNT
1.1 billion

MOST-WATCHED VIDEO
"*Minecraft* SPONGEBOB Modded Cops and Robbers"
6.6 million views

EXPECT TO SEE/HEAR
- ▶ Endless energy and enthusiasm
- ▶ In-depth *Minecraft* knowledge
- ▶ "Ooooooooooh buddy!"

SIMILAR CHANNELS

SSundee
The charismatic YouTuber

SSundee has rocketed into the elite group of top gaming YouTubers, and almost all of his uploads now rack up over a million views each. It's easy to see why—this *Minecraft* fan is effortlessly charismatic, and he always gets really involved in each gaming session. Worth a watch.

CLAIM TO FAME

JeromeASF often plays with his fans, such as with his video where he took on 200 fans in *Minecraft*.

Prestonplayz
Energetic Minecrafter

Like JeromeASF, PrestonPlayz is all about having fun. The highlights of his channel are the challenges he sets himself. Look out for the hilarious hand-mouse-keyboard challenge, where Preston plays *Minecraft* on keyboard while his friend Aiden controls the mouse.

Bajan Canadian
Minecraft, Minecraft, Minecraft

While *Minecraft* YouTubers seem to eventually spread their attention across other games as well, Bajan Canadian has eyes only for Mojang's game. He has lots of *Minecraft* video series, showcasing him playing it in unusual and exciting ways, usually using crazy multiplayer mods.

HIS BIGGEST GAMES

Minecraft
The original game

JeromeASF is still as in love with *Minecraft* now as he was when he first discovered it. He plays around with the stranger mods, like the Cute Puppy mod and the Hide and Seek mod. Seeing his delight at what the fans have created is what keeps us (and him!) coming back time and time again.

Roblox
Rampant creativity ahoy

JeromeASF's eye for creative multiplayer gameplay has led him to *Roblox*, where players create fun games for others to play through. Some of the *Roblox* games Jerome has played through include a detective mystery, a natural disaster simulator, and an amusement park builder.

Worms
Explosive multiplayer mayhem

JeromeASF dabbles with multiplayer games outside of *Minecraft,* and he's particularly fond of *Worms Reloaded*. Two teams of worms tool up with explosive weapons to take each other out, and Jerome has found the combination of tactics, mayhem, and accidental comedy too much to resist.

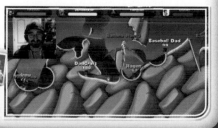

TEKKEN
ROUND 7 . . . FIGHT!

Tekken has long been home to some of the most colorful characters in gaming—it features boxers, bears, robots, sumo wrestlers, dancers, dinosaurs, and everything in between. This fighting game pits two players and their chosen characters against each other, as they attempt to punch, kick, and throw their way to victory. For *Tekken 7*, the emphasis has shifted to powerful moves. Power Crush blows through incoming opponent attacks, while Rage Arts are a spectacular series of attacks that do huge damage. With its gorgeous graphics emphasizing each hit, *Tekken 7* is a master class in one-on-one competitive gaming.

DID YOU KNOW?

Tekken characters have featured in other games too, such as *PlayStation All-Stars Battle Royale, Ridge Racer 6,* and *Pac-Man Fever.*

STATS

1994 is when the gaming series started

10 "main" *Tekken* games

3 *Tekken* movies

44 million *Tekken* games sold to date

11 brand new characters in Tekken 7

TOP 5 CHARACTERS

Akuma

1 The infamous *Street Fighter* boss makes a surprise appearance in the *Tekken* series, bringing his trademark moves with him. Akuma has his dragon punch, hurricane kick, and even his devastating "Raging Demon." He even keeps his fireball, so he's the only character with a good projectile!

Hwoarang

2 This light-footed fighter isn't for beginners, thanks to his dizzying array of fighting stances that need to be mastered. But to watch a Hwoarang pro in action can be spellbinding, as the Korean Taekwondo student fluidly dances around the arena in a blur of spins and kicks.

Jin

3 If you want to get inside your rival's head and cause mischief, pick Jin. He has plenty of attacks with awkward timing, and some convincing fake attacks too. Your opponent is never quite sure when—or where—to block. You can almost paralyze your opponent with fear!

Heihachi

4 The granddad of *Tekken* returns, and is stronger than ever, crushing his adversaries with powerful palm attacks. Heihachi might not be the flashiest fighter, but there are few better when it comes to taking huge chunks off your opponent's health bar with a handful of moves.

Xiaoyu

5 This Chinese martial artist can flip, dive, and roll around at will, using her speed to crack open the tiniest gaps in her opponent's defence. Her deadliest trick is turning her back, which makes her seem vulnerable, but actually opens a brand-new move list, just as her adversary drops its guard!

ALSO CHECK OUT . . .

Street Fighter V

The biggest fighting game around, *Street Fighter V* is the perfect 2-D alternative to *Tekken 7*. It's fast, it's frantic, and it's lots of fun.

Virtua Fighter 5: Final Showdown

Available through Xbox One's backwards compatibility, *Virtua Fighter 5: Final Showdown* isn't easy but rewards investment with a deep fighting game.

Injustice: Gods Among Us

Superman, Batman, The Flash and co. team up for a DC Comics brawl. It looks spectacular, and has some of the best-looking special moves seen in the genre.

TIPS & TRICKS

Learn combos

Some attacks will launch your opponent in the air, which lets you follow up with further attacks before they land. Learn these combos and use them.

Sidewalk and sidestep often

Tap up or down in order to sidestep, then hold up or down to walk in that direction. This is a fantastic tactic for moving out of the way of attacks.

Back dash out of trouble

Your instinct will be to block incoming attacks, but back dashing can be even more effective, as you can immediately attack back.

Alternate low and mid attacks

"Low" attacks need to be blocked low, while "mid" attacks need to be blocked high. Keep your opponent guessing by switching between the two.

SKYLANDERS
TOYS COME TO LIFE!

Skylanders **is one of the most successful gaming franchises of all time.** It was also the first game to implement the toys-to-life system that has proven so popular in the likes of LEGO *Dimensions* and Nintendo's amiibo figures. Every new game adds creative new mechanics. Whether you're racing around in cool vehicles, crushing

enemies with Giants, or even creating your very own Skylanders—a new feature in *Imaginators*—there's always something new to see or do. Best of all, each new game has full support for all existing figures. This means that your army of heroes only grows stronger with each new version of *Skylanders* that is released!

STATS

There are now
334 unique *Skylanders*
figures to collect, not including all the limited and special editions!

$$$$$
The series has made over
$3 billion

26
Skylanders Academy TV show has episodes across two seasons

Superchargers added
30 vehicle toys
which are also compatible with 2016's *Imaginators*

TOP 5 COOLEST CHARACTERS

Wash Buckler

1 We shouldn't really need to explain why a pirate octopus is awesome! Wash Buckler gets even cooler when you realize that he comes apart, allowing his tentacles to be used with any other *Swap Force* figure's torso. Perfect for letting other characters climb to new heights!

Master Starcast

2 Starcast is one of the new Sensei characters added in *Imaginators*. He's a four-armed space ninja equipped with huge, golden, throwing stars. The Dark element is extremely uncommon, making this stellar hero a great addition to any *Skylanders* team. Every good squad needs a ninja, right? Right.

Gearshift

3 Plucky Princess Gearshift uses the Great Gear as her weapon. It's that giant golden cog, which can be used both in disc form and as a pair of curved blades. She's a seriously cool character in her own right, but that amazing weapon secures her place on this list.

Fiesta

4 This magnificent mariachi band leader rolled into Skylands in his Crypt Crusher vehicle in *Superchargers*. He quickly became one of our favorite heroes! His trumpet weapon is lots of fun to use, and he can summon his Amigos too. This lets him dish out damage from a safe distance.

Shroomboom

5 The oldest character on this list, Shroomboom joined the fight in *Giants*, and—we just have to say it—he's a really fun guy! Using his custom-made slingshot, he fires various toadstool projectiles at his foes. He can even summon a larger catapult to launch *himself* as a projectile and cause maximum damage!

ALSO CHECK OUT . . .

LEGO Dimensions

Combining the build-it-yourself fun of LEGO sets with the toys-to-life thrills of *Skylanders*, LEGO *Dimensions* is superb. New figures and sets are adding to the cast all the time.

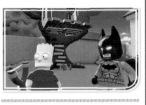

Ratchet & Clank

The main focus of this long-running series is its over-the-top weapons. These include a ball that makes enemies dance and a beam that turns them into sheep!

Knack

This PS4 launch title features a cool little character who grows bigger by collecting artefacts. Combat is a lot like that in *Skylanders*, so give it a try.

TIME LINE

2011 Skylanders: Spyro's Adventure
The original toys-to-life game, *Spyro's Adventure* created a whole new way to play.

2012 Skylanders: Giants
Introducing oversized Giants capable of accessing new areas, this added even more variety.

2013 Skylanders: Swap Force
Heroes could break in two, with sections able to be mixed and matched to create new ones.

2014 Skylanders: Trap Team
By using a Trap crystal, boss enemies could be captured and used in battle to assist your team.

2015 Skylanders: Superchargers
Vehicles were added, allowing your heroes to soar in the skies, carve up the waves, and screech around on land.

2016 Skylanders: Imaginators
Custom characters can be stored in Creation Crystals and used in the game. Make your own Skylanders!

TOP 10 UNIQUE GAMING EXPERIENCES

Rez: Infinite

1 Describing *Rez: Infinite* as a shooter doesn't do it justice. It's a visual feast, a VR roller coaster where the wireframe levels and enemies break up and re-form in front of your eyes. It's hypnotizing to watch, lulling you into a false sense of security before waves of enemies rush at you. You'll have to have fast reactions to take them down!

Sound Shapes

2 *Sound Shapes* is an enchanting mix of music and platforming. The levels pulse in time to the music, and the obstacles shift back and forth in time to the beats. If you've got any sense of rhythm in your fingers, you can dance through Sound Shapes with ease, tapping the buttons in time to the rhythm. It's fun and it's funky at the same time!

The Unfinished Swan

3 *The Unfinished Swan* is the story of a swan that escapes from a painting before it has been completed. With the game being told in black and white, except for the odd splash of color, *The Unfinished Swan* looks gorgeous. But it's the way you play *The Unfinished Swan* that truly stands out, as the world is a blank canvas until you fill it in by splattering black paint around.

HOW TO DISCOVER INTERESTING GAMES

Top tips for finding the best and most intriguing games

1 Browse the stores
Xbox One and PS4 stores have every game ever released for both systems, and you can often find gems just by browsing through the store. Search by release date to see what's new.

2 Use backwards compatibility
Xbox One now supports a wealth of Xbox 360 titles, so you can play some of the older games you might have missed out on.

3 Try Playstation Now
PlayStation Now is a streaming service that lets you revisit PlayStation classics on your PS4. It's perfect for games you didn't get to try before. Sadly, however, the service isn't free.

4 Ask your friends
This is an obvious source of information, but use it! Your friends may have different gaming taste than you but they'll be great to ask if you want to try a game you might not have considered.

5 Check popular YouTubers
YouTubers often play games just as they become popular, so you can feel like a trendsetter by discovering the "Next Big Game" and playing it first.

6 Check the sales
Sometimes the quirkier games receive hefty discounts because the developers want those games to find a bigger audience. Take a leap on games you're unsure about.

No Man's Sky

4 Your goal is to reach the center of the universe. *No Man's Sky* lets you explore space, as you investigate the unique planets and alien creatures living on them. The game has been designed in a way that you'll never see the same planet or creature more than once.

Tearaway Unfolded

5 *Tearaway Unfolded* looks like the world's biggest art class project, because everything is made out of paper. You use the lightbar and touchpad on your PS4 controller to solve the game's puzzles as you play.

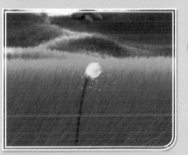

Flower

6 In *Flower*, you don't play as a person, or a robot . . . You play as a sort of spirit, drifting across fields and valleys, bringing life to the world around you. Flowers and plants bloom as you float past, in a game that doesn't have any levels to conquer, bosses to beat, or bad guys to fight.

The Swapper

7 *The Swapper* is a puzzle game where you clone yourself. You control yourself *and* the clone at the same time. Even the look of the game is unusual, with dark levels made from clay models. It sucks you into its world while confusing you with its tricky puzzles and unusual controls.

Dropsy

9 Dropsy relies entirely on sight and sound, as the character's animations and grunting tells you everything you need to know about the clown's life. It's a puzzle game where you have to figure out what to do as well as how to do it, making finding each solution feel even sweeter.

THE EXPERT SAYS . . . MICHELLE TURNER
Head of PR & Marketing, Ripstone

I absolutely love *Stick it to the Man*! The creativity in this game is so endearing, from the visual style of the world made from paper and stickers to the crazy story line involving a giant pink spaghetti arm sticking out of Ray, the main character's, head! This game has the perfect blend of puzzles and exploration, and is a great foray into the platform adventure-game genre for either the casual or hardcore gamer; people love speed-running this game, too. All this is superbly accompanied by a hilarious script—courtesy of Ryan North, the award-winning writer behind *Adventure Time*—which will have you laughing throughout.

Undertale

8 *Undertale* might not look bright and colorful, but it doesn't need slick graphics to draw players in. Every action you take in *Undertale* is considered "good" or "bad," but you won't know which is which until you've made the choice! *Undertale* makes you really think about everything you do. Even better, while you can fight all kinds of enemies in the game, you don't need violence to win. Whether you ask someone to dance or compliment them, there is always a peaceful solution!

I Am Bread

10 In video games, you can explore the farthest and darkest reaches of space. You can race the fastest vehicles known to humans. You can play as the greatest sports athletes on the planet. Or you can play as a floppy piece of bread. *I Am Bread* is one of the strangest games you'll ever play, as you control a piece of bread and try to flip your way into a toaster.

SPLIT SECOND

LEGO STAR WARS: THE FORCE AWAKENS

The best thing about this playful retelling of the seventh *Star Wars* movie isn't how closely it follows the plot of the film—it's the way it fills in the gaps around it by telling a bunch of new stories as well. One of these (our favorite of the lot, in fact) reveals how Poe Dameron originally rescued Admiral Ackbar from the clutches of the First Order. This is what helped establish and strengthen the Resistance's forces, and it plays out a little something like this . . .

1 Poe decides to sneak onto the Star Destroyer, where Ackbar is being held by stealing an imperial transport ship. The plan works, but breaking the Admiral out of his cell sounds the alarm! The First Order is quick to respond, so Poe has to think fast.

2 To escape the conflict, the group all leap down into a trash compactor (sound familiar?). Here, they're faced with several tentacled beasts and a series of devious puzzles to solve in order to avoid getting squished!

3 Back on the main deck of the Star Destroyer, Poe and Ackbar—with a little help from BB-8 and C-3PO, of course—must blast their way into the hangar and make their escape. They reach the transport and get out with just a few seconds to spare!

4 But of course, the First Order is hot on their heels. The chase runs through an asteroid field and ends on the surface of a giant rock, where Poe cunningly uses the local wildlife to help cover the group's escape. Way to go, Poe!

DID YOU KNOW?

Mario's trademark hat was originally created because his designer, Shigeru Miyamoto, apparently found it difficult to draw hair.

SUPER MARIO
GAMING'S SUPERSTAR ON THE ROAD

Whatever kind of game you want to play, Mario has you covered! Platform games are the Nintendo mascot's specialty, sure, but he does so much else, and does it really well. Racing around in *Mario Kart 8* is awesome, and so are the various sport games, such as *Mario Sports Superstars*. If you want something slower, the RPG action of *Paper Mario* and the level-building fun of *Super Mario Maker* are perfect. Out and about? Get *Super Mario Run* on your cell phone! And sometimes, you want to leap about in a classic platformer, grabbing coins, breaking blocks, and using cool powers, like in *Super Mario Odyssey*. So what are you waiting for? Let's-a-go!

STATS

6 Big Paint Stars in *Paper Mario: Color Splash*

5 sports in *Mario Sports Superstars*

120 black coins to collect in *Super Mario Run*

1 magic hat in *Super Mario Odyssey*

60 Battle Cards to choose from in *Paper Mario: Color Splash*

TOP 5 SUPER MARIO CHARACTERS

Mario

1 The hero of the Mushroom Kingdom is always ready to save the day! With the help of his friends, there's nothing Mario can't do. His new abilities in *Super Mario Odyssey* prove that you can always teach an old plumber new tricks.

Peach

2 The princess of the Mushroom Kingdom is always a tempting target for Bowser, and rescuing her is Mario's favorite pastime. Peach is fond of writing letters to Mario—we're guessing there's no cell phone reception in Bowser's dungeons.

Bowser

3 A great hero needs an equally great villain, and Bowser's latest plan is amongst his most fiendish. In *Super Mario Odyssey*, he has captured Princess Peach and is going to force her to marry him. Mario just won't stand for that, so he leaps into action to stop the Koopa King!

Yoshi

4 When Mario's in trouble, who does he call for help? You might think it's Luigi, but he can't eat enemies and doesn't allow him to ride around everywhere. Yoshi's a lot more useful like that, so our favorite dinosaur gets the nod here.

Toad

5 Of all the friendly little helpers that give Mario a hand, we like Toad and his friends the best. Why? Simple: most of Mario's other helpers don't make an awesome noise when you jump on them, but the Toads will react with hilarious squeaky dismay. It just never gets old!

TIPS & TRICKS

Soccer
If you're letting in too many goals, changing your formation to 4-5-1 puts a few more players in defense to help stop those goals.

Golf
Don't forget to always check the wind before you aim—Mother Nature can send even the straightest drive into the rough, so calculate it in.

Baseball
Don't forget that you can press X to activate a special pitch or swing if you have one charged up! It will secure you a great score.

Tennis
Sometimes, you will see a purple spot appear on the court—reach that spot in order to return a powerful smash shot to surprise your opponent.

Horse Racing
Try and explore alternative routes whenever you see them, so you can find which ones offer the quickest and easiest way to the finish.

MEET THE SUPERFAN

MITSUGU KIKAI

Who?
This Japanese *Mario* mega-fan has loved Nintendo's flagship series his whole life, as he was born in 1985, the year the original *Super Mario Bros.* was released for the NES. His collection stood at over 5,400 items back in 2010—the largest collection of *Mario* merch as officially recognized by Guinness World Records!

How?
The plan was never to have a record-breaking collection—Mitsugu simply added to it over time and it eventually grew to the crazy mountains of colorful fun that you see here over the course of many years. There's so much *Mario* stuff in total that it no longer fits in the room he has dedicated to it, meaning he has to store some of it elsewhere!

IN DEPTH

SUPER MARIO MAKER TRAPS

Tower of Terror
Take a group of normal bad guys and stack 'em high! Even a humble Goomba can become a fearsome foe when it's riding three of its friends into battle.

Flying Foes
An enemy without wings is a predictable enemy. Give Bowser's minions the ability to fly and watch them cause all sorts of havoc for anyone who plays your courses!

ALSO CHECK OUT

Sonic Mania
Mario's famous blue hedgehog rival is back in a new lightning-fast 2-D adventure, which combines the very best of his old classic hits with brand new levels and moves to try out.

Giant Goons

They might not be tougher, but bigger enemies are harder to avoid—that's a fact. Place them in narrow spaces if you feel like challenging the skills of other players.

THE EXPERT SAYS...
SHIGERU MIYAMOTO
Nintendo legend!

I'm really grateful because I think just by nature of being a creator, generally speaking, a lot of people who create—even if they make something of a high quality—make something that is really dear to them, but it's never publicized and it doesn't reach so many people. And that can be challenging sometimes. So I feel even more grateful as a creator that there are sometimes even people waiting to see my creation and anticipating it, and I just feel very lucky!

DID YOU KNOW?

Ever wonder why Luigi looks so much like Mario? His name comes from the Japanese word "ruiji," which means "similar."

Bargain Bowsers

You rarely get two-for-one deals on game bosses! One Bowser is tough enough, so putting a second one into play should be reserved for the hardest courses.

Ratchet & Clank

This remake of the original PlayStation 2 platformer is great for both old fans and newcomers, and it looks awesome. Explore the incredible sci-fi world and refamiliarize yourself with the series' unique style and quirks.

Shantae: Half-Genie Hero

After a lifetime on handheld platforms, our favorite magical platform star is now battling the pirate Risky Boots on home consoles, too. Enjoy it on the big screen and explore its magic world!

SEA OF THIEVES
A PIRATE'S LIFE FOR ME

DID YOU KNOW?
Pirates often used made-up surnames while at sea, so that their crimes would not tarnish their family name.

Being a pirate takes teamwork—which is why *Sea of Thieves* is all about working together as a crew. Someone must raise the anchor, someone needs to set the sails, and someone has to scurry up the crow's nest to give directions. All of your friends will have to play their part, and it just takes one mistake for anarchy to take over!

Sea battles are a real highlight of veteran developer Rare's new multiplayer pirate adventure. You must aim cannons, fight off boarding pirates, bail out water, make sure the ship is sailing the right way, and keep the crew calm. And this is just on the water—the pirate escapades and treasure hunting continue on land as well!

STATS

Rare formed in **1985**

4 GAMES made for Xbox One

OVER **100 MILLION** games sold to date

You Tube **910,000** YouTube views for E3 reveal

TOP 5 FOES

Your crew

1 That's right: the biggest enemies you'll face in *Sea of Thieves* are your own crew! You'll often have to deal with members of your crew who scupper your entire operation through their misdeeds. Keeping your crew straight and honest isn't easy—they are pirates, after all. Get them on your good side or expect a mutiny.

Kraken

2 This mythical sea creature roams the depths of the oceans, waiting to drag any unsuspecting ships down to a watery grave. You'll need near-flawless teamwork in order to escape its clutches; only the strongest crews will encounter a Kraken and live to tell the tale.

Skeletons

3 These bony creatures don't need grog for fuel. All they want is destruction and carnage! What these brittle foes lack in strength, they make up for in numbers. You need to decide whether to fight or flee when you meet them, and it's a decision you have to make right away, too.

Rival pirates

4 You're not the only seadogs scouring the seven seas searching for treasure. You will cross swords with other pirates too, who have a cunning plan that no other enemy can match. Be on your guard when they are around, and beware the cannon fire from their ships.

The Sea

5 You need to respect the ocean, as its crashing waves could be your downfall. Bad weather makes the open waters even more dangerous— think twice before you sail into a storm or your ship and all its precious cargo could be lost forever.

ALSO CHECK OUT...

Oceanhorn: Monster of Uncharted Seas

This bright and breezy adventure game set in a tropical paradise might not put you in the boots of a pirate, but you will still be sailing and treasure hunting.

Lost Sea

Recruit a crew of survivors to escape a mysterious island in the Bermuda Triangle, with traps and creatures standing between you and freedom.

LEGO Pirates of the Caribbean: The Video Game

The combination of Captain Sparrow and LEGO is hilarious. It will make anyone want to become a pirate!

TIME LINE

2006 Viva Piñata
Before *Sea of Thieves*, developer Rare enjoyed great success with this adorable gardening game.

2008 Banjo Kazooie: Nuts & Bolts
This return for platforming hero Banjo saw the bear building vehicles to complete races and quests.

2011 Kinect Sports: Season 2
This sequel added six new sports, including skiing and tennis.

2008 Viva Piñata: Trouble in Paradise
Taking the farming-animals-who-are-piñatas aspect as far as it could, it's one of Xbox 360's best games.

2010 Kinect Sports
Microsoft made Rare the champion of its Kinect peripheral, and this was one of its biggest games.

2014 Kinect Sports Rivals
When Kinect 2.0 launched for Xbox One, Rare had the brilliant *Kinect Sports Rivals* ready to go.

KINGDOM HEARTS

DISNEY, SQUARED!

No one could have predicted it: **characters from** *Final Fantasy* **and Disney uniting to save the universe of universes.** However, these worlds collided in 2002, and it was awesome. *Kingdom Hearts* is one of the most critically acclaimed and popular series in video gaming. The premise sounds crazy, but it all comes together into a fantastic action RPG with some unforgettable moments. *Kingdom Hearts* has an epic story, with awesome characters that will get you pumped and tug on your heartstrings. All of the mainline games and spinoffs are playable on current consoles thanks to the recent remasters, so check them out. You'll need to be ready for *Kingdom Hearts III* when that finally comes along, after all!

STATS

Nearly 5 million copies sold of the original game alone

Over 10m combined YouTube views for the E3 2015 trailer **You Tube**

14 unique entries in the series

5h 17m 31s speedrun record for the Japanese version of *Kingdom Hearts*

TOP 5 WORLDS

1 Halloween Town

Who *doesn't* like the spookiest time of the year? Halloween Town is perhaps the best-looking and most awesome-sounding area in all of *Kingdom Hearts*. Its delightfully quirky and crooked visuals are tricky to navigate, and its enemies are ghoulish and strong, making it a challenge as much as a delight.

2 Hollow Bastion

One of the more story-heavy worlds of *Kingdom Hearts*, if something is happening it's likely to be going on in Hollow Bastion. In the original *Kingdom Hearts*, this is where Maleficent reigns. It's a place where the Heartless gather, so be ready for a fight.

3 Hercules Colosseum

Where better to train than at a Colosseum under the tutorage of the mighty Hercules himself? This area hosts various tournaments you can enter, if you're feeling brave. Give it everything you've got and you may walk away with a cool prize!

4 Traverse Town

It's the first World that Sora visits after leaving his home in the first *Kingdom Hearts*. It's a place where castaways and drifters gather, and you will meet a bunch of *Final Fantasy* characters. It returns in *Dream Drop Distance*, throwing *The World Ends with You* characters in, too.

5 Hundred Acre Wood

Sometimes you need a break from the end-of-the-world nonsense to relax, and *Hundred Acre Wood* is just the place. In this colorful world, you'll spend most of your time reuniting a forgetful Winnie the Pooh with all of his friends. And eating honey, obviously.

TIME LINE

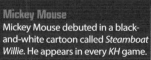

1928 Mickey Mouse
Mickey Mouse debuted in a black-and-white cartoon called *Steamboat Willie*. He appears in every *KH* game.

1932 Goofy
Introduced as Dippy Dawg in *Mickey's Revue*, he's close to Sora and Donald in *Kingdom Hearts*.

1934 Donald Duck
Appearing first in *The Little Wise Hen*, he is part of Sora's entourage in the main games.

1959 Maleficent
This wicked witch is from *Sleeping Beauty*. In *Kingdom Hearts* she thirsts for the power of the Heartless.

1999 Squall (Leon)
Squall comes from *Final Fantasy VIII*, and is the leader of Hollow Bastion in *Kingdom Hearts II*.

2002 Sora
The hero of *Kingdom Hearts*, Sora wields the Keyblade that combats the Heartless and operates locks.

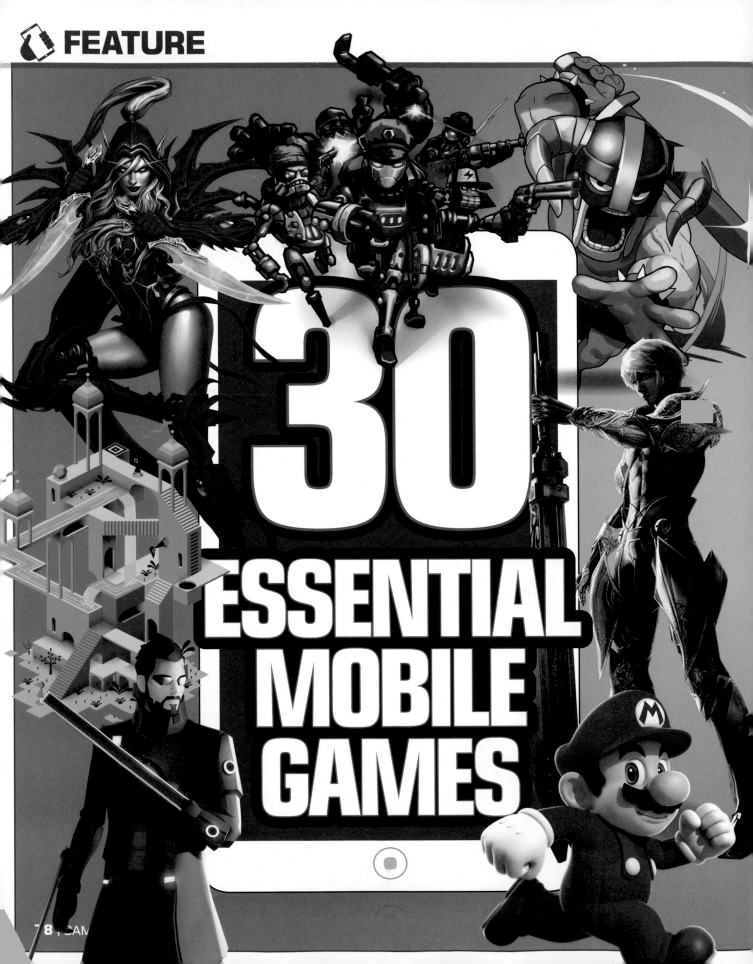

30 ESSENTIAL MOBILE GAMES

Dream Machine: The Game

iOS, Android

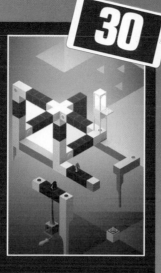

Dream Machine offers the same style of puzzles as the awesome *Monument Valley*—which you'll find later on this list. However, the number of tricky obstacles that you have to deal with quickly grows in this adventure. Most of your time will be spent staring at the screen, utterly confused, and trying to figure out a possible solution. This is definitely one for those who enjoy problem-solving and strategy games.

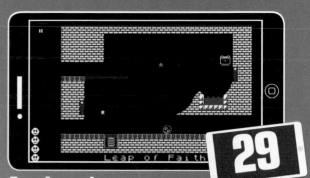

I Am Level **iOS, Android**

The creator of *I Am Level* has taken all of his favorite games and whizzed them together in a giant, retro blender. There are elements of pinball, phone-tilting, puzzling, exploring, and platforming, making *I Am Level* a gloriously unpredictable fusion of different genres that has something for everyone.

True Skate

iOS, Android

This is skateboarding for your fingers, as you flip and twist a board around a skate park using your digits rather than your feet. We should point out that learning how to pull off the cooler, high-scoring flips isn't easy, but it's rewarding once you master it. Once you start nailing those complex tricks and getting high scores, you'll feel like skating legend Tony Hawk himself.

Legend of Grimrock **iOS**

This old-school dungeon crawler revives a long-lost RPG style, as you plow through narrow tunnels and caves, trying to survive various underground horrors. The challenge is perfect throughout, the constant threat of a "game over" screen keeping you on your toes as you search for better weapons and armor in your battle for survival.

Burrito Bison: Launcha Libre

iOS, Android

Your eyes will strain to keep up with the action in *Burrito Bison*, which rockets past you like a roller coaster of colorful explosions. This is the perfect game to play in quick, short bursts. The 2-D platforming demands a steady hand as you guide Burrito Bison through the chaos, but it is such a frantic game that you will soon need a rest in order to stay sharp.

Mine Blitz

iOS, Android

You need to dig underground as quickly as you possibly can in *Mine Blitz*, dodging the spikes and bombs that are in your way. Catlike reactions are needed in order to survive, and the simple tap-to-dig gameplay makes it perfect for quick blasts of gaming. You'll revisit *Mine Blitz* time and time again in order to try and beat your scores, knowing that one small mistake could mean game over.

Mobius Final Fantasy
iOS, Android

24

Although retro *Final Fantasy* games have been ported to mobile before, there's something even better about the fact that *Mobius Final Fantasy* has been built specifically for playing on the move. Mixing complex card elements in with traditional RPG, you don't even need to be a fan of the genre to completely fall in love with its strategic gameplay.

DID YOU KNOW?
The *Final Fantasy VII* port on iOS has a cool and rather sneaky built-in cheat that instantly raises all of your stats to the maximum level possible.

23

Love You To Bits **iOS**

When Kosmo's robot girlfriend, Nova, suffers an accident, the young astronaut sets off on a journey to put her back together. This spellbinding puzzler oozes charm, as you poke and prod around places like alien shopping malls and robot discos to try to unearth pieces of poor Nova.

22

Rodeo Stampede: Sky Zoo Safari
iOS, Android

This game couldn't be any simpler to play. You hurtle through canyons and valleys on the backs of rampaging animals. You must hang on for dear life in order to try to win their hearts so that they will join your sky zoo. It's a fun test of your reflexes, and your heart will totally swell with pride as your zoo grows to show off all of your new animal friends.

Circa Infinity **iOS, Android**

21

Circles and circles and circles. *Circa Infinity* is basically a game of never-ending circles, as you try to find a safe spot to jump toward the middle of the spiraling anarchy. *Circa Infinity* is a game for those with fast reflexes, and the ability to quickly untangle a visual mess, since the game adds layer after layer of chaos. If your reflexes aren't already fast, they will be after playing this time and time again!

Knights of Pen & Paper 2
iOS, Android

20

In this unusual RPG twist, you're playing as children who are playing a tabletop RPG. While the dungeon master recites tales of goblins and treasure, you play as the party that sets out into unknown lands in order to discover it all. This game doesn't take itself too seriously, with plenty of jokes sprinkled throughout your journey. It's also easy to play in bite-size chunks, making it a perfect fit for mobile devices.

Don't Starve: Pocket Edition
iOS

19

The goal in this game is to avoid starving. That means you need to build a camp, find and cook food, keep warm, fend off attackers, and keep your mind healthy. It's a constant juggling act of assessing risk and deciding what to do next, as you try to survive the harsh *Don't Starve* wastelands.

Alto's Adventure iOS, Android

18

You play as a trick-happy snowboarder in *Alto's Adventure*, gliding through gorgeous scenery as you backflip over danger, and carve your way through the powder. Even though you need to be sharp in order to stay alive, *Alto's Adventure* is a soothing game to play if you let the serene soundtrack and dazzling art style wash over you.

17

Neko Atsume: Kitty Collector
iOS, Android

All you need to do in *Kitty Collector* is set out treats and toys in your yard, hoping to draw in local cats. However, you'll soon be sucked into the cute world of *Neko Atsume*, trying to figure out how to attract all 48 of the shy cats. It's so much fun that you'll find yourself checking in throughout the day in order to see how many feline visitors you have attracted!

16

SteamWorld Heist iOS

This turn-based shooter sees you taking command of an army of robots, trying to work out the right angles to ricochet your shots from. It doesn't matter if you have the necessary skill or not to succeed, as everyone will fall in love with the cast of charming characters and the hilarious humor.

Pokémon GO
iOS, Android

It was one of the most successful mobile game launches ever, and *Pokémon GO* is still going strong today. Ions of new Pokémon have been added to the game since it first came out, but the premise remains the same—go out and catch Pokémon in the real world, then train them up to take over Gyms. Oh, and keep an eye out for special events, when rare Pokémon are more likely to appear. You won't want to miss those! Just remember to stay safe when you're out hunting, and never go out on your own!

15

14

Real Racing 3 iOS, Android

There's no messing about when it comes to *Real Racing 3*. This is a hardcore racing simulation like *Gran Turismo*, which means it feels just like racing should in real life. This demands intense concentration and a steady hand, as you guide powerful muscle cars around each turn at top speed.

FTL: Faster Than Light iOS

13

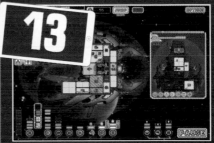

In *FTL: Faster Than Light* you control a spaceship as you try to save the galaxy, fighting rival pilots, and upgrading your ship. You have a wealth of options: re-routing power to engines to make a getaway, focusing everything on your weapons, trying to board enemy ships with your crew, and so on. With a series of random encounters making gameplay unpredictable—and death completely wiping out your progress—this is as tense as gaming gets.

Super Mario Run
iOS

12

Mario might be new to mobile runners, but *Super Mario Run* has quickly become the king of the genre. By tapping the screen, you can make Mario leap and flip through each level with style, collecting coins and bouncing on various enemies. You are even able to create your own kingdom, for those moments where you want to kick back and revel in your success. It's a lot of fun for fans old and new.

Telepaint **iOS**

11

With its tiny rooms and slow pace, you can dip in and out of *Telepaint* for quick bursts of gameplay. Don't expect an easy ride, though. Your job is to create a safe passage so a tiny pot of paint can reach the exit. The levels quickly escalate in difficulty, meaning you might find yourself thinking about the puzzles even when you're not playing.

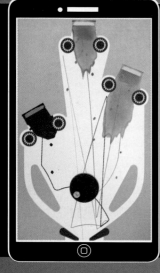

INKS.
iOS

10

It's the pinball and paint combination you never knew you needed. *INKS.* makes you feel just like an artist, as paint splashes around the table each time the ball crashes into something. You are even able to save and upload your very own messy masterpieces when you have finished them.

Hatoful Boyfriend **iOS, Android**

09

This is a dating game about pigeons. That's right— a dating game about *pigeons*. You will start playing *Hatoful Boyfriend* out of curiosity, but then stay for the story, because a surprising drama unfurls beneath its feathered exterior. This strange game certainly offers a unique experience.

DID YOU KNOW?

Hatoful Boyfriend is actually a modern remake of a Japanese dating game of the same name, which was made back in 2011.

08

Dropsy **iOS**

Dropsy is a rather sad clown who would—quite simply—like to make friends, offering warm and slightly damp hugs to those who he meets along the way. In this point-and-click adventure, you collect objects and work out the correct places to use them. From angry men in chicken suits to a dog known as "Eughh," the puzzles (and solutions) will be crazier than anything else you have played.

07

The Room Three **iOS, Android**

You're in a room with a box. You examine the box, looking at its mysterious carvings and symbols, to try to unlock the secret inside. This then leads to another room, with another box to crack, and on it goes. Spooky, mysterious, and challenging, this head-scratching puzzle game will keep you busy for ages.

The Trail
iOS, Android

This relaxing game puts you on a journey to Eden Falls, where you build a home and take up a profession. However, most of the game consists of walking, admiring the beautiful world around you, and collecting resources to build new items, such as clothing or slingshots. You can trade with other players or just enjoy a pleasant walk. It's like taking a relaxing vacation in the mountains through your mobile device.

06

05

Deus Ex GO **iOS, Android**
Deus Ex GO takes its high-paced, sci-fi action, and puts that gameplay into a tactical board game. The emphasis is on taking time to study the board, thinking a few steps ahead of the enemies. The turn-based gameplay and relatively small levels make it perfect for playing on the go.

04

Monument Valley
iOS, Android

You will want to reach in and touch this gorgeous game, with each puzzle looking just like a beautiful art print that you could hang on your wall. The captivating art style works hand-in-hand with a tricky puzzle game, which challenges everything you know about gravity, physics, and—well—common sense and logic!

Yu-Gi-Oh! Duel Links
iOS, Android

03

This free-to-play card game based on the popular series is awesome, and production values are through the roof! The simplified version of the real-life card game breathes new life into a lot of older cards, making for some clever and interesting deck ideas that you wouldn't usually see. New cards and events are added to the game frequently, too.

DID YOU KNOW?
The notion of interacting with the playing board in *Hearthstone* is an idea that came from the popular Robin Williams movie *Jumanji*.

01

Hearthstone: Heroes of Warcraft **iOS, Android**

If you have any embers of competitive fire burning in your soul, you must play *Hearthstone*. This tactical card game is built around stoking your competitive spirit until it's a raging inferno, as you obsess over the perfect playing deck to trip up your opponents. Each card has a different property—some summon beasts, some cast defensive spells, some paralyze your opponent's cards, and so on. The bigger challenge than building a powerful deck is figuring out how to stop your opponent's!

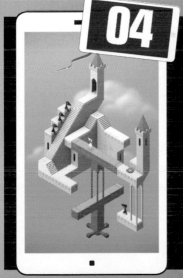

02

Crashlands **iOS, Android**

Crash landing on an alien planet, you set up camp and start exploring your mysterious new world. Far from being a hapless survivor, you soon become hostile invader, fighting back against the aggressive creatures who all want a curious nibble of your hide. It's the mystery of what might be around the next corner that makes this game difficult to put down.

CAPTURE THIS!

STARDEW VALLEY

Ship 15 of every crop

This achievement will take some diligent farming, and it'll most likely take quite a few in-game years! Different types of crops grow in each season—there are 11 unique to spring, 13 for summer, and 10 in fall. Grow and deliver 15 of each and you'll unlock a sweet cowboy hat for your character!

YO-KAI WATCH
MONSTERS ON YOUR WRIST

This ghost-chasing adventure is like *Pokémon* with a twist—literally! You spin a wheel on the 3DS to call new monsters into battle, rather than selecting them from a menu. Special moves, called Soultimate attacks, will have you playing a mini-game on the touchscreen before they're unleashed. You might have to tag spheres, or spin

dials, or break chains, or any number of things. The gameplay is highly tactical, too. Combat is automatic, but this means being powerful is more about having a mixed squad of different types than worrying about individual moves. If you like *Pokémon*, you're sure to enjoy making cool new friends in *Yo-kai Watch* as well!

STATS

6 Yo-kai Watch games

Yo-kai **manga**

11 manga volumes have been released

148 anime episodes

1 animated movie

TOP 5 YO-KAI TRIBES

Charming

1 Yo-kai that belong to the Charming tribe overwhelm their opponents with lightning speed rather than raw power. Jinbanyan is a perfect example, beating his adversaries to the punch, and ensuring he gets the first few hits in as the battle begins.

You became friends with Jibanyan.

Eerie

2 Yo-kai like Slush belong to the Eerie tribe, thanks to their spooky looks that will send a chill up your spine. They can even freak their opponents out, causing their defense to lower or their attacks to get weaker. This makes Eerie Yo-kai the perfect choice to use at the start of a battle.

Mysterious

3 Magic is the specialty of the Mysterious tribe. It's home to some of the more powerful Yo-kai in the game: Statiking, Tengu, and Frostail are a few of the characters in this impressive band of sorcerers. If you need damage, use Mysterious Yo-kai.

You found Dulluma!

Shady

4 The Shady tribe will do whatever it takes to win. To lower the stats of your opponent, use a Yo-kai from the Shady tribe to make Yo-kai easier to capture and use in your own team.

Heartful

5 These Yo-kai act as healers in combat. While it might not be the most exciting trait, it's one of the more useful abilities in the game. You should always keep a Heartful Yo-kai on standby for the trickier battles, to heal the wounded.

TIPS & TRICKS

Item fusion
You can fuse Yo-kai with certain items. One great combination is fusing Shmoopie and a Love Scepter to create Pinkipoo, a useful and adorable healer.

Yo-kai fusions
You can also fuse two Yo-kai together. Try fusing two Castelius of the same rank together to get a stronger version for your team.

Use the radar
The Yo-kai radar is perfect for helping you to track down some of those invisible critters that are sneakily hidden throughout the city.

Two tribes
You are able to use two Yo-kai from the same tribe in battle in order to receive a bonus, such as a Defense boost for your team.

Escape battle
If you are slightly worried about losing a battle, using the Getaway Plush item lets you make a speedy getaway. No need to take risks!

FINAL FANTASY
THE GREATEST RPG SERIES EVER?

Final Fantasy has long established its dominance as the biggest RPG series in the world. It outshines the competition with graphics that dazzle all who see them, as well as epic orchestral soundtracks. But it doesn't stop there, as it's the gameplay that keeps the most dedicated RPG fan on their toes. Nowhere is this more evident than *Final Fantasy XV*, a colossus of a game that is quite simply one of the biggest ever made. But there are so many different options with *Final Fantasy*. Whether it's *World of Final Fantasy*'s cute characters or the massive online world of *A Realm Reborn*, there's something in this series for everyone.

STATS

Series started in **1987**

Over **115 million** copies sold

Final Fantasy VII sold **9,500,00** copies worldwide

Final Fantasy XIII sold **1,000,000** copies on its first day on sale

Final Fantasy XIV had over **1,000,000** subscribers in its first two months

TOP 5 FINAL FANTASY GAMES

Final Fantasy XV

1 This is the biggest *Final Fantasy* of them all, combining Hollywood blockbuster visuals with a massive open world to explore. Battles turn into messy free-for-alls, with all four of your party members fighting at the same time. It's beautiful, it's chaotic, and it's the game every *Final Fantasy* fan has dreamed of.

World of Final Fantasy

2 This is the cutest *Final Fantasy* has ever been, as characters from its past and present are brought together in a celebration of the series. The gameplay twist here is that you can capture monsters and stack them on your head, inheriting their unique powers.

Final Fantasy X HD

3 This HD remaster shows that the gameplay of this classic RPG hasn't aged a day since its release. It's got tons of playable characters, plenty of puzzles, lots of secrets to discover, and some of the most colorful creations that have ever graced the series. It's well worth playing it again in HD!

Final Fantasy XIV: A Realm Reborn

4 After a lackluster launch that left fans and critics disappointed, Square-Enix made massive changes to *Final Fantasy XIV* and tried again. The relaunch, *A Realm Reborn*, is fantastic. It has a wealth of content, giant bosses, and a whole range of classes for players to choose from.

Final Fantasy: Brave Exvius

5 This *Final Fantasy* adventure was created specifically for mobile devices, with graphics that pop on the small screen and gameplay designed for short bursts of gameplay. It can be played with swipes and taps, so it's perfect for playing on the go. There are several other cool *Final Fantasy* games on mobile devices, too.

TIPS & TRICKS

Use elements wisely
Match your spells to your enemy's element. Use Fire spells on Ice enemies, Water spells on Electrical enemies, and so on.

Always pack Phoenix Downs
Phoenix Downs are feathers that will revive knocked out members in your party. Always have a handful in your inventory just in case.

Have a healer in your party
Healers have spells like Cura or Regen, which restore health to the group. It's essential you have a healer in battle.

Save MP for stronger battles
Magic Points are usually restored with items or by resting, so save them for tough battles. You don't want to run out before then.

Check everywhere
Each *Final Fantasy* is stuffed with secrets, so check every path, nook, and cranny, to look for chests you might have missed.

MEET THE SUPERFAN

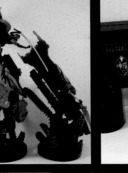

FF MUSEUM

Who?
This group of avid collectors was formed in 2006 as a way for founder Fabien Haule to share his rare merchandise with fans that may otherwise never get to see any of it. Since then, Fabien has been joined by four other superfans, and today the FF Museum team's combined collection is among the world's biggest.

What?
You name it, these guys almost certainly have it! Highlights include a full-scale replica of Judge Gabranth's helmet from *Final Fantasy XII* and a plate depicting Yoshitaka Amano's gorgeous art from *Final Fantasy VI*'s Japanese cover. Both of these super-rare pieces were limited to just 500 copies worldwide.

IN DEPTH — BEST BOSSES

Odin (A Realm Reborn)
In *Final Fantasy*, Odin often serves as a giant guardian you summon to fight by your side. In *A Realm Reborn*, however, he becomes a terrifying opponent, riding into combat in jet-black armor.

Anima (Final Fantasy X HD)
Your nemesis in *Final Fantasy X* is Seymour, but it's his powerful summon, Anima, who proves to be a far tougher battle. With a massive pool of health and some deadly attacks, outlasting her is really tough.

ALSO CHECK OUT...

Dragon Quest
Dragon Quest is a lighter take on traditional RPGs, focusing more on humor than dark story lines. *Dragon Quest Builders* is the latest entry, combining RPG elements with building.

THE EXPERT SAYS...

ALEX DONALDSON

Publisher, rpgsite.net

One of the coolest things about *Final Fantasy XV* is that it manages to do something all new with the classic series formula. Almost all of the elements that made gamers love much of the series over the past 30 years are present, but this time they've been shoved into a more open game. It's a mix of old and new that has its flaws but is most importantly fun and exciting to play, with a world that you'll lose hours exploring. In many ways, it channels the same spirit that made the original *Final Fantasy* a hit.

Behemoth (Final Fantasy XV)

Behemoth Is the first giant boss you tackle in *Final Fantasy XV*. Although later bosses are even bigger, none are as terrifying as your initial Behemoth encounter. You really feel like you're the ones being hunted as you stalk this huge beast . . .

DID YOU KNOW?

The Intelligence stat in *Final Fantasy* games indicates the strength of your magic power, but in the first game it didn't actually make any difference at all!

Vivi (World of Final Fantasy)

The adorable black mage from *Final Fantasy IX* returns for *World of Final Fantasy*. But before the sorcerer joins your team, you have to defeat him in combat and overcome his incredible magical powers.

Kingdom Hearts

The crossover between the Disney universe and *Final Fantasy* is an action-packed RPG adventure that sees you fighting off waves of magical enemies throughout the Disney kingdom. Every game in the series is stellar.

I Am Setsuna

I Am Setsuna is as close to a retro *Final Fantasy* outing as modern games get, focusing almost entirely on story and atmosphere to draw you into its world. It's a captivating game with a surprising amount of depth to it.

MINECRAFT
THE GAME THAT NEVER STOPS GROWING

DID YOU KNOW?

The version of *Minecraft* that has been modified in order to work on VR headsets is actually called *Vivecraft*.

The biggest game in the world keeps getting bigger. Mojang continues to add more thrilling content to *Minecraft*, so veterans have something new to play with, and fans have a reason to return. Those who defeat the legendary final boss, the Ender Dragon, can now head to End Cities, spooky lost ruins filled with End Ships, Chorus Plants, Chorus Flowers, and Purpur Blocks. Battling the Ender Dragon has changed too, thanks to a huge combat update that added dual-wielding. Amplified terrain also adds giant mountains and hills, and new multiplayer modes and levels make playing with friends even more fun! Who knows where *Minecraft* will take us next?

STATS

MORE THAN 121 MILLION copies of *Minecraft* sold worldwide

4 main modes

Released on **14 formats** including Xbox One and PS4

4 levels of difficulty

55 million people play every month

TOP 5 DOWNLOAD PACKS

1 Chinese Mythology Mash-Up Pack

Chinese Mythology takes elements of Far East culture and stuffs them into this mash-up pack, bursting at the seams with 41 skins and 13 new music tracks. Whether you want fearsome Chinese dragons, or to play as characters from the old Chinese tale *Journey to the West*, this pack really does have it all.

2 Battle Map Pack 3

For those who love chaos, *Battle Map Pack 3* has three arenas to fight in. Castle comes  with ramparts and banquet tables to fight on. Invasion shows off a modern city after an alien presence has destroyed it. And Shipyard is a map based on a suspended airship.

3 Tumble

Tumble is a new game mode. You must destroy the floor beneath your  opponent's feet, so they tumble to their doom. You're armed with a shovel or snowball, and must decide whether to battle from the high ground or jump down to shoot the floor away from underneath your opponent.

4 Redstone Specialists

A good *Minecraft* pack can elevate the experience massively. The cool *Redstone Specialists* skin  pack is a great example of this, since you can show your appreciation for all things mechanical by styling yourself after *Minecraft*'s technical wizards.

5 Minecon

This free *Minecon* downloadable pack is bursting with content, with four different skins to use. It has Forest Fighter, Ice Pioneer, Mesa Artisan, and our favorite, Ocean Engineer. What better way to celebrate the biggest *Minecraft* convention in the world?

ALSO CHECK OUT . . .

Terraria

Can you imagine what a 2-D version of *Minecraft* would be like? Well, you don't have to, because it already exists. *Terraria* has the same mix of crafting, building, and surviving.

Ace of Spades

If *Minecraft* were a shooter rather than a platformer, this is what it would be like. The FPS action and building means *Aces of Spades* is a game where you rarely sit still.

Cube World

It's *Minecraft* meets RPG in this unusual crossover, as you level up, battle goblins, and embark on epic quests. It's one for *Minecraft* fans who particularly love solo adventures.

TIPS & TRICKS

A sandy hint
Instead of wasting your shovel on sand or gravel, dig out the bottom block and instantly place a torch where it was to quickly destroy the sand blocks above as they fall.

Peaceful mode
If you can't find any food to eat, or you're struggling with enemies, set the game to Peaceful mode. Your health will regenerate and enemies disappear.

Creating a spawn point
If you have three wool and three wooden planks, you can build a bed. Sleep in it and it will become your new spawn point—until an enemy breaks it!

Emergency shelter
To create shelter in an emergency, find a small hill and dig a few blocks into it. Block up the entrance and place a torch to survive the night.

Enemy sensor
Surround your house with wooden planks so you can hear mobs walking on them, letting you know that you're not alone.

TOP 10 COOLEST LEVELS

One-Eyed Dragon
King's Quest

1 *King's Quest* opens with a bang, as you shimmy down a rope into a deep, dark cave that's home to a one-eyed dragon. You must outsmart and sneak past the dragon to steal the valuable mirror it's guarding. The battle of wits as you try to steer clear of the dragon's fatal fiery breath is brilliant.

Sand Slide
Journey

2 There are moments, rather than levels, in *Journey*. The standout moment is when you slide down a golden slope of sand. As the Sun shimmers across the sandy surface, the camera glides to your side, highlighting a towering mountain in the distance, breaking the horizon.

Mad Hatter's Tea Party
Batman: Return To Arkham

3 Dig deep into the secret hiding places of Arkham City and you might stumble upon the lair of Mad Hatter. The strange villain uses mind control on Batman, and the caped crusader ends up fighting Mad Hatter's goons on a giant, floating pocket watch.

6 GAMES WHERE YOU MAKE YOUR OWN LEVELS

Super Mario Maker
After decades of creating some of the greatest levels seen in gaming, Nintendo took a break and gave us a turn at creating future classics with *Super Mario Maker*.

Rocket League
You aren't really creating levels, but with the options to change settings in multiplayer matches, including how much gravity there is, you can almost create a new game.

Trackmania Turbo
This insane racer has you driving upside down, leaping massive gaps and doing flips. Build your own crazy tracks, then challenge your friends to a race!

WWE 2K17
Using its creation tools, you can put together your own wrestlers, finishing moves, and even arenas. You can build all three and create your own pay-per-view event.

Sea of Thieves
Sail the seven seas searching for treasure, create missions for other motley crews to tackle, or even create missions for your own crew to play when they go online.

Tony Hawk's Pro Skater 5
Create-A-Park mode lets you pull together rails and ramps to build your own skateboarding arena of joy.

Mount Wario
Mario Kart 8

4 Mount Wario feels like a snowboarding race that has snuck in among the *Mario Kart 8* courses. Rather than looping around a track, Mount Wario takes you down a snowy mountain, each lap indicating how far down you are. It's a thrilling chase, and the finale—where you jump from a plane and race in front of a huge crowd of cheering spectators—is gaming at its best.

THE EXPERT SAYS...
ANDY ROBINSON
Writer, *Yooka-Laylee*

My favorite level in gaming was discovering Hyrule Field in *Zelda: Ocarina of Time*. It was an incredible moment. It was one of the first epic, 3-D adventure games, so the sense of scale in this seemingly endless grassland felt amazing. The freedom to explore Hyrule felt like a breakthrough moment for games at the time, and I couldn't wait to discover what lurked over the horizon.

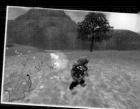

Buggy Versus Helicopter
Forza Horizon 3

5 *Forza Horizon 3* offers every possible vehicle on four wheels, which means you get to take part in odd showdowns—getting behind the wheel of a buggy to race against a Jeep, for example. *Forza Horizon 3* makes the race stranger still by having the jeep being towed by a helicopter, which means you have to drive off-road to keep up.

Fallen Rocks
Steep

7 Fallen Rocks is just under 30 seconds of pure survival. Using your wingsuit, you glide between two cliff faces with razor-sharp rocks jutting out at every angle. It's a pure adrenalin rush with no room for error, as you squeeze through every narrow gap while hoping for the best. It's a thrilling, white-knuckle ride.

Yourself
Axiom Verge

6 If you want to play this sci-fi shooter, look away, as this will spoil one of the coolest surprises in *Axiom Verge*. There's a section where you play as one of the bosses and fight against yourself. The computer controls your character while you control the boss, in a daring switcheroo that changes how you play.

Center Perks
The Escapists

8 The first of the six prisons to break out of in this game is Center Perks. It's here that you learn how to scavenge materials, create items, make friends with the prisoners, follow the daily routine, and ultimately form an escape plan. You'll know every brick of Center Perks by the time you break free.

Helicarrier Havoc
LEGO Marvel's Avengers

9 It's the scene from the first *Avengers* movie where the Helicarrier comes under attack from Loki, albeit in LEGO form. This level rockets along, capturing everything that makes the scene so frantic. Levels are rarely this action-packed.

Bullet Bill Barrage
Super Mario Run

10 Bullet Bill Barrage is World 3-2 in *Super Mario Run*, and it's really exciting. You have to hop on the back of Bullet Bills to grab all the Pink Coins hidden away in this level, leaping from bullet to bullet as Mario soars through the clouds. It's a bouncy slice of platforming fun that has more joy in its 60 seconds of gaming than most games manage in 60 levels.

TOP **10** WEIRD SPORTS GAMES

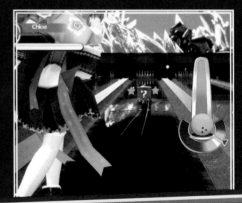

Crazy Strike Bowling EX

2 This isn't your standard 10-frame game at the local bowling alley. *Crazy Strike Bowling EX* takes the action to exotic locations like the Egyptian pyramids and adds power-ups, while each character has a pin-clearing special move to use. There's even a challenge mode if you want to test yourself, where instead of knocking pins down, you have to dodge all of the obstacles, almost as if you've become the pins yourself.

Dangerous Golf

1 You'll come for the golf and you'll stay for the mayhem, because these golf courses are set inside places like shops, art museums, bathrooms, and other areas filled with breakable objects. *Dangerous Golf* taps into our primal urge to smash things up. Here, it's actively encouraged, as you make a mess while smashing the ball into the hole with the fewest shots possible.

6 SERIOUS SPORTS SIMULATIONS

Because sometimes, you'd rather enjoy the real deal than play something silly . . .

1 DIRT RALLY
From tweaking the gear ratios to the realistic physics, *Dirt Rally* is a pure simulation of driving. *Dirt Rally* shows just how dangerous and thrilling off-road racing can be, with one small mistake sending you flying off the track.

4 GRAN TURISMO SPORT
Gran Turismo Sport is focused solely on re-creating the feeling of real driving with genuine cars, exciting racetracks based on real locations, and incredible graphics detail. It's one of the best-looking racers ever made!

2 F1 2016
Whether you're playing as Lewis Hamilton or rising up the ranks as a new driver, *F1 2016* is a painstaking simulation of the world's fastest motorsport, even down to the buttons on the steering wheel.

5 MADDEN NFL
Madden NFL goes deep into the heart of football, even allowing you to become general manager and change everything about your team, from its roster to its logo. If it's in football, it's in *Madden.*

3 PRO EVOLUTION SOCCER
From chipped through-balls to tricks like rabonas, *Pro Evolution Soccer* has always strived to capture every move seen on a soccer field. The controls are complicated but they need to be, because so much is packed in.

6 NBA 2K17
One of the best modes in *NBA 2K17* has you playing as a rookie, earning the trust of the coach through scoring points, grabbing rebounds, and sticking with defensive assignments. It feels just like the real thing might.

Kung Foot

3 What would soccer look like if you played with feet five times their normal size? *Kung Foot* has the answer. This mini-game is hidden inside *Rayman Legends* and pits up to four players against each other as they charge up their kicks and smash the ball across the field.

Handball 17

4 Handball is a relatively uncommon sport that involves players trying to throw the ball into their opponent's goal. The main skill is passing the ball around to open a tiny crack in your opponent's defense, so you can shoot at the goal. It's ideal if you want something a bit different.

Sportsfriends

5 It's four games in one! *BaraBariBall* is a fusion of volleyball and *Super Smash Bros.*, *Super Pole Riders* is a pole-vaulting showdown, and *Hokra* is a bit like hockey. There's also *Johann Sebastian Joust*—keep your controller steady while trying to make other players wobble theirs.

Rocket League

7 *Rocket League*'s perfect blend of soccer and rocket-powered cars has dominated the world of gaming. But there's more to the game than its mid-air acrobatics as you try to hit the ball into the goal. It now has basketball and hockey modes too, via a free update for all *Rocket League* owners—triple the sports fun for no extra cost.

Headmaster

9 VR allows for totally new kinds of sport games, and *Headmaster* is a great example. It's a game built around heading a soccer ball. You need to complete a series of tasks and mini-games by heading the ball. It's the perfect blend of comedy, gaming, and exercise.

Super Mega Baseball

6 There's one little gameplay trick that makes *Super Mega Baseball* ridiculously fun. You can charge your bat before the pitch is thrown. Unleashing your charge at the right time will see you smash the ball right into the bleachers.

#IDARB

8 *#IDARB* is an unusual combination of sports and platforming, as you try to outscore the other team. Long-range shots earn more points but are harder to score. *#IDARB* is at its best with lots of players huddled together, shouting at each other as everyone fights over the ball.

100ft Robot Golf

10 This is a game that does exactly as the title suggests. Since you're too big to play on normal golf courses, you have to ping the ball around a city instead. It's a lot more action-packed than traditional golf!

DID YOU KNOW?

Forza Horizon 3 is also available on PC, and is one of the few games that PC and Xbox One owners can play together online.

FORZA HORIZON 3
THE BIGGEST RACING FESTIVAL EVER

The *Forza Horizon* series has always been about fun. It doesn't get much better than behind the wheel of exotic cars in a series of racing festivals across different cities. However, the roles are reversed for *Forza Horizon 3*. This time, you're the director of a festival. You create races and events, and you get to hire the racers,

too. You can build your dream racing playground for you and your friends to enjoy, with ridiculous events like racing against freight trains, chasing helicopters through fields, or outrunning "infected" cars. With four-player co-op, you can create the kinds of stories that you all share long after you've crossed the finish line.

STATS

350 cars available from launch

4-player co-op

7 downloadable car packs available

You Tube **4,500,000** views for official E3 trailer

Map **2** times as big as *Forza Horizon 2*

TOP 5 CARS

Halo Warthog

1 The ultimate gaming crossover, the Warthog from *Halo* has arrived in *Forza* with a Twin Turbo V8 engine and 720 horsepower. It's not the fastest vehicle in *Horizon 3*, but it's definitely the most intimidating — no one is going to sideswipe you while you're racing in this monster.

2014 HSV GTS

2 For 75,000CR, you can buy a car that ticks every box in *Forza Horizon 3*. It has smooth handling, acceleration that will push you back in your seat, and a blistering top speed. Listen to the raw, throaty growl of that engine to really get your money's worth.

Ford Fpv Pursuit

3 This brute of a car is designed for off-road rallies, meaning you can shrug off impacts with trees, rocks, or whatever else is in your way. It hasn't sacrificed speed for power either, as this versatile car can hit absolutely crazy speeds on straights.

1974 Holden Sandman

4 There's nothing special about this car. It doesn't handle gracefully, it's not the fastest, and it isn't fast off the blocks. So why bother? Because there's nothing more satisfying than beating your friends in a race using this hunk of junk.

Ariel Nomad

5 A big part of the *Forza* fun is heading off-road to see what's hidden in the world, and how far you can actually *go*. The Ariel Nomad is the perfect vehicle for exploration, its bouncy suspension allowing you to jump over bumps and hills with ease.

ALSO CHECK OUT . . .

Dirt Rally

Forza Horizon 3 has a lot of off-road action in slippery fields and on gravel tracks, so why not play a racing game exclusively dedicated to off-road racing?

Need for Speed

With its multiplayer, open-world structure, *Need for Speed* lets players pick and choose where their races are and who they race with.

Project CARS

A racing game that focuses on the serious rather than the silly. *Project CARS* is unforgiving, but master its strict handling and it can be extremely rewarding.

TIPS & TRICKS

Rewind for stunts

When attempting a Danger Jump stunt, remember you can rewind if your approach isn't quite right. This effectively gives you two shots at the stunt.

Don't always listen to Anna

Anna, your sat-nav, always uses roads to track your destination. But don't forget that you can drive off-road, through fences, over mountains, and so on.

Skill songs

When a skill song plays on the radio, you get a x2 points bonus. Listen to the classical station, as these songs will last the longest.

Check the Forza Hub

You'll often earn CR or other rewards just for checking in, so make sure it becomes habit to check the Forza Hub to see what's going on.

Earning CR

Buy the Horizon Promo perk to take pictures, then at the start of each race, snap the cars bunched together for a huge CR reward.

GRAN TURISMO SPORT

THE MOST REALISTIC GAME EVER MADE

DID YOU KNOW?
The GT Awards, now in its 15th year, is a show where enthusiasts present their custom cars and the winner appears in *Gran Turismo*.

Want to know how driving a supercar feels? *Gran Turismo* is all you need. Sony's series has strived for realism ever since it began, wanting to re-create the power of sitting behind the wheel of a real car and feeling the engine's roar shaking your bones. *Gran Turismo Sport* takes it even further, letting you slip into the driver's seat of luxury cars like the Ferrari LaFerrari '13. You can drive around tracks like the NASCAR-inspired Northern Isle Speedway, the dense urban jungle of Tokyo Expressway, or the Mexican desert in Dirt Course. With a wealth of game modes and stunning graphics, *GT Sport* is everything a driver could possibly want in one gleaming package.

STATS

Gran Turismo series has sold **76.74 million** copies worldwide

5 years to develop the original *Gran Turismo*

1,226 cars in *Gran Turismo 6*

100 tracks in *Gran Turismo 6*

15 games in *Gran Turismo* series

TOP 5 GRAN TURISMO SPORT FEATURES

ALSO CHECK OUT ...

Forza Motorsport 6

Gran Turismo Sport is a PlayStation4 exclusive. Xbox One owners wanting realistic driving thrills still have the brilliant *Forza Motorsport 6* to play, though.

Gran Turismo Sport Live

1 *Gran Turismo Sport* isn't just fun to play. You can also watch other top players racing around the tracks at record-setting speed, live, thanks to *Gran Turismo Sport Live*. And, to make the experience even better, course cameras and live commentary make it feel like you're watching a real racing show.

Driveclub

Driveclub is more of an arcade racer than a realistic one, which means it's easier to play and feels like a game rather than a driving simulator.

Scapes

2 Photo Mode isn't new for racing games, but Scapes takes this to a whole new level. You can place your favorite car in more than 1,000 locations around the world, from Germany's famous Nürburgring to Japanese temples in Tokyo, before snapping the perfect shot.

Sport mode

3 Are you the next racing champion? Or do you trundle around the first corner as the pack speeds by? Sport Mode takes your skill and racing behavior into account, matching you with similar players so you never have to feel outmatched by veterans or embarrassed by the competition.

Original cars

4 Although it's not strictly a mode, *Gran Turismo Sport* has real cars that have been given fantasy twists to fit the *Gran Turismo* world. That means everything from the steering wheel to the wing has been tweaked. You'll get to drive cars that you can't use anywhere else.

Livery Editor

5 *Gran Turismo Sport* gives you a chance to get creative too, thanks to its Livery Editor. This lets you make your own decal to put on your car, and you can even swap your designs with friends. You can combine this with Scapes to create stunning, original work.

Dirt Rally

For something a little different try *Dirt Rally*, which takes the racing off-road and demands full concentration at all times for you to even finish a race.

TIPS & TRICKS

Brake early
It's better to brake early before corners and lose time that way than to brake late and hit a barrier, clip a rival, or spin out.

Take corners on the outside
Get into the habit of taking corners from the outside, so you can cut in toward the inside of the corner, making turns easier and faster.

Learn each course
Practice a course at least once before racing on it, so you know where the tricky turns are and when to slow right down.

Try different cars
Each car handles differently, depending on braking power and the type of car it is. Try them all and stick with your favorite.

SUPER SMASH BROS.

BATTLE ROYALE, NINTENDO STYLE!

DID YOU KNOW?

Despite being over 15 years old, *Super Smash Bros. Melee* is still one of the most-played fighting games at tournaments such as EVO.

For any Nintendo fan, *Super Smash Bros.* is a dream come true. It's more than just a crossover fighting game—it's a celebration of all things Nintendo. *Smash* games are packed with characters, stages, music, items, and other references from all of the biggest and best games. Unlike many fighters, *Smash* is also really easy to play. Special moves are performed at the touch of a button rather than with complex commands,

and devastating *Smash* attacks are almost as easy. Flick the stick while attacking and you'll unleash a powerful blow that can send weakened opponents flying. Blast them off the stage to win!

Every *Smash Bros.* game comes loaded with awesome content, from unlockable characters and stages, to Trophies that delve even further into the Nintendo archives. It's really fun in multiplayer, too, so grab a controller and get Smashing!

STATS

58 unique characters in the 3DS/Wii U games

5,034  entrants at the EVO 2016 tournament, across two games (*Melee* and *Wii U*) with over $50,000 total prize money!

Nearly $$40 million *Super Smash Bros.* games have been sold

72 different Pokémon can come out of the Poké Balls across all *Smash Bros.* games

TOP 5 COOLEST AMIIBO

Get more from *Smash* with some of these super-awesome figures

Greninja (*Pokémon* series)

1 The fully evolved form of lovable *Pokémon X/Y* starter, Froakie, Greninja is one of the most popular and powerful characters in the series. Leveling up this amiibo will make it a dangerous foe in *Smash,* too. It can be hard to use well due to its tricky moves, so just let the AI do it for you!

Olimar (*Pikmin* series)

2 Olimar uses his plant-like Pikmin friends to help him fight, making him a totally unique character. By using this amiibo and watching how the AI plays as him, though, you might get a better idea of how all his moves work.

R.O.B. (Famicom hardware)

3 If you don't recognize this guy, don't worry—that's just because he's really old! R.O.B. was a peripheral for the Famicom console that only came out in Japan. He just stacked things back then, but he's *much* more versatile in *Smash*!

Bowser Jr. (*Mario* series)

4 Bowser's cute son offers a completely different playstyle thanks to his Clown Car. It's packed with tools and gadgets to give him the upper hand in battle. You'll see this as soon as you power up this awesome amiibo.

King Dedede (*Kirby* series)

5 Time to bring the hammer down! Dedede, Kirby's nemesis, is one of the slowest characters in *Smash*. Still, he's able to deal amazing damage. Landing his sluggish hits might be tricky, but opponents will feel it when you do!

ALSO CHECK OUT . . .

TowerFall Ascension

An arena brawler with a focus on archery. You have limited arrows, and must pick up or catch more.

PlayStation All-Stars Battle Royale

The *Smash* formula, only with PlayStation characters, so play as Sackboy, Ratchet, Sly Cooper, and even PaRappa The Rapper!

CN Punch Time Explosion XL

Stars from Cartoon Network's best shows go toe-to-toe in this entertaining fighting game, with cooperative and competitive modes for up to four players.

TIPS & TRICKS

Edge guarding
If an opponent tries to jump back onto the stage, rolling off the edge and grabbing it yourself can prevent them from being able to do so.

Get grabbing
A lot of *Smash* players don't use their throws enough. Try throwing opponents in every direction— some lead to great combo opportunities.

Donkey Kong is here!
While playing as Donkey Kong, try to get a chain of 200 or better in solo Trophy Rush. This will unlock the silly DK Rap from *Donkey Kong 64*.

Hitstun Shuffling
Tap a direction when taking damage and you'll move slightly in the chosen direction—perfect for escaping from multi-hit moves, and for keeping close to opponents.

Mix it up
Repeatedly using the same attack will gradually make it less effective. Try to use your full arsenal in order to keep your attacks strong.

THE COOLEST GAMING SECRETS

How well do you *really* know your favorite game? You might consider yourself a fully qualified expert. You have completed it on every difficulty, you can stamp your dominance on any multiplayer match, and you could even pen a blow-by-blow analysis on the game from memory.

But games are a dizzying labyrinth of secrets, tricks, and homages, all rewards for those who have the time and the skill to seek them out. Here are some of the best secrets for the biggest games around. Can you hunt down these awesome hidden extras for yourself?

THE LAST GUARDIAN
UNLOCK COSTUMES FROM ICO AND SHADOW OF THE COLOSSUS

There are hidden costumes dedicated to the developer's previous games, *Ico* and *Shadow of the Colossus*. You can unlock them only when playing through *The Last Guardian* for a second time, though. The *Ico* costume, Horned Apparel, will appear in options after feeding 48 barrels to Trico. For Warrior's Clothes, the *Shadow of the Colossus* costume, you need to feed 64 barrels to Trico. Regardless of how many barrels you find, Trico himself will proudly display a Badge of Honor medallion on your second playthrough.

THE WONDERFUL 101
HIDDEN TAUNT MOVE

If you really enjoy showing off, you'll be glad to hear that there's a hidden taunt move in *The Wonderful 101*, which boosts your attack power considerably. Stand still in front of an enemy and hold down the X and A buttons at the same time. Taunting also allows you to create a Unite Camp immediately by pressing the Y button, which refills the Unite Gauge.

WORLD OF FINAL FANTASY
FINDING THE PHOENIX

In Valley Seven, you'll find a Murkrift in Cauldron 3, next to a gaping chasm of lava. You'll need to use three Mirages with Fire Resistance of at least 150 for this puzzle—Fritt, Bomb, and Ifrit all work here. Solving the puzzle opens up a protruding rock that allows you to cross the gaping chasm safely. You'll find the Phoenix waiting for you in the cave on the other side.

SHOVEL KNIGHT
THE SECRET BOSS FIGHT

HALL OF CHAMPIONS

1 Go to The Hall of Champions, climb the first ladder, and head right until you reach a dead end. Use a downward thrust in the right corner to reveal a new passage.

SECRET SCROLL

2 You'll find a secret scroll in this passage. If you're on PS4, it will show Kratos wandering around while Xbox One players will get a "mysterious location."

MEET THE SECRET BOSS

3 No matter the version that you are playing, you should now head on over to this new location. You will then encounter a secret boss battle against either Kratos or the Battletoads.

STARDEW VALLEY
FINDING THE GALAXY SWORD

FIND THE PRISMATIC SHARD

1 There are a few places you can find the Prismatic Shard, but the easiest method is to mine rocks outside the Quarry until you find it.

ENTER THE THREE PILLARS

2 Travel to the Calico Desert, then head over to the pillars in the top right while you have the Prismatic Shard equipped.

THE SWORD IS YOURS

3 You now have the Galaxy Sword! This level 26 weapon does 60 to 80 damage per swing, making it extremely useful. If you lose the Galaxy Sword, you can buy another from Marlon.

TOWERFALL ASCENSION
UNLOCK THE SECRET ARCHERS

There are four secret archers to unlock: Cyan, Purple, White, and Yellow. To unlock Cyan, clear Sunken City in story mode. For White, you need to play the Moonstage during VS until the purple crystal appears, so you can shatter it. To unlock Yellow, collect all seven yellow gems in Trial Mode, then head to Tower Forge 2. Head below the first dummy you see on the right on that map. Purple is the only tricky archer to unlock, since you need to keep playing on Twilight Spire until a random event unlocks him.

SPLATOON
EXPLORE SUNKEN SCROLLS SECRETS

Sunken Scrolls throughout the game let you know about the world and history of Octo Valley. But they have another secret too. See the doodle in the bottom right? Quickly scroll through the pages and you'll realize it's a flipbook animation!

OCTODAD: DADLIEST CATCH
FIND THE GAME THAT'S NOT QUITE MINECRAFT ★

When you're taken by the family to Gervason's Grocery, head to the back of the store and look at the stand by the right-hand wall, tucked away in the corner. There's a "MINTCRAFT" stand there, which is an obvious homage to *Minecraft*. Pick up the Creeper head and it will glow red before disappearing in a puff of smoke!

PES 2017
USE THE HIDDEN SOMBRERO MOVE

Most of the hidden skill moves in *PES 2017* depend on the player you're using. Only the likes of Neymar, Messi, and Ronaldo can perform certain tricks. But this hidden move is one that every player can do and it can catch defenders napping, if they aren't paying attention. Just after you pass to someone, click in the right analogue stick and while holding it in, push the left stick toward the nearest defender. This will perform the "sombrero" move. You'll flick the ball up, over your head—perfect for beating defenders who have drifted too close.

THE EXPERT SAYS...
THOMAS HAPP

Creator of secret-packed indie smash *Axiom Verge*

I was always fascinated by the "secret world" glitch in *Metroid*. If you let one of the doors close on your character, you could repeatedly jump and morph ball to go off the screen and into hidden, glitchy rooms past the boundary of the game map. It was just the game trying to reinterpret random data on the cartridge, but if you didn't know that, it felt like the game opened up to a mysterious, magical world of unlimited potential. I would spend hours trying the trick on different doors in the game. It added a lot of extra life to what was already a very lengthy game for the time.

FINAL FANTASY XV
FINDING CHOBHAM ARMOR

South of the Cauthess Coernix Station Outpost, there's a farm in the area called Saxham Outpost. There's a building here with Chobham Armor teasingly out of reach on the awning, and it looks like there's no way of reaching it. What you can do is jump on a crate just below the awning and slowly move around. Eventually, you'll find a spot on top of that crate where you can still grab the Chobham Armor, even though it still seems to be out of reach.

DESTINY
SECRET ACHIEVEMENT AND WOLVES HOWLING

There's a secret Achievement hidden in Felwinter Peak for playing the *Rise of the Iron* theme on the bells. Consider the big bell to be number one, with the other smaller bells being numbers two through six. You'll need other players to stand at some of the bells, as you need to ring them quickly to trigger the Achievement—you won't be fast enough to do this yourself. This is the order you need to ring the bells in: 1, 2, 3, 1, 5, 4, 3, 2, 3, 1, 1, 3, and 4. The secret Achievement will pop when you've done this correctly, and you'll hear wolves howling in the background, too.

★ FEATURE

THE LEGEND OF ZELDA: TWILIGHT PRINCESS HD
LINK LOOKING AT LINK

This HD re-release of Nintendo's classic adventure *Twilight Princess* contained a little surprise not many noticed. Head to Castle Town and enter Chudley's Fine Goods and Fancy Trinkets Emporium. Look at all the paintings and pictures on the container. Every single one is promotional art for the game that Nintendo released, including the first ever image of *Twilight Princess*, showing Link riding through a forest on Epona. It's a real treat for eagle-eyed fans who spotted the rare artwork!

WORLD OF WARCRAFT
FINDING THE MYSTICAL HIPPOGRYPH

It was back in 2007 that *World of Warcraft* fans first found evidence of a pink mount called Hippogryph buried deep within the game's files. Now, finally, players have figured out how to unlock the Hippogryph—but it's not easy. There are five crystals dotted around the Aszuna zone and they all need to be activated within eight hours of each other. The catch? You can't die while doing this and if someone else beats you to it, the crystals won't spawn again for a long, long time—sometimes up to a week. The crystals don't always appear in exactly the same spot either. They will show up in roughly the same area but that's as much help as you'll get. The coordinates for the five crystals are: (54, 33), (37, 32), (50, 20), (34, 35), and (47, 61).

MARVEL ULTIMATE ALLIANCE
UNLOCK BLADE

You can unlock Marvel's vampire-slayer in the fifth mission. There's a claw mini-game tucked away inside the big top. Play the claw machine and you'll see Blade inside. Lift him out of the claw machine and he'll be unlocked as a playable character.

SUPER MARIO MAKER
SECRET DEATH NOISES

Try dying in *Super Mario Maker*. No, seriously! Sometimes you'll get a new death noise, such as Mario clattering into trash cans or a long, slide whistle. There are eight in total, so keep dying until you hear them all.

AWESOME CAMEOS

ULTIMATE MARVEL VS. CAPCOM 3
MYSTIQUE

She's been a huge star in the *X-Men* movies but strangely absent from games. All except one . . . you can find the shapeshifting mutant tucked away in Magneto's ending.

STREET FIGHTER V
HAKAN

Street Fighter V's Story Mode is packed full of surprise cameo appearances. The best of these cameos has to be the return of hilarious, turquoise-haired Turkish oil wrestler Hakan, who appears in Alex's story.

DONKEY KONG COUNTRY: TROPICAL FREEZE
SAMUS

In Busted Bayou, stop when you find the collectible "K." Check the background to see Samus's ship from the *Metroid* series!

SUPER MARIO 3D WORLD
LINK

In Rainbow Run, you'll find an area with lots of blocks laid out flat. If you light them all up you will then see that these boring blocks are actually an 8-bit sprite image of *Legend of Zelda*'s hero Link.

TOP FIVE MINECRAFT SECRETS

TURN YOURSELF UPSIDE-DOWN

1 If you name any mob Dinnerbone or Grumm, ensuring the first letter is capitalized, they will then appear upside down. As an added bonus, if you're playing *Minecraft* on mobile or PC, calling yourself Dinnerbone or Grumm will make your own avatar appear upside down!

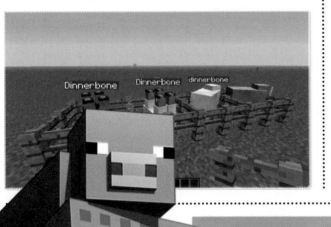

RAINBOW-COLORED SHEEP

2 There's a clever trick not many *Minecraft* players know about that will jazz up how the game looks. Name any sheep "jeb_", including the underscore, and they will appear as rainbow-colored sheep. What's more, their color will constantly change, brightening up your game.

CHISELED MOB FACES

3 This is a small detail you might have overlooked. Carefully examine chiseled sandstone blocks and you'll see the face of a Creeper staring back at you. Try a red chiseled sandstone block and instead of a Creeper, you'll see a Wither's face. Spooky.

THE EXPERT SAYS...

CAPTAINSPARKLEZ
YouTuber with 10 million subscribers!

I went through a period in middle school when I was really into finding glitches in the *Tony Hawk's Pro Skater* games. I loved those growing up. There was one with a Hawaii level and there's this Tiki thing, like a little mini statue on the side of the street. If you ollie into its mouth, it teleports you to this other "Inside the Tiki" dimension. It's incredible! I'd play hide-and-seek with other friends in split-screen mode—I'd hide in the Tiki and they'd never find me. It was the best!

MOJANG BANNER

4 You can create banners in *Minecraft* adorned with a skull-and-crossbones, and other images. But there's also a hidden banner for creating the logo of the developers Mojang! Just craft an enchanted golden apple, banner, and dye of any color you like.

STAMPY HOUSE TOUR

5 In the tutorial world, head North-East and you'll see a boat and island in the distance. This is the *S.S. Stumpy*, from famous *Minecraft* player Stampy's videos, and the island is home to Stampy's house. You can explore the boat, the island, and meet Stampy's dog.

LEGO MARVEL'S AVENGERS
UNLOCK AN AWESOME ALL-ROUNDER

One of the main features of the LEGO games is the need to switch between multiple characters and make use of their unique abilities. But some characters can do more than others, as you'll see when you unlock Korvac after beating him in the SHIELD base. He can fly, melt gold pieces, charge panels, put out fires, use computers, pass through vents, *and* use cosmic powers. Oh, and he's invincible, too!

TERRARIA
DRAG THE SUN

On the title screen, you will see that the Sun quickly passes through the sky, showing the day turning to night and then back again to day. If you're playing *Terraria* on PC, though, you can click and drag the Sun around to set the time yourself.

OVERWATCH
PLAY DIFFERENT MUSIC ON THE BELLS

At the start of Dorado, you might have noticed players shooting at the three church bells at the start of the game. Each one has a different chime. But what most players don't realize is that there are bells on the arches to the right. Using these bells as well, you can play anything from wedding music to your favorite pop songs.

STAR WARS BATTLEFRONT
HIDDEN TUSKEN RAIDERS

You'll need some patience and persistence to find this one. Play on any Tatooine map in *Battlefront*. Next, head over to the edge of the map, where you'll get a "Return to Combat Area" message when you have drifted too far. Dotted around the rocks here are Tusken Raiders, who shoot down at you and will also lift their guns in the air to celebrate, just like in the *Star Wars* movies.

ZEN PINBALL 2

The best thing about this awesome pinball game (which is also known as *Pinball FX 2* depending on what platform you play on) is the way its tables do things no real pinball table could ever do. Characters roam the play areas, complex features like RPG systems and swirling loops add to the madness, and with a huge variety of tables, you'll be spoiled with choices. One of our favorites is the cool Spider-Man table, and here's a look at how you can help Spidey deal with the evil Doctor Octopus.

1 This table is packed with cool ramps, loops, and scoops, so take a little time to get a feel for the layout. The green ramp on the right starts the Green Goblin event after a few hits, but it's the upper playfield you want if you're trying to summon Doc Ock.

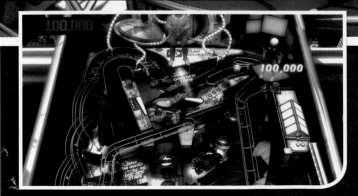

2 The purple ramp at the back left and the jump from the middle flipper to the attic are the quickest ways to reach the upper area. Here you must use the top flippers to try to get your ball into the hole directly under Doctor Octopus.

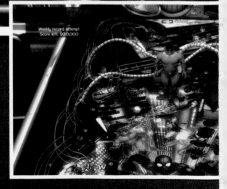

3 Do this twice and the mode will start, and Doc Ock will begin walking down the table toward you! Hitting the ramps that his tentacles are attached to will force him back a little. Let him get too close and you'll lose, so push him all the way back!

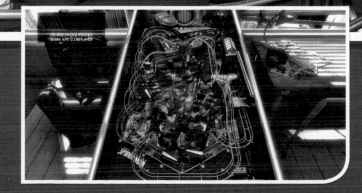

4 Be warned: you can still trigger the other villains while Doc Ock is approaching. Having Mysterio reverse flipper controls, and Goblin toss bombs onto the table while you're dealing with the tentacled terror, makes it way harder.

STREET FIGHTER V
THE WORLD WARRIORS RETURN

Capcom's *Street Fighter* series has been the leading name in fighting games for over 25 years, and keeps coming back bigger and better. Each mainline game has been excellent in its own right. They all have slightly different core mechanics too, like *Street Fighter III*'s Parry system, *IV*'s Focus Attacks and Ultras, and the versatile V-system in the most recent game.

Street Fighter V is among the easiest in the series to get into, thanks to simplified move inputs and more forgiving combo timings. If you've ever wanted to try a one-on-one fighting game, this is a good a place to start. And if you're a veteran, you should find you quickly get to grips with the cool new systems and characters. Grab a controller or a fight stick, and let the fireballs fly!

STATS

More than 80 *Street Fighter* games have been released

22 characters by the end of the first season

Veteran player Daigo Umehara has won 40 major *Street Fighter* tournaments

5,065 players competed in *SFV* at Evo (the world's biggest fighting game tournament) in 2016

36 million copies sold across all games

TOP 5 CHARACTERS

Nash

1 Charlie Nash, friend of *Street Fighter II* star Guile, was once a marine. He went missing after *Street Fighter Alpha 3*, and was presumed dead, only for him to reappear in *V*. He's changed, though—it looks like he's been pieced back together and he's no longer the nice guy he used to be.

F.A.N.G

2 A completely new addition to the *Street Fighter* roster, and Sagat's replacement as one of the evil Shadaloo organization's Four Kings. He's a master of poison, usually deploying it from a distance. He then evades opponents to let the toxins do all the hard work for him. And just wait until you see his crazy Critical Art!

Karin

3 Karin is another returning character from the *Alpha* series. She's long been a fan favorite, and her quick, powerful moves make her pretty scary to face in *SFV*. Activating her V-Trigger unlocks the full potential of her moveset. It adds loads of new options to keep opponents guessing, as well as to keep the pressure on.

Rashid

4 Rashid—or rather, Rashid of the Turbulent Wind, as he introduces himself—uses air as a weapon, and it's surprisingly effective. He can propel himself across the stage with a strong gust, for instance, or whip up small tornados to knock away airborne foes. Too bad Rashid has never heard of modesty, though!

Necalli

5 An original character created specifically for *Street Fighter V*, Necalli is an absolute beast—literally! His moves are primitive and aggressive, and his communication is animalistic—until you activate his V-Trigger, at least. This awakens some ancient power within him to make him super intelligent and more powerful.

ALSO CHECK OUT...

Guilty Gear Xrd -REVELATOR-

The graphics make this crazy fighting game look like a cartoon, but it's actually all 3-D! It plays as good as it looks, too—it's one of the best fighting games around.

Ultra Street Fighter IV

The definitive version of the fighter that brought the genre back into the mainstream. With 44 characters and 130+ Super and Ultra moves, it's a classic.

Skullgirls 2nd Encore

An indie fighter created by a former tournament player. It's a team-based game like *Marvel vs. Capcom*, and all combatants are beautifully hand-drawn.

TIPS & TRICKS

Stop jumping
The main mistake most players make is jumping too much. You're extremely vulnerable in the air, so stay on the ground as much as possible.

Learn everyone
It's not enough to know just what your character can do. In order to successfully fight the rest, it's important to know what tools they have at their disposal.

Do the Trials
As in similar games, Trials are a great way to learn basic combos. Putting these into practice in real matches is tricky, but it sure pays off!

Keep it simple
Don't rely too heavily on special moves. Most characters have regular moves that are quick, useful, and often safer than specials, so try to find a few.

STEEP
YOUR PERFECT WINTER VACATION

This extreme-sports game places you deep in the Alps, leaving you free to explore the peaks, meet other players, take pictures, and capture video. But it's the racing that will take your breath away. You can fly, snowboard, ski, or paraglide to the bottom, and each of these modes of transport feel exciting and dangerous in their own way. First-person view is exhilarating, as you hurtle down the mountain a hair's breadth away from danger, balancing your desire for speed with your need to survive. The game isn't all serious, though. Yes, you can climb mountains while basking in golden sunsets, but you can also snowboard with your friends while wearing a deer costume. Whatever you want to do, *Steep* is the only winter vacation you'll need.

STATS

4 main activities

4 different playing styles such as **EXPLORER** AND **FREESTYLER**

1st original game by Ubisoft Annecy

149 points of interest to find around Mont Blanc

Steep was in development **for 3 years**

TOP 4 ACTIVITIES

Wingsuit flying

1 No other game matches the adrenalin-pumping thrills of wingsuit flying. In no time at all, you'll be soaring through the air, and skimming the snow with your toes. In first-person view, being so close to danger is thrilling. You'll know that just one muscle twitch at the wrong time could spell doom.

DID YOU KNOW?

Steep was inspired by developer Ubisoft Annecy's proximity to the Alps.

Snowboarding

2 One of the fastest ways to carve down the mountain, snowboarding is thrilling because of the feeling that you're only *barely* in control. You are also likely to see other snowboarders wearing *Steep*'s craziest costumes when you race against them. Don't be surprised by rubber-chicken helmets, or even full-on giraffe outfits!

Paragliding

3 Although this doesn't have the white-knuckle speed of wingsuit flying, paragliding does offer the best views in *Steep*. You can soar high in the sky, and use your unusual vantage point to scout interesting-looking areas. Just remember that you'll eventually have to land safely, which is a serious challenge.

Skiing

4 Skiing is the best way to explore the Alps. It offers a combination of speed, controls, and the potential to do tricks if you want to impress. If you want to show off, you can also try skiing backwards, which adds an extra layer of style to your downhill racing.

ALSO CHECK OUT...

SSX

With little competition for *Steep* on Xbox One or PS4, the last great snowboarding game was SSX from last-gen. It's backwards compatible on Xbox One.

Forza Horizon 3

The social aspect of *Steep* can also be found in *Forza Horizon 3*, where you can drive around the world, chat to your friends, and create races on the fly.

ARK: Survival Evolved

Like *Steep*, this game is about exploring strange, unfamiliar surroundings. You must make the most of what's around you to get the most from the game.

TIPS & TRICKS

Earn credits quickly
The fastest way to earn credits is to complete Gold Challenges, so focus exclusively on those until you have a healthy amount of credits.

Turning around
If you land backwards while on skis, press the left analogue stick to the left, and the right stick to the right in order to turn around.

Pulling off tricks
Use the left analogue stick after you have jumped if you want to pull off tricks. Don't push the stick too early though, or else it won't register.

Gaining height
If you want to gain height while paragliding, make sure that you get close to the mountain so that the draft then pushes you upwards.

Turn trick safety off
This feature only lets you do tricks from a certain height. Switch it off so you have more control over your character.

MONSTER HUNTER
HOW TO SLAY YOUR DRAGON

DID YOU KNOW?

The series is growing more popular in the West, but it's still biggest in Japan, which accounts for nearly 80 percent of its total sales.

One of the best co-op games around, *Monster Hunter* **is all about teaming up to bring down gigantic beasts.** You then use their scales, fangs, and bones to create powerful new weapons and armor. Unlike similar action games, the base stats and abilities of your hunter never actually improve—only by crafting new gear can you increase your health or damage. It's all about improving your skills and knowledge of each encounter rather than leveling up.

One of the best features of the series is undoubtedly its realistic ecosystem and the way the various different species interact with one another. Monsters can grow weary during extended fights, at which point they'll often flee to another area in order to feed on smaller critters, or retreat to their nests to sleep and recover health. Only by tracking a beast are you able to keep on top of the fight, bring it down, and claim your rewards!

STATS

Nearly 800 quests to complete in *Generations* alone

Over 30 million copies sold across all games

148 different armor skills to mix and match

274 unique creatures to hunt

15 weapon styles to master

TOP 5 MONSTERS

1 Astalos

This spiky wyvern doesn't seem too difficult when you first fight it, but it has a shocking surprise in store. When angered, Astalos surrounds itself with electricity, and it starts moving much faster. This makes it tough to avoid, and even harder to hit!

2 Glavenus

This beast's tail is scary enough at the best of times, but then Glavenus sharpens it with his razor-sharp fangs. Long-range swipes, slams, and molten projectiles will really test your skills.

3 Rathalos

Rathalos has been a staple monster of the series since the very first game. It delights in spitting fireballs as it flies around. While it's airborne, the safest place to be is right below it—the opposite of its sister dragon, Rathian.

4 Lagiacrus

Monster Hunter Tri introduced underwater combat. This terrifying leviathan—and the game's cover star—was a showcase for this new system. Lagiacrus can cause serious problems with its electrical bursts. Plus, it's capable of fighting on land as well as in the water.

5 Zinogre

This large, wolf-like beast is one of the most agile foes in the *Monster Hunter* series. Leaping around arenas, it keeps hunters on their toes. Zinogre likes to charge itself up using the Thunderbugs that live in its fur—deal enough damage while it's charging and you will interrupt it.

ALSO CHECK OUT . . .

Horizon: Zero Dawn

A huge world to explore with towering robotic dinosaurs to hunt or evade. *Horizon* has a lot of familiar elements that *Monster Hunter* fans will love.

God Eater 2: Rage Burst

With an anime style, incredible creature design, and an arsenal of transforming weapons, *Rage Burst* is one of the best *Monster Hunter* style games around.

Ragnarok Odyssey

It might be bright, colorful, and cartoony, but this spin-off from popular MMO *Ragnarok Online* is a genuinely deep hunting game that will surely draw you in.

TIPS & TRICKS

Heads
Using a hammer or similar impact weapon? Focus on monsters' heads, since dealing enough damage quickly can knock them out cold.

Tails
Similarly, hunters with quick, bladed weapons should prioritize cutting off tails, which often grants additional materials and rewards.

Mad skills
Armor skills don't activate until your full set has ten or more points in an ability, so choose your gear wisely.

Bomb basics
Flash Bombs can stun monsters (and can sometimes even cancel their flight), while Sonic Bombs are able to force tunnelling creatures out from underground.

TOP 10 STRANGE STORY LINES

Voodoo Vince

1 Everything about *Voodoo Vince* is strange. You play as a one-eyed voodoo doll that has come to life, trying to save the kidnapped owner of a voodoo shop. On your journey, you battle a piggy bank of doom, a two-headed alligator, and an angry doll, amongst other foes. At one point, you even perform a duet with a skeleton! It's a wild, twisted trip through New Orleans, and you never know what's around the next corner.

Volume

2 *Volume* takes the legend of Robin Hood and transforms it into something new. It's a stealth game with a twist—most of the action plays out in the virtual world, as hero Robert Locksley sneaks around mazes to help uncover a sinister plot in the real world. Getting through levels undetected feels great, and you can make your own levels, too. The plot pinballs in unexpected directions, so you'll have to pay attention if you want to keep up.

Psychonauts

3 No game is weirder than *Psychonauts*, which takes place inside the minds of others. As psychic spy Raz, you stumble across a sinister plot at Whispering Rock Psychic Summer Camp. Each person's memories and thoughts form interesting and unique platform levels that Raz must navigate. They're surreal places but they're really fun to explore, because you've never seen anything like them!

BEST GAMES WITHOUT A STORY
Because you don't always need a great narrative to end up with a great game . . .

1 HEARTHSTONE
This competitive card battler doesn't have a story line. Instead, your time will be spent studying the cards you have unlocked and building the perfect deck to take with you into battle.

4 SUPER MEAT BOY
This platformer is extremely difficult, as you guide a piece of meat through obstacles like spinning saws and salty floors. You'll be too focused on surviving to even notice a plot.

2 HITMAN GO
Hitman GO is a series of turn-based puzzles that will have you trying to safely reach the exit, and get to your target. With no plot, the incentive to return is to get three stars on each level.

5 ALTO'S ADVENTURE
This entry into the endless runner genre is atmospheric and gorgeous to look at. It's strangely relaxing, despite the fact that it belongs to one of the most frantic gaming genres out there.

3 TRIALS FUSION
Trials is a game about balance, as you attempt to safely navigate a tricky obstacle course on two wheels. There are no cutscenes or plot revelations—it's just you and your skills.

6 JOURNEY
You could argue *Journey* has a plot, but it's threadbare and not central to the game. Instead, *Journey* is about journeying (of course) with a silent companion through deserts and mountains.

Headlander

4 You are the last human survivor on earth. It's a storyline that's been used countless times, but in this case, you're just a head! You can dock into any robot body to gain new abilities, solve problems, and access new areas. Meanwhile, a deranged computer is trying to stop you.

Lumo

6 In this retro-themed puzzle platform game, you're sucked into an arcade machine and dropped into a maze. The fixed camera can be tricky to deal with, but that only makes overcoming the labyrinth's many perils even more rewarding. Don't forget to collect all the rubber ducks!

Bastion

7 Warring factions and the end of the world collide in *Bastion*, a game that revels in its mysterious plot. Piecing together the clues leads up to a shocking revelation that leaves you to decide the fate of the world. The story is told at a slow pace, allowing each strange twist to sink in.

The Witness

9 In *The Witness*, you find yourself on an island, solving puzzles to progress. But why? What purpose does the island serve? Why are you there? Discovering the story for *The Witness* is the biggest puzzle of them all, as you piece together fragments of plot from audio logs. Can you figure out what's going on in this paradise?

Grim Fandango Remastered

10 *Grim Fandango* is the only game about being a travel agent. You're Manny Calavera in the Department of Death, sending souls to the Underworld. It's an awesome adventure with great characters, and it's really funny!

Dropsy

5 *Dropsy* is a silent clown who has been blamed for a circus fire. By talking to animals and offering warm, damp hugs to strangers, *Dropsy* sets out to find the truth about the fire and clear his name. *Dropsy* is an entirely visual game, relying on icons, grunts, and reactions to tell its story.

DID YOU KNOW?

Final Fantasy VII has 107,000 lines of dialogue, which means it has one of the longest scripts in video game history.

Final Fantasy VII

8 Shinra is using nuclear reactors to suck all the life energy from the planet, so the eco-warriors of AVALANCHE band together to stop them. That's a brief summary of a story that takes in giant meteorites, interstellar creatures, failed clones, soldiers, talking lions, giant amusement parks, and one of the most shocking moments in gaming history. There's a lot going on in *FFVII* . . .

THE EXPERT SAYS . . .
JAY THOLEN
Creator of indie oddity *Dropsy*

Dropsy had quirks that made him a fascinating (and challenging) character to design a game around. His communication difficulties, frightening appearance, and childlike demeanor allowed us to put players in the (squeaky) shoes of a unique protagonist. He's a hero, though you might not know it to look at him. After rumors of his involvement with a circus fire, Dropsy is maligned and feared by the local townspeople. Players progress by earning the trust of said townspeople one by one. Once Dropsy successfully helps a character, they'll allow him a hug. While the story does take dramatic turns, we made sure that Dropsy's methods remained grounded in his love for others.

SCORE   600
TIME 0:33
RINGS   29

SONIC THE HEDGEHOG

GOTTA GO FAST!

DID YOU KNOW?

Sonic as we know him almost didn't exist. Before the final design was decided upon, his original name was in fact Mr. Needlemouse.

It's been over 25 years since *Sonic the Hedgehog* first burst on the scene in a blur of blue and red. Since that dazzling debut, Sonic has dabbled in all sorts of genres—racing, snowboarding, pinball—but *Sonic Mania* goes back to where it all started, grabbing rings and racing round loop-the-loops. It has sprite-based graphics, which means it's pixelated like the original *Sonic* games were, and classic levels like Green Hill Zone return with new twists throughout. Best of all, it has the old crew back together again, as Sonic, Tails, and Knuckles team up once again to stop Robotnik. Along with *Sonic Boom: Fire & Ice* and a brand new 3-D game, there's never been a better time to be a *Sonic* fan.

STATS

Created in 1991

Over **87,000,000** boxed games sold

Over **335,000,000** game sales in total

Collect **100 rings** to get an extra life

Fastest time to clear the original game is just **11m16s**

TOP 5 SONIC GAMES

Sonic the Hedgehog

1 *Sonic the Hedgehog* was like nothing anyone had ever seen before. Sonic was fast, racing through loop-the-loops and rocketing off ramps into the air, while the bright and beautiful levels oozed with charm. You can revisit this classic on almost every gaming platform.

Rayman Adventures

One of the best platforming games of all time (and most fun), everyone should check out the charming *Rayman Adventures*.

Sonic Generations

2 Are you a fan of *Sonic*'s retro 2-D platforming? Or do you prefer his polarizing 3-D outings? *Sonic Generations* has both styles of gameplay, jazzed up with modern graphics and cool new moves. Every *Sonic* fan will find something here that they love.

Donkey Kong Country: Tropical Freeze

The latest in Nintendo's classic series is one of the toughest 2-D platformers of recent times.

Sonic & All-Stars Racing Transformed

3 Racing across land, sea, and air, *Sonic & All-Stars Racing Transformed* is an eye-blistering showcase of the best characters in *Sonic* and Sega's history. You can play it on almost every platform.

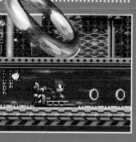

Sonic CD

5 Some love it, others hate it. The graphics were cranked up to 11, and a time-traveling gimmick was brought into the platforming. It's the most unusual game in Sonic's history! Try playing it on mobile, as the small screen makes the visuals stand out.

LEGO Dimensions

As part of the LEGO *Dimensions* crew, Sonic can use his Acrobat ability and Blue Typhoon to battle Robotnik's army.

Sonic Adventure

4 Sonic's first 3-D outing dazzled fans with its ambition, as he brought with him a new open world. The highlight is when he outruns an orca, but the different gameplay offered by his friends is cool, too.

TIME LINE

1991 Sonic the Hedgehog
With eye-popping colors, scorching speed, and running battles against Robotnik, this was an instant classic.

2008 Sonic Unleashed
A game of two parts, as you play traditional *Sonic* levels and combat arenas as his "werehog" alter ego.

2013 Sonic Lost World
This might be the fastest *Sonic* game ever, with some 3-D racing levels being almost too quick to keep up with.

1994 Sonic & Knuckles
This was compatible with *Sonic the Hedgehog* and its two sequels, adding an extra character.

2010 Sonic the Hedgehog 4
It took 16 years, but *Sonic the Hedgehog 3* got a sequel, split across two playable episodes.

2016 Sonic Boom: Fire & Ice
Sonic can command the elements to aid him in this fast-paced 3DS platformer.

OVERWATCH
OBJECTIVELY EXCELLENT

DID YOU KNOW?

There are references to *Hearthstone* all over *Overwatch*, including a number of computers and tablets shown running the online card game!

Overwatch **is a game that is best played with friends.** Communication is crucial as you either try to attack or defend each objective—letting your buddies know about incoming enemies can help you get the drop on the opposition. It's important to know what heroes the other team is using, and change character yourself if need be in order to counter them. Some matchups are easier than others!

The concept is as simple as the clean, colorful design, but there's a level of strategic depth to *Overwatch* that means it can be played to an extremely high level. Blizzard is already holding official global tournaments, and it's amazing to watch the world's best players show off their skills. Check them out and you might just learn something about how you can play your favorite characters even better!

STATS

119 million hours of *Overwatch* played in the game's first week alone!

23 unique heroes to try, across four roles

The largest prize pool for an *Overwatch* tournament to date was a cool **$300,000**

6 animated short movies so far

TOP 5 HEROES

Picking out a few of our favorite *Overwatch* stars

1 Zarya

She might have the lowest health pool of all the Tank class characters, but Zarya also has the highest damage potential and amazing utility. Shielding herself and allies can help the team survive otherwise-deadly Ultimates, while her own Ultimate rounds up enemies for her and her team to finish off.

2 Tracer

The biggest nuisance in the game! No other character in *Overwatch* can move quite like Tracer. Her health may be low, but that doesn't matter much when she's impossible to pin down. She's quite tough to play well, as everything happens at breakneck speed, but taking some time to master Tracer is definitely worth it.

3 Mercy

Mercy's potent healing skills make her a literal lifesaver. She has the added benefit of being able to swap between a healing beam and one that increases an ally's damage. This can be devastating when used to buff powerful heroes, such as Reaper or Pharah.

4 Pharah

High-flying Pharah has a primary weapon that is perfect for pushing enemies out of areas—a key part of *Overwatch*. Her explosive rounds deal high splash damage to nearby targets. Plus, thanks to her handy jetpack, it's never too difficult to find a vantage spot to start the barrage from.

5 Reinhardt

It initially feels pretty strange to play a character who doesn't have a ranged weapon, but you soon adapt. The burly Reinhardt is the most defensively minded Tank of the lot. You'll often see that big shield of his as he helps push a payload through a particularly nasty choke point. His rocket-powered hammer really packs a punch, too!

ALSO CHECK OUT...

Splatoon

Nintendo's take on multiplayer is one of the most family-friendly options out there. It's also one of the best. The goal is to control maps by covering them in paint!

Battleborn

Fusing the FPS team play of games such as *Overwatch* with MOBA elements from the likes of *League of Legends*, this is a very solid alternative to Blizzard's classic.

RIGS: Mechanized Combat League

Got PlayStation VR? Play *RIGS*! This arena combat game pits teams of mechs against one another in sport-based modes.

TIPS & TRICKS

Breaking the shield

Struggling to break Reinhardt's Barrier Field? Try Winston's Tesla Cannon and Symmetra's charged shots. Both pass through the shield to damage him directly.

The perfect team

Squad composition is key to success. Aim to have at least one Tank and one Support, with the rest based on whether you are attacking or defending.

Not so fast!

Any ability that can stun—such as McCree's Flashbang or Roadhog's Chain Hook—can interrupt and cancel certain enemy Ultimates.

Going up?

By placing Mei's Ice Wall under allies that have limited mobility, you can raise them to areas they couldn't otherwise reach.

TOP 10 BEST ESPORTS TEAMS

Wings Gaming

1 Known for its unpredictable method of map control and skilled roster of players, Wings Gaming was one of the most feared Chinese teams in all of eSports. They dominated *DOTA 2's* premier tournament, The International 2016, walking away with over $9 million—widely recognized to be the largest prize payout in eSport history—after edging out Digital Chaos in a thrilling final. The winning team's members have since left the team, now playing as Team Random.

Evil Geniuses

2 When it comes to competitive gaming, they don't come much more successful than Evil Geniuses. Founded in 1999, EG is now a feared name in the competitive *DOTA 2* circuit; for good reason too, its playstyle is electrifying. Following its victory at The International 2015, securing a $6 million prize pool, Evil Geniuses has become one of the biggest teams across multiple games.

Team SoloMid

3 Of all of the eSports teams on the scene, Team SoloMid has fostered one the strongest and friendliest communities out there. Formed in 2009, TSM fields players in every major game, including the likes of *Super Smash Bros.*, *Vainglory*, *Overwatch* and *Heartstone*. Versatile, disruptive and a constant source of entertainment, TSM is a wonderful team to follow, and to support when they play.

BEST ESPORTS PLAYERS
The biggest stars of the competitive scene

Lee Sang-hyeok
Known under his game name, Faker, Lee Sang-hyeok is widely considered to be the best *League of Legends* player in the world, currently playing as a mid-laner for SK Telecom T1.

Lee Seon-woo
Four-time champion of EVO and all-around master of *Street Fighter*, Lee Seon-woo—better known under his tag, Infiltration—signed with Team Razer in 2015 and has continued his dominance ever since.

Marcelo David
SK Gaming's Marcelo David rose to prominence through his map control and fast reflexes, helping former team Luminosity to become one of the most challenged teams in eSports.

Juan Debiedma
Juan "Hungrybox" Debiedma proved that Jigglypuff, in the right hands, is the most dangerous Pokémon of them all. A *Super Smash Bros.* champion, Hungrybox is a pleasure to watch.

Byun Hyun Woo
"ByuN" is one of the most technically gifted players in *StarCraft II*. He has risen from being an underdog to become champion, and—best of all—has an immediately likeable character.

Katherine Gunn
Katherine "Mystik" Gunn has an excellent record in competitive gaming. She was also recognized by Guinness World Records as being the highest-earning female gamer in eSports.

JAINA
Quackniix

E.T.C.
Breez

ZAGARA
Schwimpi

REXXAR
Wubby

Fnatic

4 Headquartered in the UK, Fnatic is one of the most versatile organizations in eSports. While it has teams in all of the major games, it is perhaps *League of Legends* where Fnatic has delivered its most impressive work—considered to be one of the best teams in history. Known for wild comebacks and energetic play, you can always count on this team to deliver.

FNATIC

SK Telecom T1

5 Founded in 2002, SK Telecom T1 is largely considered to be one of the most successful eSports teams of all time. SK Telecom T1 rose to prominence by dominating *StarCraft* tournaments, but later solidified its reputation in *League of Legends*. SKT's *LoL* team dominated the 2013, 2015, and 2016 World Championships.

Cloud9

6 The most successful teams in eSports have built their reputations over many years, but not Cloud9. This LA-based team arrived in 2012 and quickly rose to prominence in titles including *League of Legends*, *Smite*, and *DOTA 2*. One of the most successful organizations, it's worth investing your time and attention to these guys.

Ballistix Gaming

7 Undoubtedly one of the newest teams with the largest potential for continued success, Ballistix Gaming (formerly known as L5) has assembled a roster of top-tier talent and put them to incredible, immediate use. Ballistix's biggest victory came in the form of Blizzard's *Heroes of the Storm* Fall Championship, edging out Fnatic in a tense final to take the prize; it's a thrilling new team worthy of your time.

Immortals

8 Coming together in 2015, Immortals is proving itself to be one of the most entertaining teams to watch. Its style is unpredictable and difficult to gauge, causing upsets in the *League of Legends* NA LCS and proving themselves to be one of the most likeable and down-to-earth teams on the circuit; Immortals has great success in its future.

Team EnVyUs

9 With teams based in all major games—impressively, across both console and PC competitive gaming—Team EnVyUs is without question one of the most versatile, enjoyable, and interesting organizations in the world. Based out of North America, you should expect to see upsets, victories, and a whole lot of format-breaking play when you sit down to watch EnVyUs in action this year.

Team Expert

10 Formerly known as Team Acer, this South Korean organization finds its place on this list largely down to the success of "ByuN" Hyun Woo—formerly known as Ghostking—for his impressive dominance in the *StarCraft II* scene. From underdog to 2016 WCS champion, this Terran player amazed viewers with his lightning-fast reactions, impeccable micro control, and confidence to take on the most established players in the game.

FIFA 17
FROM RAGS TO RICHES

DID YOU KNOW?

Released towards the end of 2016, it took more than two years for EA to put the new story mode, which is called The Journey, into *FIFA 17*.

Imagine what it would be like to go from the local amateur team to playing for the biggest Premier League club in the world. *FIFA 17* now lets you find out with its story mode, called The Journey, which has you take control of 17-year-old soccer player Alex Hunter as he tries to make it big. You get to choose what Alex says, control the important decisions he makes, and play as him on the field in the big games.

A brand-new story mode isn't the only improvement though, as the physical side of each soccer game has been improved for this outing. *FIFA 17* now has more of the rough and tumble of soccer, so you can steal the ball from attackers, or hold off defenders as you power toward the goal. It makes scoring feel even more satisfying, defending even more dramatic, and multiplayer games even more competitive!

STATS

24th *FIFA* game

1st *FIFA* to use Frostbite Engine
FROSTBITE

Sales 18% higher than **FIFA 16**

17,849 different players across all leagues

650+ teams to choose from

TOP 4 PLAYERS TO USE

EDEN HAZARD

1 This Belgian attacking midfielder is a nightmare for any defense. When playing as Hazard, you'll get to do a wide variety of dribbling moves from his box of tricks, and finish with a pinpoint pass or shot. His low center of gravity makes him difficult to tackle as well.

JAMES RODRIGUEZ

2 While using Real Madrid, opponents will likely be heavily marking stars like Bale and Ronaldo. That's where James Rodríguez comes in—he's fast, and an excellent dribbler of the ball. When you get the ball as Rodríguez, you can usually create a chance out of nothing.

ANTHONY MARTIAL

3 Anthony Martial is a versatile attacker who can play on either wing or up front, where his scorching pace punishes defenders who can't keep up with him. It's that speed that makes him so much fun to play, as his pace means Martial will get plenty of chances to score.

MARCO REUS

4 Fast, direct, and strong, Marco Reus is a no-nonsense winger who likes to attack. His acceleration means you can explode into space when using him, making the most of Borussia Dortmund's tendency to counterattack opponents who have overcommitted. He's not a fantastic defender, but he's arguably the world's best winger.

ALSO CHECK OUT . . .

PES 2017

PES offers a faster game of soccer than *FIFA*, with slick passing, simple tackling, and end-to-end action. It's not quite as tactical as *FIFA* though.

NBA 2K17

Setting screens and hitting Eurostep lay-ups might sound a bit like nonsense, but they will become second nature after spending a few weeks with *NBA 2K17*.

Football Manager 2017

Placing you in the role of manager, your biggest concerns are team chemistry and balancing the budget.

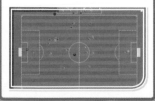

TIPS & TRICKS

Protect the ball
Holding the left shoulder button on the pad will make your player shield the ball. Use this to keep anyone attacking the ball at bay.

Corner control
Give control of your corner kicks over to the AI. This leaves you free to control a player in the box. Run into space and call for the ball.

Complete The Journey mode
Not only will you unlock plenty of awards as you play through The Journey, but you'll also receive an Alex Hunter FUT card when you're done.

Career Mode potential
In Career Mode, you can try signing some young players with good potential. Dele Alli and Ousmane Dembele are our personal favorites.

Use driven shots
To strike the ball powerfully while keeping it low, hold shoot as usual, then tap shoot as you're about to kick the ball.

DID YOU KNOW?

One year after losing out on the cover vote for *Madden NFL 16*, Rob Gronkowski appeared on the cover for *Madden NFL 17*.

MADDEN NFL 17

LET'S GET PHYSICAL

Madden NFL 17 is the perfect re-creation of the toughest sport in the world. Every huge tackle, shuddering collision with defenders, and ground-scraping dive for the end zone is just as it is in the real sport. The developers have really improved the ground game this year, so running with the ball is more fun. You have more ways to dodge desperate lunges at your legs, and you can also squirm free from a defender's grasp. Tapping the buttons to squeeze more mileage out of a running play feels like you are actually fighting for those few extra yards. The defense has been upgraded too, so cornerbacks are more likely to pick up stray throws, while safeties won't let players break free for touchdowns without a fight. If it's in football, it's in this game, too.

STATS

28th game
in *Madden* series

40 songs on soundtrack

4,800,000 Facebook followers

Available on
4 SYSTEMS

2 brand-new announcers

TOP 5 TEAMS TO PLAY AS

Pittsburgh Steelers

1 If you want fun, play as the Steelers. They are an attacking force of nature, with a quarterback (Roethlisberger) who can throw deep, a wide receiver (Brown) who can catch almost anything, and a running back (Bell) who can dart through the smallest gaps. They almost feel unfair to use.

Atlanta Falcons

2 The Falcons have talent at almost every position, allowing for just about any play style. You can air the ball out to stretch defenses thin, or run the ball and grind the opposition down on the ground. The Falcons have the superstars to get the job done.

Minnesota Vikings

3 The Vikings have really tough defenders who specialize in putting pressure on opposing quarterbacks and making interceptions from hurried passes. The defensive line strikes fear into all opponents, making them a great *Madden* pick.

Denver Broncos

4 If you like to grind out your wins by showing grit, the Denver Broncos are excellent. They have a solid defense and hardy crew of running backs—the perfect combination to play a safe, low-scoring game at your pace. Your opponent won't enjoy playing against you!

New York Giants

5 The New York Giants might not be the best team in the game, but in terms of a charismatic star who can do the impossible, Odell Beckham Jr. makes them fun to use. If you're new to *Madden*, throw the ball to Beckham and good things will follow.

TIPS & TRICKS

Developing players
When developing players for Connected Franchise Mode, make sure you focus on developing young players with quick or superstar development.

Biggest experience bonus
The biggest experience bonus when developing players is in end-of-season awards like MVP and Offensive Player of the Season.

Run with fullback
In *Madden NFL 17*, it's now easier to gain yards running with the fullback, so look for fullback runs near the end zone.

Left tackle value
Don't overpay Left Tackles in Career mode. In real NFL, they get paid a lot as they protect a quarterback's blind side. This doesn't exist in the game.

Throw on fourth down
Online, you can be brave on fourth downs and risk a throw. Humans aren't as tight defensively as the AI is.

NBA 2K17
THE BEST JUST GOT BETTER

DID YOU KNOW?
Stephen Curry is such a good shooter, the developers had to create a new shooting system for *NBA 2K17* so he wouldn't break the game.

The *NBA 2K* outings are the greatest basketball games ever made. It was hard to see where the series could improve, yet *NBA 2K17* has done it. MyGM and MyLeague modes return, with more options as you run an NBA franchise, from creating a team logo to organizing off-season activities. More dribble moves have been added, while jump shots have been tweaked. If you want an example of the amazing attention to detail in *NBA 2K17*, listen to the ball-bouncing sounds—the audio has been recorded from NBA arenas, so will vary depending on where you are. They've even added the Olympic basketball teams—it's the perfect basketball game.

STATS

93 average review score

50 licensed songs

11 different commentators and announcers

Over 7 million copies shipped

21 EuroLeague teams available for play

TOP 5 TEAMS TO TRY OUT

Golden State Warriors

1 The NBA's superteam, Golden State Warriors, is packed with talent up and down its squad. From superstars like Stephen Curry to the defensive powerhouse that is Draymond Green and the long-limbed talents of JaVale McGee, there's something here for everyone to enjoy.

Cleveland Cavaliers

2 Attack opponents with the raw physicality of LeBron James, or dazzle them with the trickery of Kyrie Irving. There's a lot to offer outside of those two, like the elite rebounding talent of Kevin Love, but the James and Irving combo is the most fun part.

Minnesota Timberwolves

3 Play as a team anchored around the most exciting player in the NBA today: Karl-Anthony Towns. This young center can do it all, from powering the ball toward the rim for an easy dunk, to drifting out to the three-point line to snipe teams from distance.

Chicago Bulls

4 With a nucleus of Jimmy Butler, Dwyane Wade, and Rajon Rondo, this is a team built around quick passes and strong drives to the basket. You won't hit too many outside shots with the Chicago Bulls, but you'll be scoring from too many spectacular lay-ups and dunks to care about that.

Detroit Pistons

5 The Pistons is a team packed with three-point shooters, and it also has one of the League's best rebounders, Andre Drummond, to grab any misses. For those who like to hurt opponents from deep, Detroit Pistons is an easy choice to make.

ALSO CHECK OUT...

NBA Jam by EA Sports

This smartphone game is more lighthearted than *NBA 2K17*. Prepare for some crazy situations, including a flaming ball!

NBA Live 16

This series skipped a 2017 entry, but *NBA Live 16* is still good fun. Authentic presentation and tons of cool game modes make this a great sim to try.

WWE 2K17

As a fellow *2K* sports series, this has more in common with *NBA 2K* than you may realize, particularly in terms of how the game looks.

TIME LINE

1999 — NBA 2K
The very first game in the *NBA 2K* series was released exclusively on Sega's Dreamcast console.

2001 — NBA 2K2
Moving away from Dreamcast exclusivity to several consoles, this saw the series' popularity explode.

2005 — NBA 2K6
Appearing on Xbox 360 for the first time, the console's power meant visuals took a huge leap.

2009 — NBA 2K10
Introducing the Association Mode, this series saw you taking control of an entire NBA organization.

2014 — NBA 2K15
Instead of creating your own likeness to use in the game, *2K15* allowed you to scan your actual face!

2015 — NBA 2K16
The previous *NBA 2K* outing had famous director Spike Lee help to develop the story in MyCareer.

SHOVEL KNIGHT

As games move forward, some of them are bravely moving backward. *Shovel Knight* is a throwback to 8-bit platformers that were made popular on Nintendo's old console, NES. Those who played *DuckTales* and *Mega Man* will recognize the same pixel-perfect platforming, stern difficulty, and chiptune music that's used here. You don't need to be a fan of those games to enjoy *Shovel Knight*, though. Just playing through the first few minutes is enough to fall in love with its quirky, retro charm.

1 Your first steps into *Shovel Knight*'s 8-bit world is learning how to play. You can shovel piles of dirt to grab gems underneath, destroy dirt walls blocking your path, and use your shovel to safely bounce on top of enemy's heads. Slowly, you begin to get familiar with your abilities.

2 As you get familiar with the world, pick apart the levels and find hidden secrets. You'll sniff out new paths and suspicious walls, and often your reward is a treasure chest. Open it and gems will tumble out, adding to your total Gold.

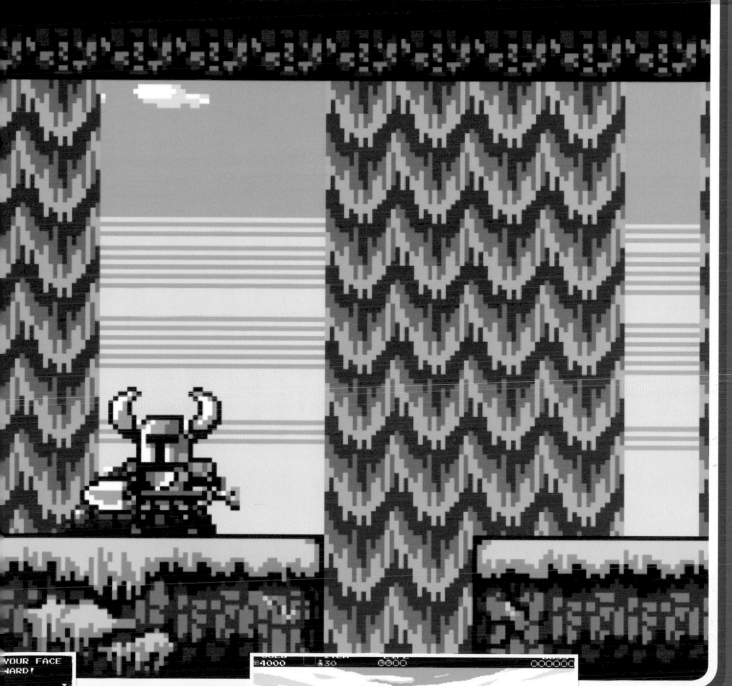

YOUR FACE
HARD!

3 Your first boss encounter is a throwback to the days of *Mega Man*. Watch Black Knight's attacking patterns, and strike when he's vulnerable. When he leaps into the air, he'll come back down, shovel first. Dodge this and quickly hit him.

4 Black Knight defeated, Shovel Knight rests, as the rest of the map opens up and the game truly begins. The world is huge! You must power Shovel Knight up and equip him with items as he continues his rescue quest.

GAMER CHALLENGE!

CAN YOU HANDLE THESE TRICKY TASKS?

How many Achievements and Trophies have you unlocked? While these virtual awards can help you show off how good at games you are, they're more than a symbol of your abilities. As you try to unlock them, you'll play in new ways that sharpen your gaming skills. They can also help with learning new techniques and clever tricks that you wouldn't have thought of before. But are you up to our challenge? Here are some of the coolest and toughest Achievements and Trophies for you to work on. Are you good enough to claim them all?

Overwatch (PS4, Xbox One)
Supersonic

You need to block 1,000 damage with Lucio's Sound Barrier Ultimate to complete this challenge. This teaches you an essential skill for dominating shooters—saving your most powerful move. In this case, that's your Ultimate, which can counteract Soldier 76, Zarya, Pharah, or Hanzo's deadly attacks.

YOUR TURN!
The Iris Embraces You

Restore 1500 health with Zenyatta's Ultimate. Timing is crucial, but use this properly and defend teammates from every offensive Ultimate.

EXPERT CHALLENGE!

NBA 2K17
(PS4, Xbox One)

Win a normal game without taking any three-pointers. This will force you to be patient, taking the ball close to the hoop for close-range two-pointers instead.

Axiom Verge (PS4, Xbox One)
Overclocked

You can't hang around if you want the Overclocked Trophy or Achievement, since you need to complete *Axiom Verge* in under four hours. Trying to complete games as quickly as possible is known as speedrunning, and that's the skill you'll learn here. No dawdling, no exploring, no taking your time—complete *Axiom Verge* once to learn where to go, then speedrun it.

FIFA 17 (PS4, Xbox One)
Offence Starts with the Keeper

This challenge teaches you how to be quick off the mark, and also how to take advantage of an opponent who is out of position. After you save the ball with the keeper, make sure that you quickly throw it up field in order to trigger your counterattack. Scoring from this counterattack will then unlock the Achievement or Trophy.

SCORE ATTACK!

Just Dance 2017

(PS4, Xbox One)

See if you can score over 13,000 points on Justin Bieber's *Sorry* to get a massive Superstar rating.

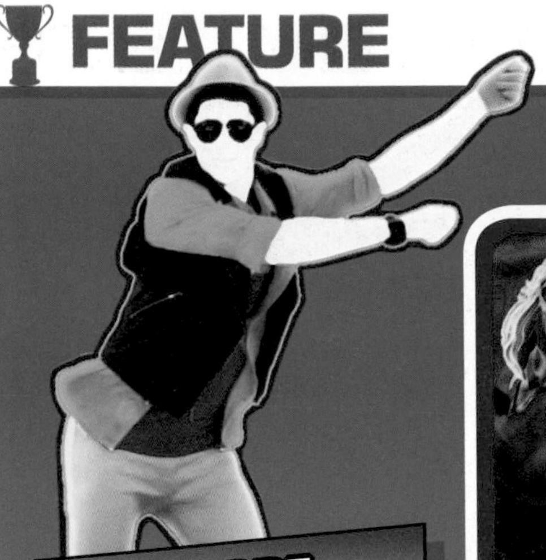

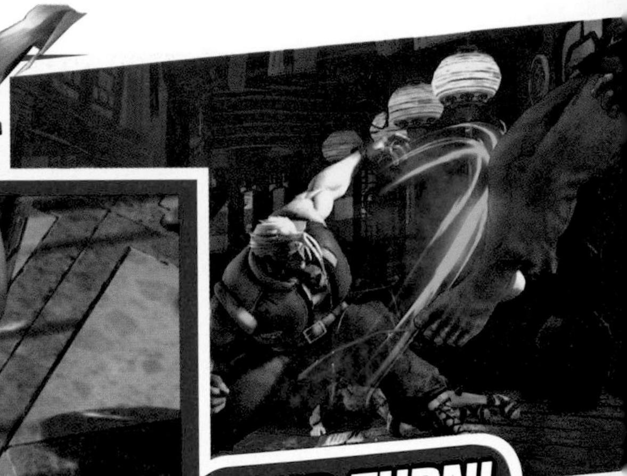

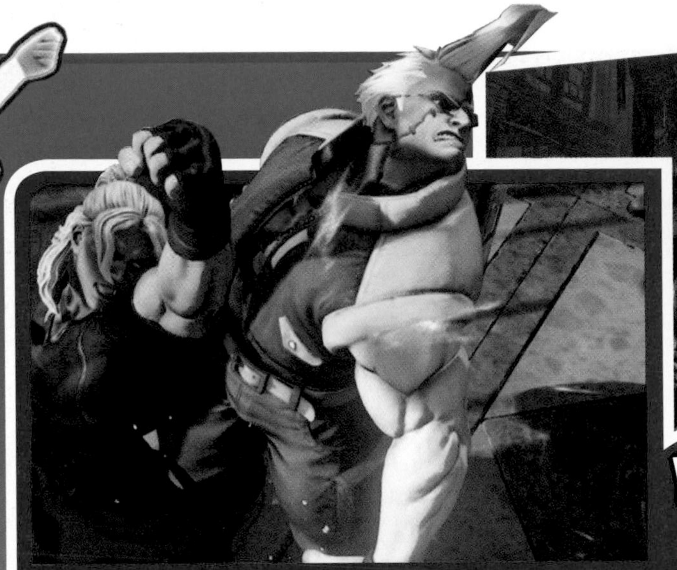

Street Fighter V (PS4)

Sudden Reversal

V-Trigger is the small, red gauge that builds while battling your opponent. When full, you can activate V-Trigger, which powers up your character. You must activate V-Trigger 100 times for this challenge—the perfect way to get used to what V-Trigger does for each character.

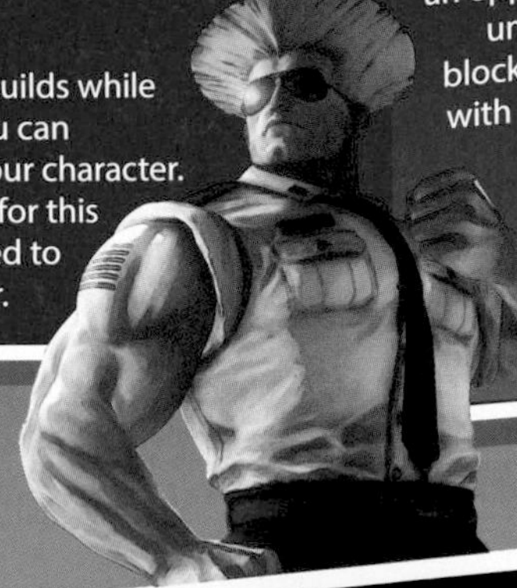

YOUR TURN!

Not over 'til it's over

V-Reversals let you knock an opponent away if you're under pressure and blocking their attacks. As with V-Trigger, activating 100 V-Reversals completes this challenge—and teaches you how to use them.

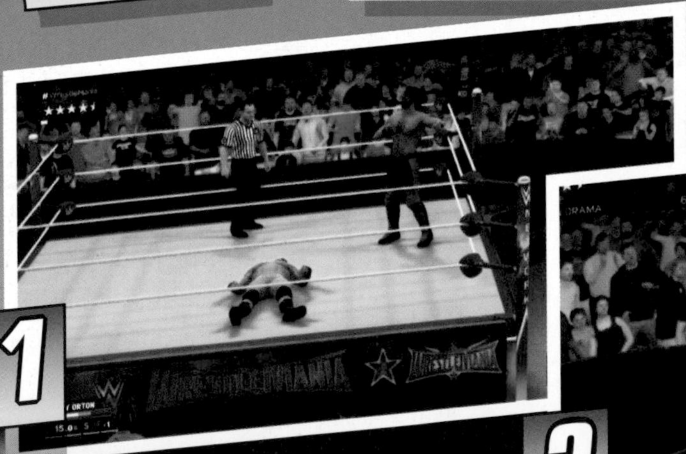

1

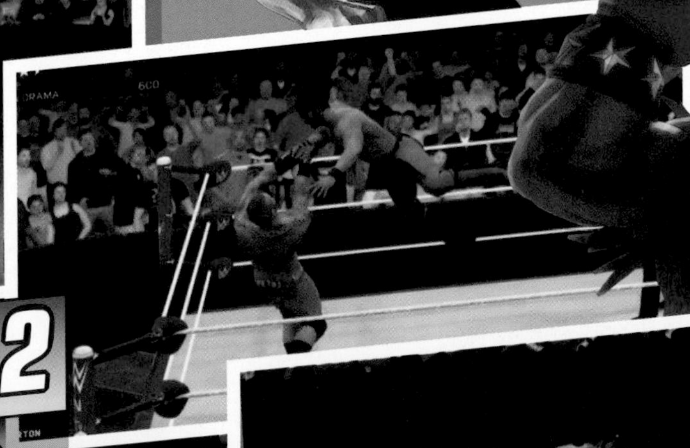

2

3

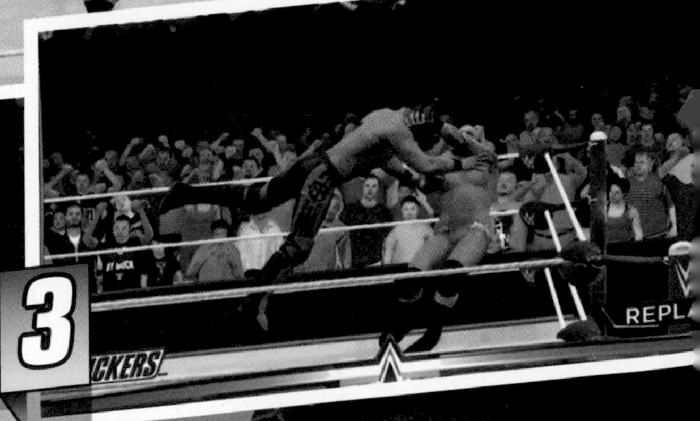

WWE 2K17 (PS4, Xbox One)

Lightning Reflexes

This *WWE 2K17* Achievement is specific in that you need to reverse Seth Rollins's finishing move with Randy Orton's finishing move. This achievement is all about seeing an opportunity and taking it. You need to build up to a finishing move with Randy Orton, then wait for Seth Rollins to do the same. Now you need to wait for Seth Rollins to try to hit his finishing move on you before immediately countering with yours. The timing isn't too demanding; you just need to be patient and wait for the right opening before you can attempt this achievement.

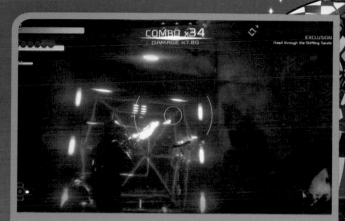

ReCore (Xbox One)
Master Juggler

When you attack and destroy enemies in quick succession, you'll create a combo. These are essential parts of any action game, and can increase your score, or—in *ReCore*'s case—damage. In the Warren dungeon, there are areas that spawn endless red, flying bots that can be quickly killed to rack up the 40 combo you need for this Achievement.

Mighty No 9 (PS4, Xbox One)
We Can Work It Out

For "We Can Work It Out," avoid firing for the first 30 seconds of any boss battle. This teaches you important skills that come in handy for all boss battles—pattern recognition, planning ahead, and most importantly, patience. It's easiest to complete this against the first boss but try it against the others too, to see how you fare.

EXPERT CHALLENGE!

REZ INFINITE (PS4)

This is arguably the most beautiful of the PlayStation VR titles so far. But can you survive an entire level without being hit and leveling down?

Velocity 2X (PS4, Xbox One)
Heavy Boots

If you feel as though your reaction times have dulled, *Velocity 2X* is a great tool to sharpen them with. Heavy Boots unlocks when you complete any level without letting go of the boost button. The blistering speed of your ship when boost is applied means you'll only complete this if your reflexes are up to the job.

YOUR TURN!
High Flier

Once you've honed your reaction times, you're ready to tackle High Flier. This Achievement unlocks when you earn a PERFECT medal on any level. You need to collect all the rescue pods and crystals, and beat the Gold time.

Rocket League
(PS4, Xbox One)
Still A Show-Off

You need to learn how to score goals in a wide variety of ways if you want to get anywhere in *Rocket League*. For the Still A Show-Off challenge, you need to score a goal while reversing. Despite the name, this isn't just showing off, as you might need to score while reversing in a tight spot during an actual game.

YOUR TURN!
Break Shot

You need to score a goal by hitting your opponent into the ball for this Achievement. Again, this teaches you how to score in a variety of ways, because you never know when that unusual way of scoring might be needed.

Worms W.M.D **(PS4, Xbox One)**
The Worm That Turned

In this worms-versus-worms showdown, the more worms you can hit during a single turn, the better. This challenge is for killing four worms in a single turn, and the fourth level—Chop Suey—is perfectly set up for such a dramatic maneuver. Keep practicing, and take this newfound skill into multiplayer.

SCORE ATTACK!

OlliOlli2: Welcome To Olliwood
(PS4, Xbox One)

Score more than 5,000,000 points on the very first level, 1-1. You'll need to master manuals if you want to have any chance of beating that score.

TOP 5 HARDEST ACHIEVEMENTS

Dreamcatcher
Tumblestone (PS4, Xbox One)

You need to win a Battle match against three Nightmare bots at the same time in order to get this Achievement, which might be the toughest challenge ever.

On The Ball
Star Wars Battlefront (PS4, Xbox One)

On The Ball unlocks when you complete any Survival mission on Master difficulty in 35 minutes. It takes skill, stamina, and a plan of what to do.

Goose Egg
NHL 17 (PS4, Xbox One)

Recording your first shutout in Be A Pro mode unlocks Goose Egg, but it's not as easy as it seems. Playing as a goaltender is difficult, and there's no room for error.

The End
Minecraft (PS4, Xbox One)

Slaying the Ender Dragon undoubtedly remains the toughest task in *Minecraft*, not only because it's difficult to kill, but simply finding it can cause you real frustration.

The Ball Is Free
Madden NFL 17 (PS4, Xbox One)

You only get to attempt this Trophy when the other team chooses to punt. You'll deal with the pressure of making the most of a limited chance.

Dirt Rally (PS4, Xbox One)
I Am The 5%

Have you ever used the in-car camera view for racing games? It certainly makes racing much harder, but also far more authentic. For the I Am The 5% challenge you are forced to use it since you have to win a rally event using the headcam view from start to finish. It will teach you how to use the trickiest camera in racing games.

Ittle Dew 2 (PS4, Xbox One)
Dizzy

You need to roll continuously for five seconds with a single roll to unlock this Trophy. This means you'll have to explore your surroundings thoroughly to find a good area to roll in. If you want to speed things up, head to the North-West corner in Fluffy Fields, and you'll find the perfect spot there.

No Man's Sky (PS4)
Stranger in a Strange Land

Survive 20 continuous days on a planet with extreme conditions for this Trophy. Since each planet in *No Man's Sky* is randomly generated, the challenge is picking the right planet. Upgrade your suit with life-support modules, add deflector upgrades, and check the planet conditions are shown in red (indicating a dangerous climate) when you leave your ship.

YOUR TURN!
The Sentinel

Once you've unlocked Stranger in a Strange Land, you're then ready for The Sentinel, where you need to survive for 32 days. Again, the trick is finding the right planet—ideally one with extreme weather that your upgraded suit can handle.

EXPERT CHALLENGE!

PES 2017
(PS4, Xbox One)

For a real challenge, try winning the league with West Glamorgan City. The lack of star players will force you to learn PES inside out to succeed.

Final Fantasy XV (PS4, Xbox One)
Angling Expert

This one serves as proof that mini-games can sometimes be just as fun as the main event. Angling Expert unlocks when you reach the maximum level in *Final Fantasy XV*'s fishing mini-game. Head to Galdin Quay, buy fishing equipment from the merchant, and use the mini-map to cast your lure. Remember to let fish respawn if you've caught a lot.

Project CARS (PS4, Xbox One)
Selfie

It's tempting to dive straight in to the main game and stick to that, but this Selfie Achievement teaches you to explore the menus. You unlock Selfie by taking a picture of your car, and you'll find Photo Mode only by pausing the game and poking around the menus. It's always worth seeing what options are available, so check out the menus in every game you play.

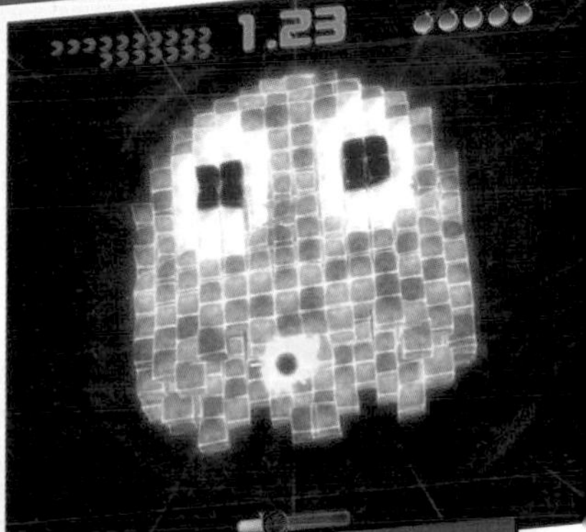

World of Final Fantasy (PS4, Xbox One)
Reigning Champ

Games aren't just finished when you see the credits roll. Some of them have a further test of skill for you, such as *World of Final Fantasy*. To unlock the Reigning Champ Trophy, you must defeat every opponent in the Coliseum. Don't try and complete this right away, though—you won't unlock all the Coliseum opponents until you reach the end of the game.

YOUR TURN!
Turn Those Corners Up

The *true* ending in *World of Final Fantasy* starts by selecting "No" in the final conversation. Perform tasks like battling Ifrit, catching Ramuh, and finishing quests from The Girl Who Forgot Her Name.

SCORE ATTACK!
PAC-MAN CHAMPIONSHIP EDITION 2
(PS4, Xbox One)

This game is built around chasing high scores. Can you score over 3,000,000 on the mountain course? You'll need to figure out the best route around the maze.

1

2

King's Quest (PS4, Xbox One)
Misteak

Sometimes it's worth doing things that don't make sense, just to squeeze a little extra enjoyment out of your games. It also pays to be observant. When you run past the bushes on the way into town during the first episode of *King's Quest*, you'll notice wolves in the bushes. Shortly afterward, you grab raw meat from the trap in the forest . . . what if you took it back to those bushes? Using the meat here will see the wolf spring from its hiding place, taking you to a "game over" screen. Even so, a Trophy will unlock for your efforts.

3

EASIEST ACHIEVEMENTS/TROPHIES

Overcooked
Overcooked (PS4, Xbox One)

Let any food burn, then put the fire out with a fire extinguisher. Trophy unlocked! You can complete this challenge on the very first level.

Victory
World of Tanks (PS4, Xbox One)

You just need to survive and win a multiplayer battle to unlock Victory. Team battles are so big, there will be games your team will win without you even having to play!

Listen . . . do you smell something?
Ghostbusters (PS4, Xbox One)

Collect 100,000 Ecto. Despite the daunting number, gathering all the Ecto in a single level is enough to complete this.

Welcome
UNO (PS4, Xbox One)

You just need to complete your first-ever round of *UNO* to unlock this Achievement. You don't even need to win. Just participate and it's yours.

In a Rocket Built For One Person?
Dragon Ball Xenoverse 2 (PS4, Xbox One)

When in Conton City after beating Raditz in the first mission, jump in a vehicle!

LEGO Dimensions
(PS4, Xbox One)
Forever Alone

Forget teamwork for this Achievement, which asks you to complete a level while keeping just one character active on the Toy Pad. You can do this quite easily on the opening level, Wizard of Oz: Yellow Brick Road. Using the original crew of Batman, Gandalf, and Wyldstyle, progress through the level as normal, ensuring you only ever have one character on the Toy Pad.

Minecraft: Story Mode (PS4, Xbox One)
Leveraging Resources

Messing around and being creative can yield rewards. When you're introduced to the workbench in chapter two of the first episode, you must build a sword. Instead of doing that, build a lever and the Trophy will unlock.

THE EXPERT SAYS...
HAKOOM
Unlocking the most PS4 Platinums in the world

Unlocking Trophies has improved my skills in many ways. Because I play every type of game to chase Platinums, I get experience in every type of game, and the more I play, the more I sharpen my skills. I am a better gamer now than I was in the past because I have more experience with games and online due to the sheer amount of games I have played—I've played over 1,700 games. It's like a job—the more you work, the better you get at it, and then you get promoted to a manager, then a GM, and so on.

EXPERT CHALLENGE!

Street Fighter V (PS4)

Win an online match without jumping even once. Jumping is a bad habit in *Street Fighter V*, so doing this will teach you strong fundamentals.

Ratchet & Clank (PS4)
Super Trader

You need to complete every Holocard set to unlock this Trophy. That means digging into each deep and dark corner of *Ratchet & Clank* to unearth the nine RYNO Holocards needed, on top of the 99 standard cards. It's a lesson in learning level layouts and how to sniff out secrets.

YOUR TURN!
Ultimate Explorer

Once you've collected all the cards in *Ratchet & Clank*, the next step is to collect all the gold bolts. You can use a Map-O-Matic from planet Kalebo III to help track them down—but again, level knowledge will trump all.

45

08:35 - Morning Roll Call (Day

THE ESCAPISTS

SPLIT SECOND

All you have to do is break out of jail in *The Escapists*. It's a goal that's tantalizingly just out of reach, as you can see the outside world through the barred windows of your prison cell. But slowly and surely, you start to formulate a plan. You might start a prison riot and escape in the mayhem. Perhaps you steal keys from the guards. Maybe you even dig a tunnel to freedom. New levels keep getting added to the game, and the new London Tower prison is the best yet.

Someone st
wardens t

1 You've been accused of treason, locked up without trial at the London Tower. The evidence against you has mysteriously gone missing, so it looks like you're doomed to spend the rest of your days in prison. Time to make an escape plan . . .

2 First learn the daily routine. There's a morning roll call, afternoon roll call, and evening roll call. Miss any, and you'll be in trouble with the guards. They'll find you, search your cell, and maybe put you in solitary confinement.

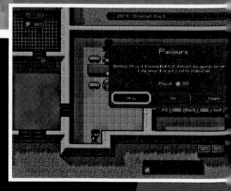

3 The trick is to learn when you can sneak off and gather resources for your escape. One of the jobs you have in the London Tower is to clear out weeds, so explore the area while you do it, talk to prisoners, and get items to hide in your cell.

4 Ultimately, you decide what to do and how to achieve it. Maybe walk out of the front door disguised as a prison officer, or fight your way out with inmates helping you. With so many escape options available, which will you go for?

TOP 10 ULTIMATE PARTY GAMES

DID YOU KNOW?

The ghost that appears in *Spelunky* when you spend too long in a level seems invincible, but it isn't. Lava pits deal some damage to it, but it takes ages to kill!

Overcooked

1 Stop! Move! Get out of my way! Quick! If you've ever been annoyed at watching someone else play games badly, try playing games *with* them. *Overcooked* is a game designed for maximum chaos, as you try and work with a friend to cook orders on time in a tiny kitchen. You don't even need two pads for this one, as two players can share the same pad to play.

Spelunky

2 Although it's widely loved as a single-player game, *Spelunky*'s hidden weapon is its four-player co-op mode. Having four adventurers try and coordinate a safe route to the exit in *Spelunky*'s deadly tombs is anarchy, and there's always the potential to "accidentally" whip another player into a pit of snakes.

Guitar Hero

3 *Guitar Hero* is the perfect party mix. You get a rocking soundtrack, the chance to perform, an audience, and everyone gets to have a try. You don't need two guitars to get the most out of *Guitar Hero*, as passing the guitar round a group of friends is enough to get the party started. Just don't be the player who ruins the song and gets booed off stage . . .

DIGITAL PARTY GAMES

Pass the tablet around and have a great time!

Heads Up!
You hold the tablet to your head and your team has to describe the word on the screen while you guess what the word is. The quick-fire rounds make this game hilarious fun!

Jenga
The best thing about *Jenga* on tablet is it gets rid of the only annoying aspect of the game—you don't have to rebuild the tower after each round. A steady hand is definitely needed.

Party Doodles
Other players have to guess the word based on doodles you've drawn. The worse you are at drawing, the more fun *Party Doodles* becomes, so if your drawing isn't great, don't worry!

Bounden
In this two-player game, each player grabs one end of the tablet. You must work together to tilt the device, to move an on-screen sphere through rings. It's exhausting but fun.

Ticket To Ride
It might not be the most glamorous of party games, but this digital take on the popular board game is perfect for if you want to play something a little slower to chill out.

Sing! Karaoke by Smule
Who needs a karaoke machine? Fire up this game and sing along to awesome songs by artists that cover all kinds of genres.

Worms W.M.D

4 If you want multiplayer fun but don't want to buy another controller, *Worms* is ideal. Players take turns to inflict damage on the other team using weapons including carpet bombs and exploding bananas. It's tactical but in a hilarious way, so it never gets *too* serious.

Peggle 2

5 All you do in *Peggle 2* is fire a ball into a table full of pegs, scoring more points as it hits more pegs. With more players involved, the element of luck makes *Peggle 2* surprisingly tense, as you end up screaming at the screen for the ball to hit *one last peg* for you to take the lead.

Nidhogg

6 *Nidhogg* takes the noble art of fencing and strips it of all nobility. It's played with neon colors, at blistering pace, and with more momentum swings than a pendulum clock. You have to reach the end of the level to win, but that means defeating your opponent multiple times.

Rocket League

7 With four players flying around the arena at once, split-screen multiplayer is *Rocket League* at its best! Two-on-two is the standard way to play, but there are others as well—you can add in bots for extra chaos, or pit one skilled player against three opponents in a thrilling handicap match!

Mario Party 10

9 Designed like a board game, players compete against each other in a race to see who can grab the most stars. Each turn throws up a new mini-game, ranging from dodging Bullet Bills to snowy mountain races. In *Mario Party 10*, a fifth player can join as villain Bowser, chasing the four players!

THE EXPERT SAYS ...
KELSEY CHRISTOU
Events marketing manager, Twitch

I love *Super Smash Bros. Brawl*. I'm a huge Nintendo fangirl so it is great to be able to have so many of my favorite characters to pick from, but of course I would always play as Pikachu! There are tons of modes to choose from but my favorite way to play is inviting over a bunch of friends to play in group mode and turning the items onto unlimited. It results in a very hectic and entertaining match as you compete with your friends to be the winner. Just don't forget which character you are playing as and accidentally walk off the edge of the platform . . .

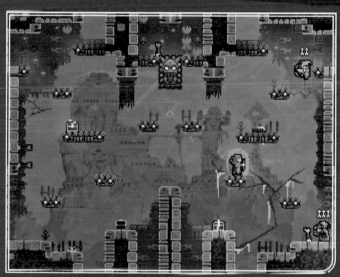

TowerFall Ascension

8 Put four players in a small arena, give them a bow with three arrows, then watch the anarchy unfold. *TowerFall Ascension* is a quick-fire showdown where you have to scramble for the best position to fire on your rivals and make your shots count. The fast rounds and easy-to-learn gameplay make this a guaranteed hit whenever you have friends over who are itching for some multiplayer action.

Divekick: Addition Edition+

10 *Divekick* is a fighting game anyone can play, as it has just two controls—jump and divekick. The controls are simple, but the tactics aren't. You need to consider when to jump, when to gamble on a divekick and what your opponent is going to do . . .

PIKMIN
ALIEN ANT FARM

DID YOU KNOW?
You can buy three short animated films about *Pikmin* from the Wii U and 3DS store to watch on the move wherever you are!

In *Pikmin*, you don't just control one character— you control 100 of them! Playing as Olimar and Louis, or Alph, Brittany, and Charlie, you look after the Pikmin, a strange army of small alien creatures that look like plants. Using the unique powers of the different-colored Pikmin, you have to find food sources to save the starving people of Koppai. The Pikmin are so small that the biggest challenge is overcoming the natural world, which seems enormous for the ant-like horde. You have to build bridges over flowing water, destroy barriers like cardboard boxes, and fight enemies like giant worms and swarms of bees. Most video games go big but *Pikmin* proves that it's just as much fun to go small. This brilliant game turns nature into a huge adventure.

STATS

87% average score for *Pikmin 3*

Control up to 100 Pikmin

Series began in 2001
4 games in the *Pikmin* series

YouTube 1 mln YouTube views for E3 trailer

TOP 5 PIKMIN

Pink Pikmin

1 These special winged Pikmin can fly, which makes them useful in specific situations. They can attack airborne enemies, fly over water, and even lift objects. Pink Pikmin are perfect for getting something done in a hurry.

Grey Pikmin

2 These rock-like Pikmin were new in *Pikmin 3* and they're useful in a ton of situations. They can smash through barriers, are immune to being crushed by heavy objects, and do more damage when thrown.

Yellow Pikmin

3 Yellow Pikmin are immune to electricity, so they can survive electrical hazards. This also means they can solve puzzles by linking hands and connecting severed wires. They can also throw bomb rocks and dig very fast.

Red Pikmin

4 These little red terrors are immune to fire, so are valuable in fire rounds. Red Pikmin also have the highest attack power. This means they are the quickest at tearing down obstacles like dirt walls.

Blue Pikmin

5 Blue Pikmin are the most balanced. They're durable, they're mobile, and they pack a punch, without really excelling in any category. They can swim, though, making them the best for beating aquatic enemies.

ALSO CHECK OUT . . .

New Little King's Story

Like *Pikmin*, but with people rather than alien ant creatures. You need to gather villagers and use them to build, attack enemies, mine resources, and so on.

Plants vs. Zombies 2

Grow plants to do your bidding as you try to stop zombies from reaching your house. The first game is lots of fun, too!

Super Smash Bros.

Captain Olimar shows up with the Pikmin by his side. He can pluck them out of the ground, throw them, and order them to carry him around.

TIPS & TRICKS

Leave planted Pikmin underground
Hold off plucking Pikmin from the ground for as long as possible so they have more time to grow into more powerful flower Pikmin.

Remember to charge
Shaking the Nunchuk or pressing B will make your Pikmin charge. This is your go-to move if you need to destroy an obstacle in a hurry.

Use the gamepad map wisely
An easy way to control Pikmin is to slide the stylus across the Gamepad, which sends your controlled Pikmin to the map area shown.

Beat butterflies
They aren't really enemies, but red and yellow butterflies contain nectar that you can use to power up your Pikmin. Take them out!

Use Wii Remote, Nunchuk, And Gamepad
This is the ideal control scheme for Pikmin on the Wii U. You can use the Wii Remote to aim at areas on-screen and the Nunchuk to closely control the camera. The screen on the Gamepad will act as a useful map.

DID YOU KNOW?

The Last Guardian was inspired by the union between Wander and his horse in the developer's previous game, *Shadow of the Colossus*.

THE LAST GUARDIAN

THE GAME THAT ALMOST DIDN'T HAPPEN

It's a game most gamers thought would never come out. But after years of development, it's finally here, and you can finally play it. The good news is that *The Last Guardian* has been worth its eight-year wait. It's about the friendship between a little boy and a strange creature called Trico, as they help each other to escape the castle they're trapped in. Controlling the boy, you need to earn

Trico's trust, helping him when he's injured, feeding him when he's hungry, and using his huge body to access new areas and solve puzzles. You'll slowly get drawn in to this odd friendship with the strange bird-mammal hybrid, as it turns from wild animal into your best friend. From its delicate art style to its fantastic setting, *The Last Guardian* is every bit a gothic fairy tale come to life.

STATS

2007 is when development first started

4 studios worked on the game

You Tube

5,700,000 YouTube views for E3 2015 trailer

4,200,000 YouTube views for launch trailer

440,000 YouTube views for 2010 trailer

TOP 5 WAYS TRICO HELPS YOU

Giving you a boost

1 Use Trico's huge size to your advantage by scampering up his neck, and climbing on top of his head to reach new areas. Think of Trico as a portable ladder, albeit one with a mind of his own and a tendency to wander off at times.

Smashing through doors

2 Work your way through the labyrinth, and you'll find areas you can't access, such as doors that are locked or rusted shut. Trico can use his bulk to smash through those doors, and his strength to reach other areas too.

Protecting you in battle

3 Trico can stand up to the guards in the castle. *The Last Guardian* isn't a game that features a heavy emphasis on combat, but when you're forced into a fight, Trico can turn the odds in your favor with swipes of his claws.

Reaching lower areas

4 Just as you can climb up Trico's neck to reach higher areas, you can reach areas lower down with the magnificent creature's help. Just encourage Trico to dangle his tail, and you can use it as a makeshift rope.

Finding hidden areas

5 Like a curious animal, Trico will sniff around when left alone, and sometimes uncover a hidden area. This works best in wide, open areas where Trico has room to explore and poke around. Just sit back and watch what happens!

ALSO CHECK OUT . . .

The Ico & Shadow of the Colossus Collection
The developer's previous two games, packaged together in HD, focus on you trying to survive a surreal and unusual world.

Papo & Yo
Just like *The Last Guardian*, you have to learn how to tame an unusual creature in this game, and use its animal behavior to your advantage.

Journey
Together with an online companion, you travel through the enchanting world of *Journey*, crossing deserts, walking valleys, and climbing mountains.

TIPS & TRICKS

Remove spears
Trico won't listen to you if he's in pain, such as if he's got spears stuck in him. Remove them with the Circle button.

Making Trico follow you
If you want Trico to follow you, call out to him by pressing the R1 button. He won't follow you if he's in a bad mood or hungry.

Keeping Trico happy
If Trico isn't listening to your commands, try feeding him more barrels. To do this, bring barrels in front of Trico and wait.

Calm Trico down
If Trico is acting erratically (jumping and roaring), you'll need to calm him down. Climb on his back and hold the Circle button.

Let Trico lead the way
If you become stuck, climb on Trico's back and see what he does. Sometimes he will point out the way ahead.

TOP 10
BEST GAMING ACCESSORIES

Recording microphone

1 If you're 13 or older, maybe you've got your eye on creating Let's Play videos or invading YouTube with your own take on the best and worst video games that are out there? Then you're going to need fantastic audio recording. You'll get better audio quality from a standalone mic compared to a headset, and a mic is great for Let's Plays, or just chatting to friends.

RAZER SEIRĒN MICROPHONE

Webcam

2 Everybody knows that there's more to gaming than just, you know, *playing* the games these days. If you have your eye on vlogging and creating awesome videos, a webcam will help you create great content and build your audience. Video quality is king in these situations, so it may be good to have a camera that can support 1080p recorded and streaming video.

Streaming microphone

3 For the budding video superstar, a high-quality microphone is always helpful. You can use Kinect or the PlayStation Camera or a headset. But you might want one of the latest batch of mics that are designed specifically for vloggers who want great audio and cool design. There are loads of great ones to choose from.

STREAMING STARTER GUIDE

Six essential things you'll need to start broadcasting your gaming sessions to the world!

1 STREAMING SERVICE
With two main streaming services available, we recommend quickly choosing between Twitch and YouTube Gaming, if you're 13 or older.

4 A CAMERA
If you really want to raise your profile, a solid camera will do a world of good. There are a variety of different options available, so do some research online. Ideally you want a 1080p HD camera, but 720p would be okay, too.

2 DIGITAL ACCESSORY
Once that's out of the way, you'll want to look into enhancing your broadcast. A few digital accessories are available to transform your PC streams.

5 ADD LIGHTING
Not a gaming accessory per se, but investing in lighting will really improve the quality of your streams. You can buy beginner lighting rigs online, and these will bring a new dynamic to your streams.

3 A GOOD MICROPHONE
Getting good audio quality is key. If you're gaming on console, a headset will work, but a dedicated microphone will provide superior audio quality.

6 BE A PRO
Now you just need to impress people. While nothing can replace genuine skill, a pro controller (or equivalent mouse and keyboard for you PC gamers) can make a big difference. Time to get practicing!

PS4 pro controller

4 While Sony doesn't offer an official PS4 equivalent to the Xbox One's Elite controller, you can still get a pro-level controller that can help you up your game. Some controllers come equipped with advanced customization options and unique ergonomics, to help keep you at the top of your game.

Xbox One pro controller

6 If you've got serious intentions of going pro—or at the very least improving your leaderboard positioning— you should consider something like Microsoft's own Xbox One Elite Controller. Controllers like this allow you to customize buttons, add extra paddles to the back of the controller, and edit stuff like sensitivity.

Capture kit

7 This little box plugs in to your PC or Mac and helps you capture game footage and screenshots. A high-end capture device will be able to record footage at 1080p, and can even stream your games.

Wireless gaming headset

9 For some great multiplayer gaming, you're going to want to get yourself a wireless headset. You'll be able to hear the action in crisp surround sound, and the quality microphone will help you communicate with your friends as you play together.

Pokémon GO Plus

5 With Niantic and The Pokémon Company increasing the number of new Pokémon to catch and hatch out in the wild, accessories like the The Pokémon GO Plus are really useful. They connect to your smartphone to help you catch Pokémon and collect items from PokéStops without having to pull out your device.

THE EXPERT SAYS ...
KEITH HENNESSEY
Communications Director, Turtle Beach

Developers spend a great deal of time and money on sound design, including casting voice actors and scoring music, in order to create detailed and realistic soundscapes. So in many ways, the game audio is just as important to the overall experience as the visuals. That's why a good gaming headset is so vital. Not only does it immerse you in the game world in the way the development team intended, but it can also give you a competitive advantage in multiplayer games, enabling you to hear the enemy sneaking up behind you or communicate with your teammates during a frantic battle.

Gaming Keyboard

8 If you love playing games on PC, you can take your play to the next level with a dedicated gaming keyboard. Keyboards like this have super clicky "mechanical" keys to offer better feedback, and are designed specifically with gaming in mind. They often have key labels specific to gaming genres, meaning an upgrade like this can often take your play to the next level.

Customized controllers

10 While having a pro controller is pretty cool, it's also possible to get a personalized gamepad. Some companies sell customized versions of official controllers, and Microsoft is letting Xbox One owners design and customize their own through Xbox.com, with the service letting you put together custom colors and even add your Gamertag. Alternatively, you can pick up some decals or special grips for your controllers to make it feel unique.

Sunny
OK

Happy
GOOD

Funky
OK

Crazy
PERFECT

Bab
GOO

DID YOU KNOW?

If you don't have a motion controller for your PS4 or Xbox One, you can also play *Just Dance* with an app, turning your smartphone into the controller.

JUST DANCE 2017
DANCE, DANCE, DANCE

Sometimes it's fun to just shake loose. *Just Dance 2017* is the perfect dance partner. It gives you some awesome tunes and moves to copy, so you look like you've slid right out of a YouTube music video. You can get competitive by tackling Dance Quests, take on the world with Just Dance TV, or prove your fitness with Sweat mode. There are 40 songs to dance through, from Beyoncé to Maroon 5, but *Just Dance Unlimited* lets you stream songs from previous games. It also adds new tracks to the series, like DJ Snake and Justin Bieber's *Let Me Love You*.

STATS

40 new tracks

200 extra songs through *Just Dance Unlimited*

Released for 7 different consoles

8 games in main *Just Dance* series

11 spin-offs including *Just Dance Kids*

TOP 5 SONGS TO DANCE TO

ALSO CHECK OUT . . .

Dance Central Spotlight

The staggered difficulty slowly introduces players to new dance moves, making it a great choice for those who don't have the confidence to jump right in.

Sorry—Justin Bieber

1 It's no surprise to see Justin Bieber's worldwide hit on this list—it's just so easy to move to! Not only is *Sorry* a crowd-pleaser when you have friends over, as they'll want to sing along (hopefully in tune!), but it has a great mix of slow moves and quick dancing.

Xbox Fitness

If you love working up a sweat while dancing, *Xbox Fitness* is the logical step, as it's strictly focused on staying fit and healthy. It's also completely free.

PoPiPo— Hatsune Miku

2 A virtual pop star joins the party! Hatsune Miku, star of the Sega rhythm-action games, brings a particularly high-energy slice of electro-pop with this catchy tune. A lot of the moves are over-the-top or a bit silly, making it all the more amusing to dance around to.

What Is Love— Ultraclub 90

3 It's an all-time classic song, but that's not what makes this such a fun choice. There are lots of moves where you slide side to side, so clear some room before you start playing and enjoy dancing to a cover version of a nineties classic!

Run The Night— Gigi Rowe

4 Pure pop is the order of the day here! Up-and-coming artist Gigi Rowe delivers a great song that sits alongside the hits of much bigger stars just fine, and it's really fun to dance to—all the repeated patterns mean you can learn the moves and ignore the screen!

Wherever I Go— OneRepublic

5 This one makes a nice change of pace, a slightly slower track that serves as a great warm-up. Don't let the lower tempo catch you out, though—there are still some quick and tricky moves thrown in, so stay on your toes.

Fruit Ninja Kinect 2

For something a little more frantic, your dancing skills could make you a *Fruit Ninja* pro as you slice the fruit that flies across the screen at lightning speed.

TIPS & TRICKS

Stretch first
Stretch your limbs before you get started to decrease the chance of hurting yourself or pulling a muscle while dancing. It happens!

Clear the area
Make sure you move any furniture out of the way, or anything that can be damaged. You'll be moving around a lot!

Start slow
Pick one of the slower tracks to get warmed up, rather than an up-tempo one, and play on Easy to learn moves.

Exaggerate your movements
It's better to exaggerate your dance moves, so the game is more likely to recognize them, and to help you get into the song, of course!

Focus on the lower-right
The dancing movements you need to perform appear on the bottom-right of the screen, so look at those and not the actual dancer.

CUPHEAD
WHEN OLD MEETS NEW

DID YOU KNOW?

All of the graphics in *Cuphead* are carefully drawn by hand, and the studio went through hundreds of pens every month!

Stop and gape at the screenshots. Look at the lush, vintage, cartoon style oozing from these pages. *Cuphead* is beautiful, but don't be fooled by its retro charms—*Cuphead* is a lean, mean, running-and-gunning machine. This fast-paced shooter puts you up against a series of bosses that have sprung from the wildest of imaginations. From owl wizards in magician garb to boxing frogs, you'll have no idea what you're fighting next, and the big, bad bosses just keep on coming. *Cuphead* throws in a few platforming levels, but puts the emphasis on its standout boss battles, which offer the perfect platform to show off that beautiful art style. An ideal mix of old and new, it's a treat for your eyes, and a challenge for your thumbs as well.

STATS

2 brothers created *Cuphead*

150 attempted designs to create main character

Development started in **2010**

Over 30 bosses to fight

TOP 5 BOSSES

Do you have what it takes to bring down *Cuphead*'s most imposing enemies?

The evil plant

1 Many years of experience in tackling boss fights teaches you that keeping your distance will keep you safe. That is not the case here, because you can be struck anywhere at any time, making this a rather tense test of your reflexes.

The boxing monster

2 There's no time to relax in this fight. The boxing monster wants to get close so it can swing at you with its fists, keeping you on your heels as you try to strike the balance between attacking and running away.

The flying gentleman

3 *Cuphead* isn't limited to fighting on the ground. Some of the larger-than-life bosses—such as this dapper gentleman with a vicious tongue—can only be tackled by taking to the skies.

The pirate ship

4 You'll feel exhausted when this boss battle is done. You have to survive the pirate firing at you, the pirate ship itself spitting projectiles, and even deadly barrels dropping in from overhead.

The ghost train

5 The guardian of this train is a ghost, which shoots eyeballs out of its hands at you. These eyeballs slowly hone in on you, adding a constant threat as you try to fire back at the ghost.

ALSO CHECK OUT ...

Resogun
One of the best games on PS4, this fast-paced arcade title also has the beauty to match its brawn. Good luck keeping up with the action!

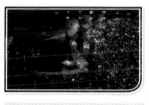

Super Time Force
This smart, side-scrolling shooter game blends time travel alongside its run-and-gun antics, as each level piles up the visual chaos and anarchy.

Shovel Knight
If you're looking for tough platforming gameplay with a retro style, there are few better options out there than this pixel-art gem.

TIPS & TRICKS

Don't be afraid to die
Take risks to see how close you can get to the bosses, which areas of the screen are safe, and so on. It's worth losing lives to get that information.

Keep moving
Always keep moving in *Cuphead*. You never know when a boss is going to quickly fire a projectile your way, and if you're moving, it will probably miss.

Play with a friend
You can have a second player join you, playing as Mug Man. Not only is the extra pair of hands useful, but you'll also have someone to discuss strategies with!

Never stop firing
Even if it doesn't seem like you're hitting anything, you never know when the boss might accidentally stray in your line of fire.

Try again the next day
Sometimes fatigue will be your biggest enemy, especially as *Cuphead* is so relentless. Don't be afraid to take a break and try again tomorrow.

DRAGON QUEST BUILDERS

AKA SLIMECRAFT!

If you love games that let you use your imagination to create homes, towns, and even castles, *Dragon Quest Builders* is for you.

The good news is that you don't need to dig through a guidebook to figure out how to play, since *Dragon Quest Builders* gives you all the information you need to get building. Upon discovering a material, for example, your character learns exactly what kinds of things they can make with it straightaway, letting you focus on what really matters: making awesome buildings and creations. And that's what this game is all about—building. Characters that you meet will give you building tasks to complete, and a few guidelines for what the building should include. From there, it's totally up to you how you build, so you can make a tiny hut out of wood, or a huge castle out of stone!

That's not all, though: the game has a compelling story, with tough bosses, all wrapped up in *Dragon Quest*'s fantastic visual design.

STATS

Over **1** million copies sold

Dragon Quest is **31** years old

84 average score for *Dragon Quest Builders* from 54 scored reviews (source: opencritic)

32 games in the franchise

3.5 percent of players who have earned the

Platinum Trophy

TOP 5 SURVIVAL ESSENTIALS

Weapons

1 It is dangerous to go out into the wilderness with nothing to defend yourself. There are monsters and all sorts of dastardly creatures out there, so you better arm yourself with something. This could come in the form of a club, a hammer, or a sword.

Food

2 In *Dragon Quest Builders*, you have to keep your character's hunger meter topped up by chowing down on anything from burgers to berries. You can whip up food by building a kitchen.

Armor

3 You shouldn't go out into the wilderness without protection. Create a forge and smith yourself some decent armor. We recommend spiked armor, which looks awesome, but also reflects damage back at enemies when they attack.

Knowledge

4 Having a weapon and armor is good, but useless if you don't know what you're up against. Each monster behaves differently, so you must react accordingly. Take these rock-like creatures: they won't attack right away, but store up energy, then explode!

A trump card

5 There will be times when it seems that all is lost, and that's when you need to pull out that special item that will bring you back from the brink. Our choices are a good old-fashioned bomb, or an impregnable shield —these are especially helpful against Golems.

ALSO CHECK OUT . . .

Minecraft

The definitive crafting sandbox; the LEGO of video games. *Minecraft* needs no introduction, it's clear just how much this game has influenced gaming.

Terraria

This 2-D world-building game packs magic, monsters, and creation into a randomly generated world. Exploring is tense, but great fun.

Don't Starve

If you like the idea of survival while being chased by weird and wonderful monsters, then *Don't Starve* is the game for you. You'll need to plan well and find resources if you want to survive.

TIPS & TRICKS

Escape to the country

Explore! Who knows what you may find out in the wilds. Whatever you find out there will help you, regardless.

Spin to win

You can utilize your spinning attack in order to quickly amass materials. Take a hammer, dig down underground, and spin away to mine quickly!

Making a point

Lay down spikes around your settlement, and you will find that monsters will get caught on them and lose life very quickly.

Double stack

You can hold down the Square button to place two blocks in quick succession, one on top of the other, which is useful for saving you time.

Salt of the earth

Make your buildings using regular old dirt, and you can later craft items that modify the dirt into stone blocks.

TROVE
WORLD OF WARCRAFT GETS BLOCKY

DID YOU KNOW?

The servers had to be restarted by the developer three times on launch day due to the high number of people playing *Trove*.

What happens when you cross *World of Warcraft*'s gameplay with cool pixel graphics? *Trove* is what happens! It's an online sandbox game that pits you against a horde of blocky monsters as you level up and hunt better loot to equip. You pick from classes, such as Ice Sage and Neon Ninja, before venturing forth into *Trove*'s blocky world, with portals separating each area by difficulty.

Unlike most MMOs, *Trove* is a fast-paced game, against weird and wonderful adversaries like giant lollipops and zombie miners. It isn't weighed down by hundreds of menus or slow, laborious gameplay, as you leap and bounce around enemies while popping off your special moves. Bright and breezy, fast and furious, *Trove* is the perfect blend of co-op gaming, action, and humor!

STATS

15 different classes

3 crafting professions

250 maximum level for each profession

5 cool rewards for inviting friends

1,270,000 YouTube views for *Mantle of Power* trailer
You Tube

TOP 5 CLASSES

What will you do in this crazy new world?

1 Chloromancer

Chloromancer is *Trove*'s commander of color, with an array of spells that light up the screen and blind opponents with their dazzling beauty. Attack from a distance or up close with this flexible class; just put your sunglasses on, as the colors are super-bright!

2 Dino Tamer

If you want to play a class that's oozing with fun, Dino Tamer is the only choice. Not only do you have an array of traps to catch the wandering dinos with, but you can also clamber on the back of these prehistoric beasts and ride them around. Now that's traveling in style!

3 Fae Trickster

The playing style is centered around staying out of harm's way. Avoid taking damage, and your own attack increases, plus you can teleport away from danger, leaving a decoy that enemies attack instead. Combine the two and you can quickly rack up damage.

4 Tomb Raiser

Tomb Raiser shows it can be fun getting others to do your dirty work. You can summon a small minion army from the ground, as they quickly climb all over your target, chomping away at their health.

5 Candy Barbarian

With his crushing leap attacks and moves that suck enemies towards him, Candy Barbarian is perfect for plowing through an army of weaker minions.

ALSO CHECK OUT . . .

Bastion

This incredible fantasy adventure sees you controlling "the Kid," a hero who travels through a fractured world defeating enemies to find a safe haven.

Zelda: Breath of the Wild

If you love adventuring, battling monsters, and finding cool weapons and armor, Link's latest adventure is a must.

World of Warcraft

It's still the world's biggest MMORPG, and those who find the online aspect of *Trove* super-fun are guaranteed to love *World of Warcraft*.

TIPS & TRICKS

Remember to dodge

Most enemies have a windup animation for their most powerful attack. Learn the animation and dodge when you see it.

Take out ranged enemies first

When fighting a big group, take out ranged enemies first. They're usually quick to kill, but can cause a lot of damage if left alone.

Avoid summoned monsters

Some bosses summon monsters, but these give you no experience points when killed. It's usually better to just ignore them.

Don't build your house right away

Make sure that you hold off from building your home (known in *Trove* as a "cornerstone") until you have found a few recipes to build it with.

Play with friends

It makes the game much more fun, and you don't have to split your loot or experience points with friends.

CAPTURE THIS!

WIPEOUT: OMEGA COLLECTION

Win a clean race in the highest speed class

One for the true future racing masters! *WipEout* games get incredibly fast—in order to lead the pack, you'll need expert course knowledge, quick reflexes, and solid air-brake skills. If you can put all three together, be sure to get a screenshot or video of your glorious moment, and share it with all of your friends!

POOCHY & YOSHI'S WOOLLY WORLD

CUTENESS OVERLOAD

Remember Mario's lizard sidekick, Yoshi? He gets to shine in his own outing when the evil Magikoopa, Kamek, has turned all the other Yoshis into yarn. That means running and jumping your way through six worlds of platforming mayhem while falling in love with the world around you. Everything is made from yarn and cloth, giving it a gorgeous look that makes you want to stroke it. In *Poochy & Yoshi's Woolly World*, a 3DS port of the Wii U original, you can even design your own Yoshi patterns to use in the game. There are also brand-new levels designed around fresh-faced Poochy, Yoshi's canine friend. It all adds up to the cutest game of the year—if not ever!

STATS

Over 1,370,000 copies sold worldwide

6 different worlds

20 Stamp Patches hidden in each level

5 Smiley Flowers hidden in each level

5 Wonder Wools hidden in each level

TOP 5 ENEMIES

DID YOU KNOW?

In *Super Smash Bros.* there is a battle stage based on *Yoshi's Woolly World* featuring yarn platforms.

Shy Guy Tower

1 It's one of the classic *Mario* foes, but Yoshi doesn't have to fight one of them, or even two, or three. Yoshi is against *four* of the bad guys, stacked on top of each other, as they use the power of teamwork to put a stop to your journey. Take them out one at a time!

Goonie

2 This flapping bird patrols the skies in *Yoshi's Woolly World*, and you often need a well-placed yarn shot in order to clear the way. However, you get more than one Goonie variation to deal with here. There are also Flightless Goonies, Skeletal Goonies, and Flightless Skeletal Goonies—creepy.

Stalking Piranha Plant

3 This classic *Mario* enemy is usually hiding in warp pipes, snapping at the plumber's heels as he leaps overhead. Yoshi must deal with a trickier version of the Piranha Plant here, as this one stalks you, and backs you into a corner.

Giant Nep-Enut

4 Of course, not everything is adorable on Yoshi's journey, as Giant Nep-Enut is the closest the game gets to something ominous and scary. It's the outline of yarn and size of Giant Nep-Enut that make you stop in your tracks, as you try to work out how to safely sneak past it.

Bomb Guy

5 Proof that anything can be cute in *Yoshi's Woolly World*, Bomb Guy is dwarfed by the explosive device he's carrying around. It doesn't seem all that threatening when it's made of yarn, but don't be fooled—this will still harm Yoshi if you get reckless as Bomb Guy closes in.

ALSO CHECK OUT . . .

New Super Mario Bros. U

It's a faster, trickier platforming beast than *Yoshi's Woolly World*, and the perfect next step up for those who have conquered this fun adventure.

Super Mario Maker

If you have your own ideas for 2-D Nintendo platforming fun, *Super Mario Maker* lets you get creative on both Wii U and 3DS.

Captain Toad: Treasure Tracker

The only game that can rival *Yoshi's Woolly World* in the cuteness stakes, this 3-D platformer is slow and steady.

TIPS & TRICKS

Don't hunt secrets immediately
Play through a level before returning to find the hidden Stamp Patches, Smiley Flowers, and Wonder Wools.

Use yarn balls on collectibles
Using yarn balls is an excellent way to grab collectibles that are just out of reach. Just make sure you remember to aim your shot first!

Save yarn balls for bosses
It's always a good idea to hold on to a few yarn balls for bosses, as attacking from a distance keeps Yoshi safe from harm.

Eat enemies for yarn
If you need some yarn and there are no yarn blocks around, eat an enemy and press down on the D-pad. This gives you a single ball of yarn.

Fly through it
If you get really stuck, switch to Mellow Mode and you can fly through the level. It might even help you to figure out why you're stuck.

★ FEATURE

SUPERHERO ROUNDUP

I NEED A HERO

DID YOU KNOW?

LEGO *Marvel Super Heroes* isn't just a video game—it also has a mini-series that you can watch online, and a TV special as well.

Being a superhero is the best job in the world. You travel the world, save people, gain adoring fans, and work alongside the likes of Batman, Iron Man, and The Hulk. Okay, maybe not The Hulk—it's difficult to deal with his bad days at work. Even so, whether it's stomping evil on the streets of New York or going toe-to-toe with a supervillain in an explosive display of eye-popping powers, games that help you feel like a true hero are lots of fun. Superhero games cover every genre, from platforming to fighting games to MMORPGs, either placing you in the shoes of a well-known hero or allowing you to create your own. These games are the pick of a mighty genre.

STATS

8 Marvel games on PS4 and Xbox One

5 DC Comics games on PS4 and Xbox One

424,000 *Injustice* sales in first month

18 min registered *DC Universe Online* players

180 characters in LEGO *Marvel Super Heroes*

TOP 5 SUPERHERO GAMES

LEGO Marvel Super Heroes

1 The biggest Marvel party ever, this brings 180 characters together from the farthest corners of the Marvel universe. There are the big names like Iron Man and Hulk mingling alongside the lesser-known faces like Squirrel Girl and Toad. You all join forces to solve tricky puzzles, and fight bad guys on your quest to stop the planet-eating Galactus.

Injustice 2

2 Dark, moody, and mysterious, this one-on-one fighting game nails the DC Comics vibe with its grungy look and gritty brawling. It has a fantastic story line that draws on DC Comics's rich history, and battling your friends online is great, competitive fun.

Transformers Devastation

3 Created by Platinum, the masters of action games, this brawler is packed with explosive colors, fast cars, and enormous robots fighting each other. Underneath the shiny surface beats the heart of a complex fighting game. Only those who take the time mastering *Devastation* will get to face Megatron . . .

Marvel vs. Capcom Infinite

4 The crazy crossover series returns! This two-on-two fighter pits your favorite Marvel icons against Capcom's bravest warriors. Over-the-top special moves and super attacks still explode off the screen, but it's been made a little easier for newcomers to get into this time.

DC Universe Online

5 This MMORPG has players all around the world creating superheroes (or villains) before swooping through Gotham and Metropolis, fighting iconic DC characters—and even each other. Thanks to its huge amount of quests and secrets to discover, this massive game will last you hundreds of hours.

TIME LINE

2011 — DC Universe Online
DC Universe Online became one of the first major console MMOs and is still going strong to this day.

2013 — Injustice: Gods Among Us
This game surprised everyone when it brought DC's deadliest together for a huge brawl.

2015 — LEGO Marvel's Avengers
Tying in with the movie release *Age of Ultron*, LEGO *Marvel's Avengers* mixed platforming, action, and humor.

2013 — Marvel Puzzle Quest
This clever puzzle game combined tile-matching with the need to pick the right special moves at the right time.

2014 — Marvel: Contest of Champions
This mobile fighter game included Marvel characters not usually seen in gaming, like Rhino and Colossus.

2016 — Batman: Return To Arkham
This pack brought the critically acclaimed *Arkham Asylum* and *Arkham City* games together.

MEET THE SUPERFAN

DOMINIQUE "SONIC FOX" MCLEAN

Who?
Sonic Fox emerged as the best *Injustice* player in the world, winning tournaments from Winter Brawl to EVO with ease. In fact, after winning his 13th tournament, he even set a world record for the most tournament victories in *Injustice*.

Why?
Sonic Fox used Batgirl in *Injustice* to great effect, using her speed to bully opponents and unlock their defense. No one else put the time into *Injustice* that Sonic Fox did, and his game knowledge and confidence powered him to the winner's podium in almost every tournament he entered.

IN DEPTH TOUGHEST BOSSES

Giant Superman (LEGO Batman 3: Beyond Gotham)
As LEGO *Batman 3* rumbles towards its dramatic conclusion, Brainiac turns Superman against your crew. Not only that, Superman grows in size, adding huge bulk to his already incredible power!

Shredder (TMNT: Mutants in Manhattan)
Shredder is an intimidating foe, thanks to his suit of armor covered with razor blades. He slowly stalks the Turtles to try and push them into a corner, before lashing out with his razor-tipped fists.

ALSO CHECK OUT...

Overwatch
From cyborg ninjas to gritty cowboys, *Overwatch* has a huge cast of great, colorful personalities with their own unique abilities for you to choose from in this team shooter.

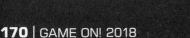

Galactus (Ultimate Marvel vs. Capcom 3)

This enormous boss towers over every Marvel hero and villain in *Ultimate Marvel vs. Capcom 3*. You have to slowly whittle down his health bar while dodging his giant, earth-shattering attacks, which takes some stamina.

THE EXPERT SAYS ...

RYAN & JAKE NEAL

AKA "Ketchup & Mustard," *Injustice* commentators

Injustice is a perfect opportunity to introduce a new audience to fighting games. For those looking for casual fun, the game has a wide selection of offline modes to keep you entertained. For those looking to take their skills to the next level, there's a wide variety of in-depth mechanics and attributes that made *Injustice* a unique competitive experience. A notable addition is the ability to use the stages to your advantage, and the way characters interact changes depending on your selected hero or villain.

DID YOU KNOW?

The developers of *Injustice: Gods Among Us* used a Twitter poll to decide which extra characters to add to the game.

Megatron (Transformers Devastation)

The final showdown in *Transformers Devastation* pits you against Megatron in an arena sealed off by deadly lasers. You need to face the powerful Decepticon leader in a one-on-one battle and triumph.

Marvel Ultimate Alliance

This gaming classic has been re-released on Xbox One and PS4. While the graphics might not blow you away, the fast-paced action is perfect for playing with friends.

Batman: Arkham Underworld

In this unusual twist on the caped crusaders adventures, you play as the villain. You'll need to build an underground lair and defend it from other players in this strategy game.

TERRARIA
FIND PEACE IN AN ENDLESS SANDBOX

Terraria has risen to prominence as one of the biggest indie game successes ever. First released in 2011 by developer Re-Logic, the game found success through its unique blend of exploration, crafting, and construction, letting gamers build wild worlds in procedurally generated 2-D spaces. It's a beautiful game, with its 16-bit graphical style being wholly reminiscent of the SNES era of gaming, though its mechanics and systems surpass anything anyone thought games could be capable of back in the nineties.

Terraria offers a deep sandbox that truly lets players carve out their own mark and story on the world; whether you are diving into dungeons, building beautiful structures, or crafting an array of awesome weapons and items, there's always something new to do and discover here. If you're looking for a game full of depth, one that becomes bigger and more varied the longer you spend with it, then *Terraria* will be the perfect game for you—it's a 2-D *Minecraft* with elements of classic platformers peppered in for good effect.

STATS

18 million copies of *Terraria* sold across all formats

3,646 items can appear in the game

Over 1 million average YouTube views a week

5 different layers to the main overworld

Features over **192 block types**

TOP 5 COOL THINGS TO TRY

Gold Ore (3)

Get lost in the jungle

1 While it's easy enough to get distracted by the NPCs and dark descent to Hades in *Terraria*, you should never ignore the jungle region. It's a huge, sprawling part of the game world, requiring multiple trips to resupply and harvest all of the secrets that lie hidden in its tangled web of danger.

ALSO CHECK OUT...

Minecraft
Exploring caves, gathering materials, building shelters and fighting monsters? There are some obvious similarities between *Minecraft* and *Terraria*!

Starbound
Essentially *Terraria* in space, *Starbound* has a sandbox built around reactive play and randomly generated items, quests, and weather cycles. It's really quite awesome.

King Arthur's Gold
Create freeform constructions, fight in big sword battles, or snipe enemies as an archer in a combat-focused take on the *Terraria* spirit.

Craft some Obsidian

2 Obsidian is used to craft some of the game's more significant items, but coming across it can be a challenge. You might want to build wild construction lines between surface water pools on the top layers and the lava pools in the lower Stratas of the game world.

Explore the skies

3 Floating, and hidden by the clouds, are islands containing precious metals and loot, locked away by keys that can be found only in the dungeons. These islands are hard to locate, but building a solid sky bridge is the best way to locate them.

Enter the dungeon

4 Head as far east or west in your procedurally generated game world to find the Old Man. Return at night, and he will transform into Skeletron, a powerful creature guarding the dungeon. This boss battle and the dungeon is one of the game's toughest challenges.

Going down?

5 The deepest subterranean level of *Terraria* is Hades, and it's awesomely horrible. To get there, you'll need potions crafted from Obsidian, fire-resistant items, and enough inventory space to gather up the epic loot to be found, guarded by *Terraria*'s most disgusting monsters.

TIPS & TRICKS

Get wood
Don't overlook the basics! Store up as much wood as you can, since it is vital for building structures and workbenches.

Beware the night
Terraria operates on a day/night cycle, and the scariest beasts come out in the dark. Stick to your shelter until you're sufficiently geared up.

The essentials
Eager to explore? First make sure that you build yourself a Furnace and an Iron Anvil in order to expand your crafting options.

Have a stock of torches
Killing Slimes for the gel that they drop will let you create torches, and should ensure that you have a ton on you at *all* times.

Build even more houses
Building empty houses will invite local NPCs to come and take up residence, offering a number of useful services in return.

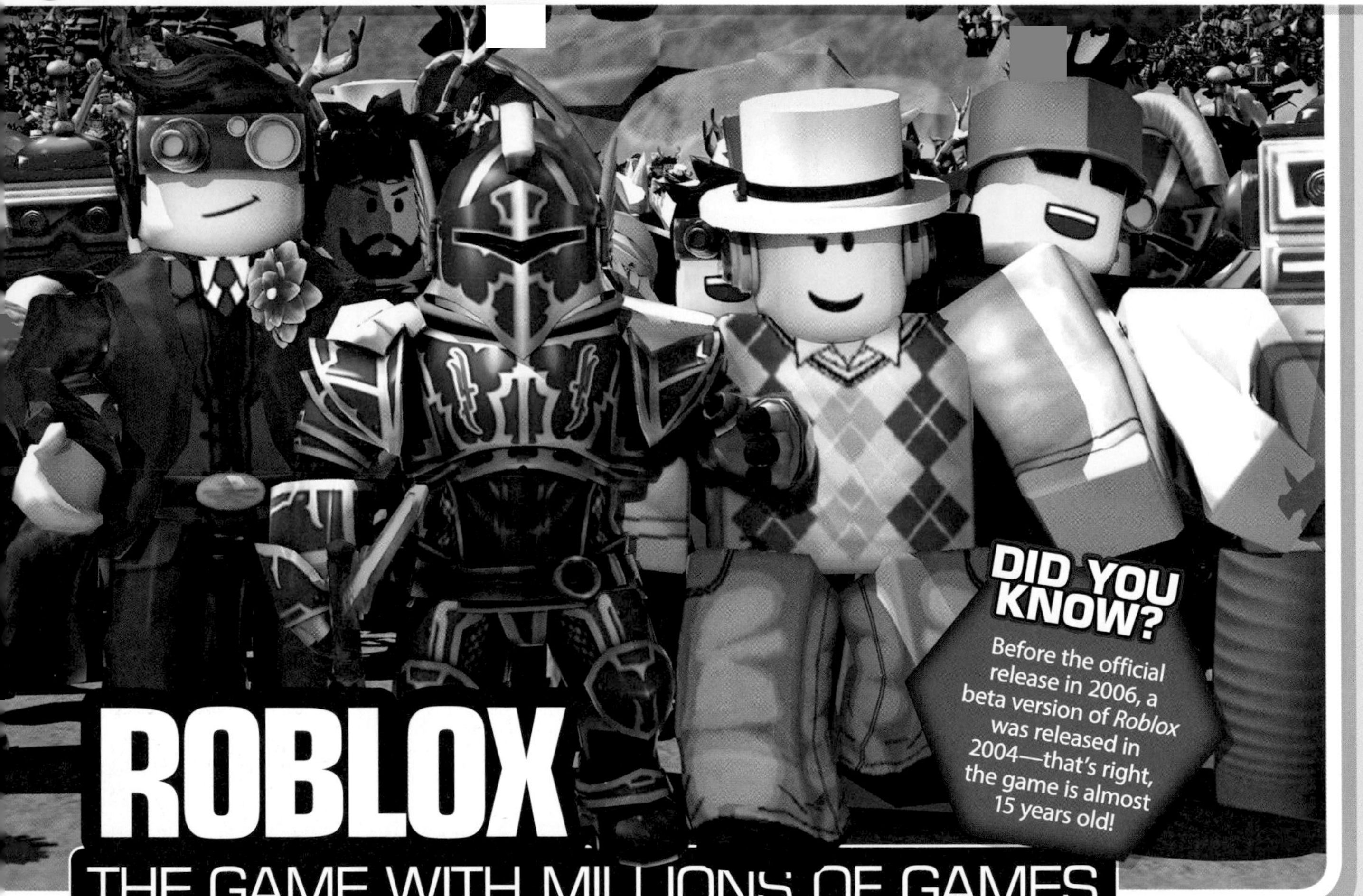

ROBLOX

THE GAME WITH MILLIONS OF GAMES

DID YOU KNOW?

Before the official release in 2006, a beta version of *Roblox* was released in 2004—that's right, the game is almost 15 years old!

Roblox isn't really a game itself. It's a toolkit that can be used to create new games or play in ones made by others, and there are over 15 million of them so far. Whatever kind of game you want to play, you can more than likely find it in *Roblox*. There are thousands of genres and ideas crammed into it, and more are being added and updated on a daily basis. It has everything from dodgeball to paintball, from bird simulators to natural disaster simulators, from running a wood business to working at a pizza parlor. *Roblox* games might not have the visual sparkle of *Final Fantasy XV* or the depth of *Minecraft*, but they don't need to. After all, what others games offer you the chance to play whatever you want, whenever you want?

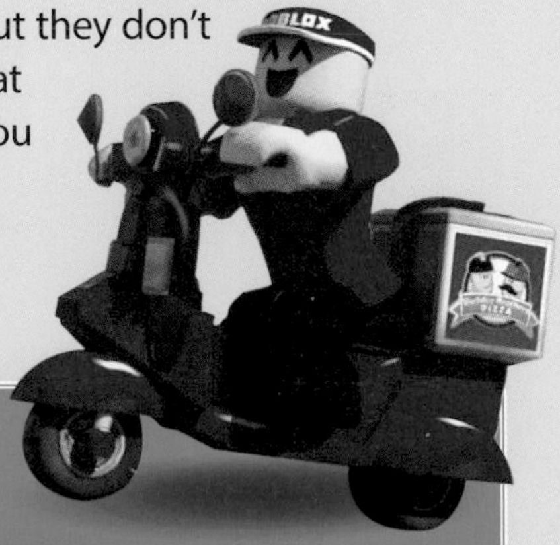

STATS

Originally released in **2006**

Up to **100** players online

2 player co-op online

Over **15 million** games created to date

44 million active players every month

TOP 5 ROBLOX GAMES

Wins:

Super Bomb Survival

1 Bombs are raining down from the sky and you need to survive until the time runs out. That means avoiding tumbling dynamite, towers falling over from bomb blasts, and players themselves being thrown across the level by the huge explosions.

Hide and Seek

2 Sometimes the simplest games are the best ones. You have 30 seconds to find somewhere to hide, before the player chosen as "it" gets to move. What starts as hide-and-seek often ends as a frantic chase, as you desperately avoid "it" touching you until time runs out.

Natural Disaster

3 In this crazy game, every player gets transported to a small island where various natural disasters, like earthquakes or tsunamis, occur. You simply have to survive for as long as possible, which is made harder as players scramble around in a blind panic. It's a lot more fun than it sounds!

Dragon's Rage

4 Trapped on a small island with other players, you need to survive as dragons swoop past and smash through the ground beneath you. As you fight over the remaining space with the other players, more dragons fill the sky. The last few seconds can be absolute anarchy.

Bird Simulator

5 It's not all madness and mayhem with *Roblox*'s games. *Bird Simulator* does exactly what the name suggests. You can glide around with the other birds, peck at food, or just walk along the forest floor. It's tranquillity in game form and it's very relaxing.

Trove
This blocky MMO looks like *Roblox* and has the same creative spirit as it, too, since players can create dungeons and items for others to use.

Minecraft
Just like *Roblox*, there's a lot of fun to be had playing through the creations of others, as you see what the creative minds of *Minecraft* fans have cooked up.

Super Mario Maker
For the first time ever, you get to build *Mario* levels. You can see how your own creations stack up against those of Nintendo creator Shigeru Miyamoto.

TIPS & TRICKS

Watch others first
Some *Roblox* games offer a spectator mode. This is a good way of seeing what you're supposed to do, ahead of playing the game yourself.

Collect coins
Some games, such as *Hide and Seek*, have coins dotted around for you to collect as you play. Grab these to buy extra items in those games.

Find a game for your mood
Feeling tired? Play something relaxing that doesn't need quick reactions, like *Lumberjack Tycoon 2* or *Bird Simulator*.

Unlock all games quickly
Load five separate games from the recommended list and quit out. This will unlock the full set of *Roblox* games.

Keep playing!
New games are constantly being added to *Roblox*, so it's worth checking back regularly to see what's new.

CAPTURE THIS!

HORIZON ZERO DAWN

Bring down a Thunderjaw

Horizon's huge world is overrun with vicious robot dinosaurs, and the Thunderjaw is easily one of the most dangerous. You won't be able to tackle it head-on until you have upgraded your gear and abilities. Even then, you're going to need a lot of skill and plenty of cunning. Try using traps, and aiming to dislodge its powerful disc launcher, which can then be used against it for crazy damage!

TOP 10 COOLEST COMPANIONS

DID YOU KNOW?

Ratchet and Clank don't always work together. In *Secret Agent Clank*, the plucky little robot becomes a solo spy to rescue Ratchet from jail!

TRICO
THE LAST GUARDIAN

1 You find Trico locked up at the start of *The Last Guardian*. It's a towering creature—a curious mix of dog, bird, and cat features. After setting the beast free, Trico becomes key to escaping the strange prison you both find yourselves in. Your blossoming friendship with Trico is heartwarming—this is a journey of kindness and trust.

THE TORCH
ABZÛ

2 This mechanical sidekick can be found on the seabed in *Abzû*. Once activated, it will follow you around, illuminating dark areas and cutting through walls of coral to let you pass. You'll grow fond of the curious little device, as it scoots around the ocean of its own accord. Unfortunately, the relationship doesn't last quite as long as you might want it to . . .

CLANK
RATCHET & CLANK

3 Ratchet and Clank have been causing trouble on the PlayStation scene since 2002. Ratchet gets all the glory, as he's the one with his finger on the trigger of all the cool sci-fi weaponry. But Clank is the one who provides the humor, his running quips keeping the mood light as the duo smash and shoot their way through a near-endless army of robots and aliens.

GAMES TO PLAY WITH YOUR FRIENDS

Why make do with an AI buddy when you have *real* buddies?

1 **TMNT: MUTANTS IN MANHATTAN**
Instead of one companion, you get three as you fight against Shredder alongside the other Ninja Turtles.

2 **OVERCOOKED**
Cooking has never been so chaotic, as you and a friend try to get orders out of the cramped kitchen on time while scrambling past each other. It takes real teamwork to succeed.

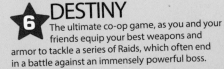

3 **LITTLEBIGPLANET 3**
LittleBigPlanet 3 takes companionship farther than having your friends play alongside you. You can play through levels your friend has created or even create them together.

4 **LEGO JURASSIC WORLD**
Team up with any two characters from the movies while playing this game with your friends!

5 **FORZA HORIZON 3**
Racing games are always super-competitive as you try to screech over the finish line first. But *Forza Horizon 3* gives you a co-op option, as you help each other complete objectives.

6 **DESTINY**
The ultimate co-op game, as you and your friends equip your best weapons and armor to tackle a series of Raids, which often end in a battle against an immensely powerful boss.

IGNIS
FINAL FANTASY XV

4 He's the driver, taking Noctis and his crew all over Eos. He's also the chef, cooking up recipes that ensure the group land critical hits on enemies. He's useful in battle as well, curing teammates with Regroup and using Venom Strike to poison foes.

TURRET
OVERWATCH

5 Torbjorn treats his turret almost like a pet, showing pride when it eliminates the other team and crying, "my turret!" when it falls in battle. The Swedish engineer's partnership with his sentry makes any *Overwatch* team a much tougher nut to crack.

LAYLEE
YOOKA-LAYLEE

6 Just like Banjo had Kazooie, Yooka has Laylee. Laylee clings to the back of Yooka's head, but she isn't just decoration. She can flap her wings to help Yooka with jumps, and is also useful in battle. Her sonar blast knocks out nearby enemies.

LUIGI
SUPER MARIO 3D WORLD

7 Mario and Luigi have been a team ever since they made their debuts in *Mario Bros.* Even though they sometimes go head-to-head in games like *Mario Kart*, it's hard to picture Mario without his brother by his side.

EPONA
THE LEGEND OF ZELDA: BREATH OF THE WILD

9 Epona is such a big part of Link's tale, Nintendo created an amiibo showing Link with his equine companion. There's no sight more thrilling in gaming than watching them ride headfirst into battle.

THE EXPERT SAYS ...
JOHN RIBBINS
Creative director at Roll7, the studio behind the *OlliOlli* games

My favorite companion character has to be Agro, the horse from *Shadow of the Colossus*. While other game companions are there for comic relief, or as a kind of tutorial that's pretending to be your friend, Agro felt like a genuine companion. *SOTC*'s world is barren, and Agro is your only means to traversing the giant plains on which the game is set. It's not often that you get to ride a horse in a game, and *SOTC* made it feel really cool—you can stand on her back and shoot arrows, or do cool flips off her. There's even a dedicated button to whistle and call her if you lose her!

DONALD DUCK AND GOOFY
KINGDOM HEARTS 3

8 Sora's companions for his *Kingdom Hearts* adventures are Disney heroes Donald Duck and Goofy. It's impossible to choose a favorite. Donald Duck brings his hilarious angry squawking. Goofy has his lovable charm and a shield for battle, adding defensive steel to your team. They both make your journey an unforgettable one and they're the perfect companions to have by your side.

SLIPPY TOAD STAR FOX ZERO

10 *Star Fox* fans will know Slippy as the companion everyone loves to hate, thanks to his squeaky voice and the shrill way he tells you off for shooting him by mistake. However, you'll grow to love the quirky team member, as he pitches in with dogfights, and bails you out of trouble.

FARMING SIMULATOR 17
CREAM OF THE CROP!

There's more to farming than planting crops and driving a cool tractor. Much more. *Farming Simulator 17* takes you behind the scenes of one of the hardest jobs in the world, as you're in charge of everything on the farm, from the crops to the animals. The level of detail here is astonishing. You'll learn about different types of soil, fertilizing fields, weeding crops, setting tractor routes, buying farming equipment, animal reproductive rates, farming finances, and so on. If

that all sounds a bit much, don't worry. You can set AI Helpers to assist you and learn everything at your own pace.

It's not all as stressful as it sounds, though—in fact, many players find the game rather relaxing, the perfect way to wind down after playing something more action-packed and stressful. If you want, you can just plow the fields during the day and turn in when night falls. Just don't call a farmer's life easy!

STATS

8 main *Farming Simulator* games

2 *Farming Simulator* **mobile games**

5 downloadable JCB vehicles

75 different **manufacturers**

250 **farming vehicles**

TOP 5 THINGS TO DO

Go crazy with your farmland

1 Because *Farming Simulator* is a game, you obviously don't have to play by the rules. You are able to place conveyor belts, animal pens, wood chippers, and more in any arrangement you want. Go crazy and experiment—you never know, you might even stumble upon a new type of farm that works well.

Specialize in an area

2 When you start playing *Farming Simulator 17*, you'll learn how to do it all, from foresting to raising farmyard animals. It can be productive to focus all your attention on one area, rather than several, and truly hone your craft. How successful can you be as an expert?

Play online

3 You don't have to suffer the sweat and toil of a farmer's life alone. You can team up with your friends online, which not only makes *Farming Simulator 17* more fun, but it also makes things easier. Best of all, 16 of you can play together at the same time.

Try out a few mods

4 The developer has created *Farming Simulator 17* in a specific way, so fans can add content to the game. These extra bits of content—known as "mods"—do everything from improving the graphics to automatically taking care of some farming jobs for you.

Take some pictures

5 With its stunning views stretching on for miles, and lush sunsets bathing the fields in light, it's nice to take a break from farming and start snapping away instead. Pick the right angles, and you will be able to take some artistic shots of your beautiful farm.

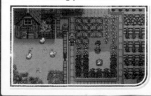
TIPS & TRICKS

Play the tutorials
It can be tempting to skip through the tutorials and get straight to the action, but *Farming Simulator 17* is far too complex for that.

Buying the right tractor
When buying a tractor, look at its horsepower, price, and maintenance cost above all other categories. A high max speed is a good bonus, too.

Keep an eye on the AI
When you set the "Helper AI" to perform a task for you, such as plowing the fields, watch them work to begin with in order to make sure they are doing it properly.

Personalize your farm
If you want to make your farm look nice, buy sheds and trees. It's the easiest, most cost-effective way to spruce up your farm.

INDIE ESSENTIALS

Proving that you don't need a team of thousands and a million-dollar budget to make a fantastic game, these essential indies are some of the best and most original video-game experiences out there. Whether you're into heart-pumping action, puzzles, or platforming, there's an indie game out there to suit your tastes.

20

No Man's Sky

If you love exploring, this is the perfect game for you. The game offers you a universe full of more than 18 quintillion planets for you to explore! You can upgrade your ship, trade resources that you discover, and meet alien races as you move from one solar system to the next.

19

Press ⊗ to Retry

N++

This tricky platformer has tons of quick-fire levels for you to play through that will test your skills to the limit (thankfully with quick restarts for all the times you'll fail). If you can get a friend to join you, there are also levels specially built for multiplayer, but you'll both need to be very precise.

18

Enter the Gungeon

With guns that fire rainbows, fish, lasers, and a whole lot more, this isn't a game that takes itself seriously. Expect plenty of humor and fun along with the intense action it offers. The game mixes procedurally generated dungeon crawling with awesomely frantic battles.

17

Day of the Tentacle Remastered

There have been a few great remakes in recent years and this remastered version of adventure game classic *Day of the Tentacle* from Double Fine is one of them. Solve puzzles and travel through time to stop Purple Tentacle from taking over the world in this colorful point-and-click full of quirky characters and crazy puzzles.

16

Cuphead

With an amazing art style inspired by the cartoons of the 1930s, *Cuphead* looks like no other video game out there. The game has a big focus on awesome boss battles and offers a co-op mode if you want to play through with a friend.

15

American Truck Simulator

It might not be for everyone, but the hugely successful *Truck Simulator* series proves that there's fun to be had hauling cargo to its destination. This entry lets truck fans travel along many of the most famous highways in the US, and is surprisingly fun—it has a massive fanbase, too.

14

Thumper

As your ship moves along the track, you have to react with lighting speed to the prompts that appear in time with the music to get the highest score possible. The game's combination of fast-paced music and cool visuals makes it one of the most intense rhythm-action games you'll ever play.

13

Job Simulator

One of the best VR games released so far is from indie studio Owlchemy Labs. It is set in a future where human jobs have been made obsolete by robots. The Job Simulator lets you experience what they used to be like. Unfortunately, the simulator gets it hilariously wrong . . .

12

Quadrilateral Cowboy

One of the most original games we've played in a long time, *Quadrilateral Cowboy* teaches you how to hack with basic computer code so you can pull off cool capers. Successfully sneaking your way through a restricted area by hacking open doors and turning off security cameras makes you feel like a cool super-spy!

11

Ittle Dew 2

Ittle Dew 2 is a real treat of a game, and worth exploring. Inspired by the *Zelda* series, the game has you battling monsters, solving tricky puzzles, and exploring the island you are trapped on to find loot, as well as the eight raft pieces needed to escape the island. Not only is it fun to play, it will make you laugh, too!

10
Kerbal Space Program

In *Kerbal Space Program*, you are in charge of a space program operated by some adorable aliens called Kerbals. You must build and then fly spacecraft to try and meet a series of objectives—half the fun is in meeting them, the other half is in how hilariously things can go wrong when you fail.

9
Yooka-Laylee

A spiritual successor to the *Banjo-Kazooie* series, *Yooka-Laylee* follows in its footsteps by delivering colorful 3-D platforming, funny characters, and loads of collectibles. The chameleon Yooka and bat Laylee both have cool abilities that you must combine to progress and defeat the evil Capital B.

8
Abzû

Explore a mysterious underwater world in this beautiful game where you play as a lone diver. There are loads of amazing creatures to admire, as well as secrets for you to uncover, in one of the prettiest and most relaxing video game experiences you can find on the market today.

7
Keep Talking & Nobody Explodes

In this game, one player looks at the screen (or a VR headset) and can see a bomb. The other players can't see the bomb, but they do have the instructions to defuse it. Cue some frantic back-and-forth as you work together to try and defuse it before the timer runs out.

6
Minecraft: Story Mode

An absolute pleasure for fans of *Minecraft*, Telltale's story-based take on the *Minecraft* world is full of references to the main game that are sure to delight veterans among you. In combination with a fresh cast of characters that we've come to love, *Minecraft: Story Mode* is a runaway success.

COOLEST INDIE CHARACTERS

Red Transistor

She may lose her voice as part of the story, but you still learn enough about Red to make you care. She just so happens to have awesome time-freezing combat abilities, too.

Thomas
Thomas Was Alone

Who knew a little red block could be a great character? *Thomas Was Alone* proves that with some good narration, it is possible.

thomas was alone

Gomes Fez

The fez-wearing, dimension shifting Gomez doesn't speak during the course of Fez, but his adorable design makes him a character that you can't help falling in love with nonetheless.

The Kid Bastion

As you make your way through *Bastion's* ruined world, your actions as The Kid are explained by a narrator who reacts to what you do. It's a clever storytelling device.

Shovel Knight
Shovel Knight

Shovel Knight's simple and distinctive design makes him instantly recognizable. With his trademark weapon helping him bounce through each stage, he's a classic platforming hero.

5

Owlboy

Owlboy sure has been a long time coming, after starting development way back in 2007, but it was worth the wait. This clever platformer, inspired by retro games, has you controlling Otus, who is able to fly and carry allies with unique abilities that help you progress on your journey.

4

What a lovely occasion... It's always a joy to visit Stardew Valley.

Stardew Valley

In this farming simulation game, you have to clear land, plant crops, and raise livestock to earn in-game cash and grow your farm. There are also characters to interact with in the small town nearby, and mines for you to explore. Down there, you can collect resources and battle against monsters!

3

Overcooked

Overcooked is a multiplayer cooking game that's all about teamwork. You and your friends will receive orders at a rapid pace, so you have to divide the chopping, cooking, and cleaning. But with kitchens set on moving trucks, icebergs, and even the deck of a pirate ship, that can be pretty tricky!

THE EXPERT SAYS...
ROB FEARON
Developer of indie shooter
Death Ray Manta

Take a few people sitting on the sofa, ask them to prepare, cook, and serve some meals, and let the giggles flow. *Overcooked* takes mere moments before it descends into chaos—someone's trying to wash pans, someone else is trying to serve, you're trying to put onions in a stew, everyone is in everyone else's way, and you're all on a truck that's just split in half, because this is a video game, and now everything is on fire. Now you're in space and a dog has the most amazing eyebrows. The dog is called Kevin. It's ridiculous, and totally awesome.

* (Playfully crinkling through the leaves fills you with determination.)

2

Rocket League

Since *Rocket League* has been released, developer Psyonix has kept the updates rolling, with new modes, cars, and even hats to keep the game feeling fresh. Even without updates, *Rocket League's* exciting take on soccer, where giant rocket-powered cars replace human players, is enough to keep us coming back.

1

* Froggit and Whimsun drew near!

Undertale

This smash-hit RPG has earned itself a dedicated fanbase, and with good reason. You explore an underground region filled with monsters, towns, and puzzles. The game's battle system is a blend of turn-based RPG and action-packed shooter—you select an attack from a menu, but must then play a mini-game to execute it. What really makes the game stand out, however, is the level of choice offered and how your decisions can change the story. You don't have to attack and defeat any of the monsters if you don't want to. Instead, it is possible to "beat" every monster you meet by making friends with them!

CRASH BANDICOOT

SPIN TO WIN!

DID YOU KNOW?
Crash Bandicoot was created by Naughty Dog, who would go on to make the Uncharted series.

Nintendo has Mario. Sega has Sonic. Sony had Crash Bandicoot, a Wumpa Fruit-eating bandicoot mascot of its own, who was out to stop Doctor Neo Cortex's plans for world domination. Just like Mario and Sonic, Crash built his name on fast-paced platforming. The difference is, the bandicoot's adventures didn't just see him run left to right. He also ran *into* the screen, a mind-blowing 3-D trick back when *Crash Bandicoot* came out, and it's still his calling card for platforming gameplay. You spin and stomp on everything in your path, while avoiding traps and grabbing secrets. The *N. Sane Trilogy* brings the original three games back in sparkling HD.

STATS

1996 is when the series started

★★★★ Crash has had **6 different developers**

20 Crash Bandicoot games in total

7,130,000 sales for *Crash Bandicoot 3*

Crash Bandicoot 3 is the 8th best-selling PlayStation game of all time

TOP 5 CRASH BANDICOOT GAMES

Crash Bandicoot 3

1 The highlight of the series, as Crash and sister Coco go back in time to stop Doctor Neo Cortex. The time-traveling plot means you race through incredible stages, like riding a tiger on the Great Wall of China, spinning through pyramids, or battling across a medieval castle.

Crash Bandicoot

2 Along with *WipEout*, the standout launch title for Sony's brand-new PlayStation. Platforming was simple, with Crash running into the screen or from left to right. Simple gameplay meant the spotlight was on the antics of Crash and his funny animations.

Crash Team Racing

3 Nobody expected to see Crash Bandicoot and the gang jumping into karts for a race to the finish line. Yet this surprising left-field turn was a masterstroke for the series, as Crash's capers and huge cast of supporting characters worked perfectly on the racetrack.

Skylanders: Imaginators

4 After six years without a single game, *Crash Bandicoot* returned for *Skylanders: Imaginators*, keeping his trademark spin attacks and somersault jump. He even has his own levels, styled after his debut outing on PlayStation, and his nemesis is playable as well!

Crash Bandicoot 2: Cortex Strikes Back

5 Although it didn't have the novelty of the original, nor the honed-to-perfection gameplay of *Crash Bandicoot 3*, *Cortex Strikes Back* still had its charms. The biggest twist is that Doctor Neo Cortex now wants to save the world rather than destroy it, although his intentions aren't quite as noble as they first appear.

ALSO CHECK OUT...

Yooka-Laylee
This is as close as you can get to *Crash Bandicoot* without the fur and the Wumpa Fruit. It tilts slightly toward puzzles and exploration over fast platforming.

Sonic Mania
Another blast from the past, *Sonic Mania* goes right back to the blue hedgehog's roots. The lightning-fast 2-D gameplay echoes *Crash*'s early days.

Sea of Thieves
With its big, bright, and bold sea adventures, *Sea of Thieves* might not be a land-based platformer, but it has the same mix of cartoon mayhem that *Crash Bandicoot* does.

TIME LINE

1996 Crash Bandicoot
The first one was a huge hit as a PlayStation launch title, showing off the console's visual power.

1999 Crash Bandicoot 3: Warped
Three years later came the second sequel and best game in the series, as Crash teamed up with sister Coco.

2007 Crash Bandicoot: Crash of the Titans
With co-op and a huge variety of mini-games, this was Crash breaking free from his old platforming roots.

2010 Crash Bandicoot Nitro Kart 2
The last *Crash* game before the mascot went into exile was a racing game only released for mobile devices.

2016 Skylanders: Imaginators—Crash Edition
Crash Bandicoot's dramatic return after six years away came through the famous *Skylanders* series.

2017 Crash Bandicoot N. Sane Trilogy
Crash Bandicoot relives his glory years as the first three games in the series are remastered in HD.

TOP 10 FUNNIEST GAMES

Octodad: Dadliest Catch

1 Cooking, cleaning, shopping, taking the family out. All easy enough—unless you're an octopus disguised as a human! The simplest of tasks becomes a nightmare when attempted with octopus tentacles rather than arms. To make things worse, you're being hunted by a chef, who wants to see you served on a plate to his customers.

LEGO Star Wars: The Force Awakens

2 It's *Star Wars* but in LEGO form, injected with a healthy dose of humor. From bickering Stormtroopers to faulty lightsabers, LEGO *Star Wars* takes everything from *Episode VII* and gives it a new comedic twist. If you've seen the movie, you'll love the thrill of being surprised as the dramatic action movie gets turned into a hilarious video game.

Roblox

3 Home of the weird and the wonderful, *Roblox* is where amateur game developers get to show off their creations to the world. With imagination being the only limit, there are all sorts of hilarious adventures in this toybox of fun. Our particular favorite is *The Elevator*, where each floor brings something new . . . from cat memes to potatoes lying on the ground!

6 HILARIOUS THINGS TO DO ONLINE
A few fun pranks to play on your friends while playing together

 Drive the wrong way
Some racing games won't allow you to do this. For those that do, just turn your car around, and start driving the wrong way down the track to cause chaos on the roads.

 Take it to the corner
When playing *FIFA* or *Pro Evo*, you can protect a lead by taking the ball into the corner of the field, and holding it there. The other player will desperately scramble to get the ball back.

Hit enemies off cliffs
In *Overwatch*, Lucio has Soundwave and Pharah has Concussive Blast, abilities that knock opponents back. You can actually hit your opponents off cliffs or high drops for an easy kill!

 Hail Mary
In *Madden NFL*, a Hail Mary is a desperation play where you gamble everything on an unlikely touchdown. Use it as a normal play, and hear the frustrated cries of your opponent if it works!

Block the way
Sometimes, it's the simple acts that are the funniest. Just standing in someone's way, blocking a doorway or path, can cause panic in others. *Overcooked* is almost designed around this.

 Spook other players
There are all sorts of hilarious and inventive ways to scare other players online, from playing as Darth Vader in *Battlefront* to jumping up on unsuspecting players in *Splatoon*.

Goat Simulator

4 Of course a game where you play as a goat couldn't be serious, but *Goat Simulator* takes the humor to extreme levels. You can kick a gas station to blow it up, or strap on a Jetpack and fly. It's a game that's proud to be crazy!

Guacamelee!
Super Turbo Championship Edition

5 *Guacamelee* is a platforming game, but more than that, it's packed with humor from start to finish. There are jokes about *Minecraft*, O RLY owl, *Wreck-It Ralph*, Grumpy Cat, and more.

Overcooked

6 This game is tailor-made for multiplayer mayhem, as you try to work with your friends to keep orders coming out of a cramped kitchen. You'll laugh at how things quickly spiral out of control, with food even catching fire if you do especially badly.

Worms W.M.D

7 There's a deliciously dark streak of humor running through *Worms W.M.D* as you try to eliminate the other team. You start with dynamite and bazookas, but the longer rounds go on, the stranger the unlocked weapons are. You can use anything from exploding bananas to flying sheep!

Grim Fandango Remastered

9 You play as Manny Calavera, a travel agent for the undead. A suspicion about the quality of his clients leads Manny to sniff out major corruption, leading him on a hilarious adventure to put things right.

THE EXPERT SAYS ...
VIKKI BLAKE
Games writer, IGN/GamesRadar+

It's hard to believe that a game with just three characters and a completely mute heroine can be fun to play, let alone hilarious, but few have made me giggle as much as *Portal 2*. I didn't think any character could top the horribly brilliant GLaDOS for laugh-out-loud one-liners, but then came the lovably inept Wheatley, your guide through GLaDOS' monstrous maze. From the moment you meet to the moment you break out of the test chambers, Wheatley and GLaDOS keep you entertained with their withering wit. It doesn't matter how many times I play *Portal*, it still makes me laugh out loud. An honorable mention goes to *Animal Crossing: New Leaf*. Oh, how I love Kapp'n!

DID YOU KNOW?
Four years after it was originally released, *Skate 3* re-entered the video game charts in 2014 after a series of popular YouTube videos showcased the game.

Skate 3

8 This Xbox 360 game is now available on Xbox One through backward compatibility, and it's definitely worth checking out. A skateboarding game shouldn't be funny, but the crashes are hilarious, and almost encouraged thanks to a "bail" button. Send your superhuman skateboarder tumbling down stairs, into rails, and up ramps. The more creative you are, the funnier the results.

Headlander

10 The entire human race has been turned into robots and it's up to you—a floating head—to save them. You can take over robot bodies, which is where the odd story makes sense for the gameplay. The strange plot gives the developers lots of easy opportunities for ridiculous jokes, which they pepper throughout this sci-fi-themed adventure.

SLIME RANCHER
HAPPINESS IN GAME FORM

DID YOU KNOW?

Slime Rancher is the first game that was created by Monomi Park. The studio consisted of just two people when development first started in 2014.

Can you imagine trying to tame and befriend a bunch of cute, slimy creatures? Such is the bizarre life of Beatrix LeBeau, the space farmer whom you control in *Slime Rancher*. Using a vacuum gun, you need to suck up objects—such as food and slimes—that you find out in the wild, before spitting them out on the slime ranch that you have built. Slimes produce plorts, which is currency in *Slime Rancher*'s world, but you'll find that slimes are constantly hungry, and tend to fight each other. You need to create pens for the right type of slimes, find the right food, and scour the world for food and other slimes to add to your farm. Then you need to consider protecting your slimes from outside threats and building teleporters, upgrading your jetpack to explore the world around you to catch bigger slimes for bigger rewards.

STATS

2 developers created *Slime Rancher*

4 developers currently on the *Slime Rancher* team

200,000 copies sold while in Early Access on PC

52 Steam achievements to unlock

TOP 5 SLIMES YOU'LL MEET

Giant slimes

1 Known as Largo Slimes, these massive bouncing balls of goo are the result of two slimes fusing together. They have an insatiable hunger, and pose a physical threat if you get too close, but their giant size also means the plort payout is huge, if you manage to tame them.

Slime explosion

2 Boom Slimes can cause mayhem if not handled with care. Should these slimes become irritated, they'll crackle with energy and explode, sending other slimes scattering all over your ranch. It's worth doing at least once to see what the carnage looks like.

Angry slimes

3 Even in a game that radiates happiness like *Slime Rancher*, not everything is happy. Slimes become angry when they're hungry for too long, and they'll start to actively hunt for their own food. They'll even accept you as a snack if they have to!

Happy slimes

4 How do you feed slimes? By firing food into their mouths, naturally, or—at the very least—firing food into their pens. Watching the delightful creatures munching away on carrots and beets while little hearts float above their heads is very cute.

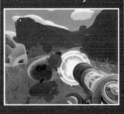

Slimes together

5 The happiest sight in *Slime Rancher* is seeing a group of pesky slimes all tucked up in one of your pens, well fed and happy. It's the sign of a good rancher, and you'll get to enjoy (and spend) all the juicy plorts they produce as a result of your hard work.

TIPS & TRICKS

Fly around
Try to buy the jetpack as soon as you can, as this will enable you to find well-hidden slimes and food.

Head high
Secret crates are often hidden higher up in the nooks and crevices of large hills. Make sure you poke around to see what you find.

Air roofs are vital
Air roofs will help to protect your slimes from antagonizing Tarrs. Make them a priority, and build them up high for added security.

Keeping largos under control
Although largos produce a lot of plorts, they tend to fight each other, so make sure you limit them to three or four per pen in order to prevent chaos.

Feed starving slimes
If you see an angry or upset slime, feed it! It's starving and needs food. Separate it from the other slimes if you have to.

POKÉMON GO
THE GAME THAT CAUGHT US ALL!

When this mobile game first launched, it was a huge phenomenon. Massive crowds of players chased after rare Pokémon and everywhere you looked, people had their phones out in the hope of finding something new and exciting. Developer Niantic continues to build on the original game too, adding new Pokémon to catch and train, offering new items, and hosting special events where rare Pokémon can be caught.

As an augmented reality game that turns the real world into a land full of PokéStops, Gyms, and Pokémon nests, *Pokémon GO* isn't just really fun—it's also good for you. The game promotes getting out and walking around. So as long as you remember to stay safe while playing—and always watch where you're going—you might find that playing turns you not only into a great Trainer but a healthy one as well!

STATS

Dragonite is the most powerful non-Legendary Gen1 Pokémon, maxing out at **3581 CP**

Around launch, the game was downloaded more than **80 times per second**

By the end of 2016, *Pokémon GO* players had walked nearly **9 BILLION KM,** catching around **90 BILLION** Pokémon in the process!

$ $ $ $
$100m made in just 20 days, passing $500 million around 40 days later

TOP 5 THINGS TO DO

Catch Pokémon

1 Gotta catch 'em all! This is the core element of the game—finding Pokémon hiding out and about in the real world, and snagging them for yourself in your Poké Balls. There's no need to fight over them, though. Every Pokémon can be caught by every Trainer, so you can all have fun!

Spin PokéStops

3 If you find yourself running low on supplies, it's time to get spinning. These places are scattered around the real world and by approaching and interacting with them, you can get Balls, Berries, Potions, and Pokémon Eggs. You can even place Lures to attract more Pokémon!

Raise Pokémon

5 Powering up your companions is extremely important. As you feed them Candies and Stardust, their CP (Combat Power) will increase, making them more effective in battle. You'll also need to evolve them to their final forms in order for them to be as powerful as they possibly can, but that costs a lot of Candies!

Hatch eggs

2 Almost every Pokémon can be found in the wild, but many can also be hatched out of Eggs. These come in three kinds—2km, 5km, and 10km—each requiring those distances to be walked before they hatch. Make sure you've always got plenty of Incubators running.

Battle at Gyms

4 When you've got some battle-ready Pokémon, you can either take on Gyms that are owned by enemy teams to try and claim them, or train up friendly Gyms so that they can hold more defending Pokémon. Either way, the fast-paced battles are great fun, so get training!

ALSO CHECK OUT...

Pokémon Shuffle
This puzzle game is really fun, and it's constantly updated with more stages and special events. You'll never run out of puzzles to solve, but they can be tricky!

SpecTrek
Similar to *Pokémon GO*, only with ghosts and a greater emphasis on fitness. If you're into all things spooky and like being up and about, give it a go.

Temple Treasure Hunt Game
Go in search of hidden riches in augmented reality! You can take on randomly generated trails, or share existing ones with friends in the fun multiplayer mode.

TIPS & TRICKS

Catch 'em all!
Capturing extras of Pokémon you already have is important, since you need as many Candies as possible to power up and evolve your squad.

Evolve first
If you've got a solid Pokémon, always evolve it before powering it up—it might learn poor moves when it evolves, making it weaker in battle regardless.

Winning streak
There's a huge bonus reward if you can catch a Pokémon or spin a PokéStop seven days in a row.

Countering types
Just like in the core games, using super-effective moves does extra damage to enemy Pokémon. Learn your matchups!

Don't forget to stay safe!
The most important thing is to always play safely. Never go out alone, and pay attention to your surroundings at all times.

WORMS W.M.D

SPLIT SECOND

This classic party game is always a blast in multiplayer, and games can get really competitive! While it's fun to test your skill using a limited selection of tools, sometimes you just want to let loose with the craziest weapons in the game and unleash havoc! The latest version allows for huge six-player skirmishes, with up to four worms per team. Things quickly descend into pure chaos, as you can see from this play-by-play breakdown of one particularly crazy game.

Hot

200

Boffins

Heroes

Team Gav

1 Things start off relatively calm, all six teams feeling one another out with basic grenades and rockets. Sweet and Gavin seemed to be fighting over that *Rocket League* car, and rightly so—those things are totally awesome!

2 The fight quickly picked up, though, and it wasn't long before explosive Concrete Donkeys started raining from the sky! These things are devastating, bouncing around and blowing stuff up whenever they hit the ground.

Spicy
200

Sweet
200

Gavin
200

Plodder
200

3 If you thought *that* was bad, one silly worm decided to take things even further. He pushed the red button (*never* press the red button!) and activated Armageddon, summoning a seemingly endless shower of meteors to destroy the entire stage!

G-Dog
28

4 Only two worms survived the chaos—one from our mighty squad, The Teamsters, and one from the evil Team Gav. We wanted to finish this properly, so we reached for our trusty baseball bat and pushed poor G-Dog into the sea to steal the win!

TOP 10
HIGH SCORES AND SPEEDRUNS

DID YOU KNOW?
The letters "TAS" mean "Tool-Assisted Speedrun," where the character is programmed to make the most efficient moves possible.

Super Mario Bros.
The best speedrun ever

1 When it comes to speedruns, Nintendo classic *Super Mario Bros.* is king. Thanks to its huge number of clever tricks to shave milliseconds off your overall completion time, fans have been tackling the platformer for over 30 years. With deft use of glitches, speedrunner and record-holder Darbian completed the game in 4 minutes, 56 seconds, and 878 milliseconds.

Guitar Hero
Hardest rhythm action song completed

2 "Ghost Walking" is the hardest song in *Guitar Hero*, according to Mike McLafferty, the audio designer on the game. That didn't stop *Guitar Hero* player Alexzis from completing the song on Expert without a single note missed, becoming the first player in the world to nail the difficult feat. He did this just days after the game was released!

6 OTHER AMAZING GAMING FEATS
Yet more incredible examples of skillful gaming

 Biggest Gamerscore ever
Stallion83 has been the world Gamerscore leader for several years now, and is in no danger of slowing down any time soon. The dominant Xbox gamer ended 2016 with a monstrous Gamerscore of 1,467,000.

2 **Most platinums ever**
Most PlayStation 4 owners are proud of the few Platinums they've unlocked for mastering specific games. Hakoom, the worldwide leader for Platinums, has unlocked an astonishing 1,165 of the Trophies!

3 **Blindfolded Zelda**
It has to be one of the most impressive ways to complete any game. Using just sound and his own immense knowledge of the game, Runnerguy2489 beat *Ocarina of Time* while blindfolded. We don't know how he did it either!

 Longest win streak
Fighting game legend Ryan Hart saw off 260 opponents in a row on *Street Fighter V*, setting the longest winning streak in gaming history. The staggering feat took him 11 hours to accomplish. We bet his fingers ached afterward!

5 **Longest *Minecraft* session**
The longest ever *Minecraft* marathon is impressive, and definitely unhealthy. Joseph Kelly played the game for 35 hours, 35 minutes, and 35 seconds nonstop. Better yet, he streamed it all and raised money for charity.

 Biggest gaming tournament
Dota 2 players can look forward to the biggest prize fund in the world when they enter The International, which put $18.5 million up for grabs in 2016.

Pac-Man
The unbeatable world record

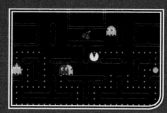

3 The world record score of 3,333,360 for *Pac-Man* can't be beaten. That is the highest possible score after beating the 255th level, after which the game crashes. So the world record has shifted to how quickly players can reach that score. The appropriately named Dave Race holds that current "unbeatable" record: 3 hours, 33 minutes, and 12.69 seconds.

4 No matter what your skill level, *Spelunky* is a tough nut to crack. The sheer number of enemies, traps, and deadly drops is overwhelming at times. Which is what makes BananaSaurus Rex's feat so impressive. He had to stay alive for seven and a half hours, finding every bit of treasure to collect a record total of $3.1 million.

Spelunky
The most gold ever

THE EXPERT SAYS ...
DARBIAN
Current Super Mario Bros. world record holder

"My favorite game to speedrun is *Super Mario Bros* for the original Nintendo. It contains a fantastic mix of speedrunning elements—such as frame-perfect tricks and wrong warps—and flashy tricks like the flagpole glitch, and the bullet bill glitch. Additionally, it lacks any lengthy cutscenes outside of the fanfare that occurs when completing a level which lasts for only a few seconds. Any speedrunner can choose to take this game from a "easy every time" to a "I'm only human!" difficulty level based on how many tricks they decide to attempt."

Portal
The dizzying speedrun

5 It takes roughly eight hours to complete *Portal*, Valve's dizzying puzzle game. Four speedrunners got together and figured out how to break the game down, putting together a completion time of 8 minutes and 31.93 seconds. It took two weeks to record the speedrun, which they broke down into segments.

Legend of Zelda: Ocarina of Time
The most discussed speedrun

6 There are lots of different routes you can take through *Ocarina of Time*, and a lot of glitches that can be used. Because of how flexible it is to attack, speedrunners are always discussing how to tackle it in the fastest time. The record holder is Skater82297, who set a time of 17 minutes and 31 seconds on his birthday.

7 When Lori Baker set the *Tetris DX* world record on the Game Boy Color release of the game, considered the gold standard for *Tetris*, it triggered a fresh wave of record attempts. Japanese player Tao Kitamoto is the current *Tetris* master, with an astonishing 5,164 lines cleared. It trumped Harry Hong's nine-year-record of 4,988 and looks like an unbeatable record . . . for now.

Tetris DX
The best Tetris player in the world

8 A perfect example of a modern speedrun game, *Bastion* has lots of tips and tricks that can be used, speedrun YouTube tutorials, and a healthy community of players helping each other out. Vulajin is the current record holder, with a blistering time of 12 minutes and 40 seconds. His run combines game knowledge, skill, and a healthy dose of luck as well.

Bastion
The modern speedrun

Shadow the Hedgehog
Longest speedrun ever

9 BlazinZzetti set a new type of speedrun record when he 100% completed *Shadow the Hedgehog*. He collected all A-ranks, Keys, and Paths, which meant having to play through the game 326 times. His overall time was 181 hours, 14 minutes and 47 seconds; Unsurprisingly, he doesn't plan on tackling the feat again any time soon! We can't say we blame him.

Journey
Strangest speedrun

10 Proving that any game can be used for a speedrun, French player Azama has been relentlessly attacking the tranquil adventure that is *Journey*. After months of practice, he managed to beat the game in an incredible 19 minutes and 40 seconds. This is now the record that any new speedrunners will have to beat.

DID YOU KNOW?

If you want an even bigger adventure in some of your favorite worlds, why not give the *Kingdom Hearts* series a try? It's really good!

DISNEY MAGICAL WORLD 2
STEP INSIDE YOUR DREAMS

If you've ever imagined what life is really like in a Disney kingdom, you can finally find out for yourself. Everyone loves the Disney movies, but Disney games haven't always managed to capture the same movie magic. Playing through this game feels like you're ticking off a dream Disney checklist, as you explore the magical world of Castleton. You can dance at the Castle Ball.

Check. Build snowmen with Elsa. Check. Hula dance with Lilo. Check. You don't even have to find Disney characters to have fun. You can play dress-up with clothing you've created, or even build Disney furniture. This is the game that all Disney fans have dreamed of—whether you're a fan of Alice or Aladdin, Pinocchio or Peter Pan, *Disney Magical World 2* has it all.

STATS

Over **100** Disney characters

6 Disney-themed worlds ★★★

Over **250** items to find

Mickey Mouse's first appearance was in 1928

9 AR cards to scan on the official website

TOP 5 THINGS TO DO

Meet Disney characters

1 Venturing around Castleton and bumping into Disney characters is a thrill that never gets old, especially since you're never sure who you're going to meet next. You'll see all sorts of faces, stretching from *Tangled* to *Pirates of the Caribbean*, from *Winnie the Pooh* to *Frozen*.

Decorate your home

2 You have your own home in Castleton, so you can decorate it how you want. You're not limited to buying furniture either. You can create your own Disney-inspired items to liven up your house, using material that you find on your adventures.

Run your own cafe

3 Nothing is free, even in the magical world of Castleton, but you have one of the best jobs in the world. You run a café, where Disney characters are the customers! Serve cake to Aladdin, ice cream to Elsa, and sandwiches to Minnie Mouse.

Dress-up

4 When you first arrive in Castleton, you need to create a character. You can try to create yourself, or perhaps someone else, but whoever you create, you have to dress them up. You can then make new clothing, as long as you find the items.

Explore Castleton

5 There's so much to do, and finding the activities is a big part of the fun. You can watch concerts, dance with Disney characters, build snowmen, go shopping—every day in Castleton brings new surprises, and it's up to you to find them!

Animal Crossing: New Leaf
Let this life simulator seep into your bones for a tranquil experience. Whether you're catching bugs or talking to the villagers, everything is peaceful.

Tomodachi Life
By creating Miis and leaving them to interact with each other, *Tomodachi Life* is like a human zoo, where you get to laugh at their crazy antics!

Fantasy Life
Fantasy Life combines elements of life simulator with RPG. If you'd like a challenge, not only is *Fantasy Life* difficult, but it'll take over 100 hours to fully complete!

TIPS & TRICKS

Alternative ways to get items
If you're struggling to find an item you need, remember that every item in *Disney Magical World 2* can be unlocked in two different locations.

Growing food
For the seeds you have, take them to Rabbit's Garden and you can grow them there. You can use the food for new café recipes.

Use the Notice Board
The Notice Board in Castleton will let you know about what's happening and what activities to play if you get stuck.

Collect stickers
You'll be given stickers as rewards for completing certain tasks during the game. Stickers unlock further items, like new recipes and so on.

Explore and have fun!
Don't get caught up chasing items. Just walk around Castleton, talk to the characters, and simply enjoy yourself!

THE RETRO COLLECTION

THE BEST CLASSIC GAMES YOU CAN PLAY TODAY!

There's no doubting that modern games are pretty cool. They have the best graphics, online play that lets you connect with friends all over the world, and massive, detailed worlds to map out and explore. But with all that current generation excitement, it can be easy to forget that there are tons of awesome retro games to play. Whether it's the old-school classics, remasters, and remakes, or brand new games that borrow from yesterday's favorites, there is definitely something fresh waiting for today's up-and-coming army of gamers.

20

Voodoo Vince Remastered

What do you get when you combine burlap, stitches, a button and a healthy dose of black magic? Voodoo Vince, of course! He's an adorable voodoo doll that hurts himself to hurt his enemies. Guide this tiny Louisiana hero through haunted bayous and crypts to save his creator, Madam Charmaine.

HOW TO PLAY Xbox One

19

Jet Set Radio

We all know that graffiti is illegal in real life, but it's all part of the fun in this awesome cel-shaded Dreamcast remaster. Choose from several punk skaters, and rollerblade the streets of Tokyo-to, collecting spray-paint cans, tagging buildings, doing tricks, and dodging the cops. The soundtrack is one of the coolest you'll ever hear while gaming!

HOW TO PLAY Xbox One Backwards Compatibility, PS Vita

18

Wave Race 64

Easily one of the best water-racing games of all time, *Wave Race 64* has slick jet skis to ride, nine aquatic courses to navigate, and ocean waves that still look wet enough to drench your controller. Just watch out for buoys. If you're really skilled, you can even unlock a dolphin to ride instead of your jet ski!

HOW TO PLAY Wii U Virtual Console

17

Beyond Good & Evil HD

This cinematic adventure lets you play as cool photographer Jade, whose sidekick just happens to be a talking pig named Pey'j. Explore the futuristic fantasy planet of Hillys while taking pictures of weird creatures and fighting against the DomZ, a race of life-draining aliens. You don't even need a license to drive the hovercraft!

HOW TO PLAY Xbox One Backwards Compatibility

15

Final Fantasy VII

Join the resistance with Cloud Strife and fight against the evil megacorporation Shinra in one of the biggest RPGs of all time. Summon incredible beasts in battle, play arcade games at the Golden Saucer, ride giant birds called Chocobos, and stop Sephiroth in this truly epic tale. After you've saved the world, try out *Final Fantasy VI*, *VIII*, and *IX* from the series on the PS3 and Vita.

HOW TO PLAY PS4, Steam, iOS, Android

16

Adventure Island

Skateboards aren't just for city sidewalks—they're also for remote tropical islands! Play the role of Master Higgins on his quest to rescue Princess Leilani and her sister Tina from the Evil Witch Doctor. Dodge snails, jump over cobras, outrun boulders, and duck underneath bats in this fun action platformer. You can even ride a dinosaur in *Adventure Island II*.

HOW TO PLAY Wii U Virtual Console/3DS Eshop

14

Golden Sun

Originally released on the Game Boy Advance in 2001, this 2-D fantasy RPG is filled to the brim with monsters and magic. Take control of Issac and his friends on their journey through the world of Weyard as they cast incredible spells in rotating battles, collect helpful creatures known as Djinn, and use mysterious Psynergy to solve exciting puzzles.

HOW TO PLAY Wii U Virtual Console

DEDICATED RETRO MACHINES

13

Ape Escape 2
(and other PS2 on PS4 titles)

There's only one objective in this colorful 3-D platformer: to catch all of the monkeys! Take on the role of Hikaru and use cool gadgets like the RC car and Bananrang to track down all those pesky apes. And when you're done monkeying around, try other PlayStation 2 on PlayStation 4 games, like mind-reading adventure *Psychonauts* and city-destroying fighting game *War of the Monsters*.

HOW TO PLAY PS4

12

Mega Man Legacy Collection

Need a good challenge? Look no further than this collection of NES platformer-shooters! Guide Mega Man through challenging levels teeming with Dr. Wily's reprogrammed minions. Then defeat the Robot Masters (like Bubble Man, Snake Man, and Dust Man) so you can use their powers. The Blue Bomber has never looked better!

HOW TO PLAY PS4, Xbox One, 3DS, Steam, iOS, Android

NES Mini

Ever wonder where certain popular game series started, like *The Legend of Zelda* and *Final Fantasy*? Ever wondered where the Ice Climbers in *Super Smash Bros.* originally came from? The NES Mini is home to a whole bunch of classic 8-bit Nintendo titles. It comes with an authentic NES controller and 30 pre-installed games, most of which are a real blast.

KEY GAMES Bubble Bobble | The Legend of Zelda

Retro-Bit Generations

This all-in-one console is for adventurous gamers who want to try out a ton of lesser-known games. The Retro-Bit Generations has over 100 built-in retro games from the NES, SNES, and even the Game Boy. It comes with two USB controllers, so playing with a friend is an option. Plus, with the SD card slot and internal memory, saving games is super-easy.

KEY GAMES Holy Diver | Super Ghouls 'N Ghosts

Sega Genesis Classic Game Console

This plug 'n' play is a proper tribute to Sega's awesome 16-bit console. It comes pre-loaded with some of the greatest games ever released for the system. Two wireless controllers are also included, and it can even play old Genesis/Mega Drive cartridges! Though it should be noted that it can only be connected using an AV input.

KEY GAMES Sonic the Hedgehog 2 | Streets of Rage 3

Atari Flashback 7

Flashback 7 has everything you need to go back in time and experience some of the earliest video games. It comes packed with a bunch of the classics like *Pong* and *Frogger*, two wireless joysticks, and enough video-game history to make your head spin. Don't let the simple graphics fool you—these games are awesome!

KEY GAMES Asteroids | Centipede | Missile Command

THE BEST OF NEW RETRO

COOL NEW GAMES INSPIRED BY THE CLASSICS

Shovel Knight

Inspired by *Mega Man*, *Zelda II*, *Super Mario Bros. 3* and *Castlevania III*, this 2-D sidescroller puts you in the armored shoes of Shovel Knight as he digs, bounces, and smacks his way through a huge world map. Tight controls and great music make this one retro-themed quest worth taking.

Fez

To one odd little fez-wearing dude named Gomez, everything around him seems as flat as paper. That is, until he discovers a special item, and suddenly he can see in all three dimensions. If you think about it too much, the whole concept will blow your mind!

3D Dot Game Heroes

What happens when you take the old-school, 8-bit video games and give them a modern graphical makeover? *3D Dot Game Heroes*, an awesome adventure inspired by *The Legend of Zelda* and *Final Fantasy*! Fight through dungeons, collect items, and upgrade your sword until it's enormous.

Owl Boy

Part bird simulator and part Super Nintendo game, this excellent *Kid Icarus* and *Super Mario Bros. 3*-inspired Steam release took nine years to make. You play as Otus, who saves his sky village from pirates. Meet characters along the way and pick them up to use their weapons.

Adventures of Pip

When the evil Queen DeRezzia starts turning all the townspeople into single pixels, young hero Pip sets out to stop her. Funny and easy to control, this *Super Mario* and *Zelda*-style platformer will have you replaying levels to collect everything long after you've finished it.

SEGA 3D Classics Collection

What can make retro games even cooler? Playing them in 3-D! The original *Sonic the Hedgehog* leads this pack of six games, followed by colorful shooter *Fantasy Zone II*. There's also *Power Drift* for racing fans and the arcade beat em' up *Altered Beast*, a game for anyone who has ever wanted to transform into a werewolf or a dragon.

HOW TO PLAY 3DS

10

Rez Infinite

This HD remaster of a 2001 Dreamcast rail shooter has you playing as a hacker trying to reboot a supercomputer before it shuts itself down for good. Locking onto viruses and firing adds notes to the pulsing electronic soundtrack, and if you have a PSVR headset, you can even play the game in virtual reality!

HOW TO PLAY PS4

9

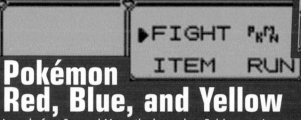

Pokémon Red, Blue, and Yellow

Long before *Sun* and *Moon*, the legendary *Pokémon* series started with three famous Game Boy titles. See where Nintendo's ultra-popular monster-catching franchise began with *Red* and *Blue*, which contain the original 151 Pokémon (like Charmander, Diglett, and Geodude). Then try *Yellow*, which gives you Pikachu at the very beginning of the game.

HOW TO PLAY 3DS Virtual Console

8

Nights into Dreams . . .

Ever wondered where dreams come from? Travel to Nightopia with Claris and Elliot in this strange and psychedelic 3-D journey. Glide through rings and gates to complete each imaginative level before the timer runs out, then tackle the bizarre bosses. Flying has never been so fun!

HOW TO PLAY Xbox One Backwards Compatibility

6

EarthBound

After a meteorite crashes into their neighborhood, young Ness and his friends set out to investigate, and that's where this Super Nintendo role-playing game begins. An emotional story, interesting places to discover (like the neon city of Moonside), and some really weird enemies make this great for gamers who want something a little different.

HOW TO PLAY Wii U Virtual Console/3DS Eshop

7

Super Mario 64
(and Super Mario World, Super Mario Galaxy)

The Nintendo 64's ground-breaking *Super Mario 64* is perhaps one of the most important retro games you can play, simply because it was one of the very first 3-D platformers—*ever*! And once you've tracked down and collected all the hidden stars, travel back to *Super Mario World*, hop on Yoshi's back, and experience some of the best 2-D platforming ever made. Or, for something a little more recent, check out *Super Mario Galaxy* and go planet hopping.

HOW TO PLAY Wii U Virtual Console, 3DS

5
Kirby's Dream Collection

Experience the famous pink puff-ball's first set of platforming adventures in this excellent Wii collection. From the original black and white *Kirby's Dream Land* to the more modern *Kirby 64*, the gameplay stays simple: get through the levels by sucking up enemies and taking their powers. It's easy to learn, and Kirby never gets indigestion!

HOW TO PLAY Wii U Backwards Compatibility

4
Earthworm Jim HD

This hilarious and totally weird sidescroller stars an earthworm inside a spacesuit trying to save Princess What's Her Name. Blast through odd and gross levels (one is inside a monster's intestines!) and battle against bosses like Professor Monkey-for-a-Head. You can also launch cows using refrigerators, which is just as funny as it sounds.

HOW TO PLAY Xbox One Backwards Compatibility

3
DuckTales: Remastered

A remake of the classic NES title, this 2-D sidescroller puts you in control of Scrooge McDuck on his search for five hidden treasures. Bounce on Scrooge's cane to defeat enemies and reach special areas within levels. You'll also meet different characters from the old *DuckTales* TV show.

HOW TO PLAY Xbox One Backwards Compatibility

2

Donkey Kong 64

Nintendo's lovable gorilla stars in this massive Nintendo 64 collect-a-thon. Choose from several Kong family members in a quest to stop the evil crocodile King K. Rool. There are tons of bananas to track down (even golden ones!), and once you hear the *Donkey Kong* Rap, you'll never be able to stop singing it. You've been warned!

HOW TO PLAY Wii U Virtual Console

1

Wind Waker HD
(and Oracles, Ocarina of Time 3D)

Back on the Gamecube in 2003, Link went on a breathtaking cel-shaded journey, and now you can experience it in full high definition while using the Wii U's gamepad. Sail the open seas on a talking boat in search of your sister, who has been kidnapped by the evil Ganon. There are islands to hop, dungeons to conquer, and musical melodies to learn using the Wind Waker baton. After you're done sailing, go ahead and try out *Ocarina of Time 3D* on the 3DS, which was Link's very first third-person adventure on the Nintendo 64. And finally, for something a little more retro, try out *Oracle of Seasons* and *Oracle of Ages*, a pair of time-traveling Game Boy Color titles.

HOW TO PLAY Wii U, 3DS

THE EXPERT SAYS …
DARRAN JONES
Editor, Retro Gamer magazine

I'm really glad that plug-and-play devices like the NES Mini exist and continue to get made. They not only represent fantastic value for money in many cases (imagine having a brand-new console come with 30+ of your favorite games) but they also act as an important tie to gaming's past. These cool devices are typically packed with lots of amazing games, including *Sonic*, *Mario*, *Zelda*, and more, and many older gamers would argue that they're as fantastic to play now as they were when they first came out.

ABZÛ

Games aren't always adrenalin-soaked pursuits of evil villains and mischievous bad guys. *Abzû* is a magical adventure that takes you into the ocean and leaves you free to explore its watery depths. You can cling onto the backs of passing turtles, swim with schools of fish, or poke through underwater ruins to decipher the mysterious markings on the wall. It's a game shrouded in mystery, enticing you to dive deeper and deeper into its enchanting world and untangle its secrets.

1 As you swim through the ocean, you'll come across passages that are sealed off by red webbing. This means you'll have to root around and explore the nearby area to find a camera on the seabed, as this has the means to cut through it.

2 Your camera friend will float alongside you, with a curious mind of its own. It will swim off to investigate new areas, and use its flashlight to point the way ahead. Take it to the webbing and it will start to cut through.

3 You're off! You're then sucked into the ocean's currents and pulled along for a ride, along with all the sealife caught alongside you. It's one of the magical, mesmerizing moments of the game, as you're free to look around during the rush.

4 And relax. You'll eventually spill out into a new area, ready and waiting for you to explore all over again. With it comes new sealife, new secrets, and possibly more red webbing for you to slice through with your camera companion.

TOP 10 PLATFORM GAMES

Super Mario Maker

1 If you've got a 3DS or a Wii U, you might never need another platform game. Not only does *Super Mario Maker* let you make your own levels based on classic *Super Mario Bros.* titles, it allows you to download and play thousands of levels made by players around the world. With so many levels out there—many of which are really tough—it could last you forever.

`00000000` `8488`

Ratchet & Clank

2 The original *Ratchet & Clank* is a PS2 classic, but this remake means that you won't have to hunt down an old console. Apart from being visually pleasing, it's a blast thanks to the weapons Ratchet uses when trying to protect planets around the galaxy and the special abilities, like gliding and diving, that Clank provides.

Sonic the Hedgehog 2

3 The second *Sonic* platform game has entertained players for over 25 years with its classic combination of incredible speed, bright and colorful levels, and tricky traps. That is why you can still get it on consoles today. With control of Sonic's faithful sidekick Tails, a second player can either help you to complete each stage, or race you to the finish line.

SIX SCARY HAZARDS
You'll want to watch out for these . . .

Spikes
☠ If you're Sonic, they're just an inconvenience, but for guys like Mega Man, the sight of spikes is terrifying. Falling into a pit full of them may even cause instant death. Best avoided!

Fire
☠ Sometimes you'll see pits of fire, and other times it'll shoot out of the walls or floor. Sometimes, enemies will breathe fire—but no matter where it comes from, fire is always dangerous.

Water
☠ Some platform-game heroes can swim, and they're the lucky ones. Poor guys like Sonic can't stay underwater for too long or they'll drown, causing you to lose a life and some of your progress.

Poisonous Sludge
☠ No matter who falls into a nasty pit of poisonous sludge, they're going to have a bad time. It might be green and slimy, or purple and mysterious, but it's not nice.

Electricity
☠ Whether it's random lightning strikes, electrified barriers, or even projectile balls of electricity, you'll find that the amount of damage you take from high-voltage accidents can be shocking.

Bottomless Pits
☠ Why do platform-game heroes always hang out in places where bottomless pits are so common? One slip and they die immediately. No wonder they're rare!

Shovel Knight

4 It might look old-school, but *Shovel Knight's* retro styling is just one of many reasons to love this quirky title. The game was only released in 2014, but with deep gameplay and fantastic design, it quickly became a classic. Leaping through pixellated levels is still so much fun.

Rogue Legacy

5 Every time you enter the world of *Rogue Legacy*, levels are created from scratch. Not only that, but you'll play as a different hero with new abilities each time, as you play as the previous hero's child. Gradually, you'll get closer to beating the bosses and solving the mystery of the castle.

Banjo-Kazooie

6 If you love a treasure hunt and you've got an Xbox One, this 3-D platform game should keep you happy for a long time. The strong bear and sassy bird help each other to collect musical notes in hard-to-reach areas, as they try to rescue Banjo's sister from the evil witch Gruntilda.

Yooka-Laylee

7 There aren't many 3-D platform games out there these days, and *Yooka-Laylee* is trying to revive the genre. The game comes from many of the team that made classics like *Banjo-Kazooie*. Large levels are packed with collectibles for this chameleon and bat team to discover.

Shantae: Half-Genie Hero

9 As the guardian genie of Scuttle Town, Shantae has to keep the pirate Risky Boots at bay as well as protecting the town from other threats—whatever they are. It's a classic 2-D platformer that explores the character's past.

Oddworld: New 'n' Tasty

8 If you like to fire up your brain while playing platform games, the *Oddworld* games are always sure to satisfy. Abe has to rescue his fellow Mudokon workers from Rupture Farms, often by directing them around so that they can help him to solve puzzles. It's not easy, but it's really satisfying when you finally solve a problem that has been bugging you for ages.

Umihara Kawase

10 If you like really difficult, retro platform games, you need to pick up this PC game. Based on a game from the nineties, you play as a sushi chef who makes her way through levels with an elastic fishing rope while avoiding walking fish. It's weird, but it has some really dedicated fans because of its unique gameplay.

TOP 10 MASSIVE WORLD-BUILDING GAMES

Minecraft

1 It's the biggest world-building game of them all. You can build a simple log cabin with a front garden or a towering castle. Some players have built whole cities to live in and explore, while others have re-created famous gaming levels from *Mario* and *Pokémon* titles. In Creative Mode, you can fly around the world with all the blocks you need, making the only limit your imagination.

Terraria

2 *Terraria* is much more than a 2-D version of *Minecraft*. Both games are about collecting resources to build, but *Terraria* is slanted towards exploration and combat. Dig down into the earth and rock and you can explore dangerous new areas, filled with valuable resources. Soon, you'll craft powerful new tools, and eventually, the game world becomes a playground for you!

The Sims 4

3 *The Sims 4* is home-building rather than world-building, as you create the dream house for your family of Sims. From picking the furniture to choosing the right things to say in conversation, you're the unseen puppetmaster. Any small change you make can have a drastic effect on the house, which is what makes *The Sims 4* so much fun.

6 WAYS TO PLAY WORLD-BUILDING GAMES

1 Start small
It's easy to become overwhelmed with the sheer amount of choice at the start. There's so much to build and explore. Start with a small building and slowly work your way outwards on the map.

2 Build defenses
In a world-building game that surrounds you with hostile creatures, you need to make sure your base is safe. Build an entrance that only you can use, or a weapons bench so you can defend yourself.

3 Gather resources
You'll need resources to build, and the challenge with most world-building games is gathering those resources. Make a note of what you can gather nearby and what you can build from it.

4 Plan ahead
The longer you play, the more you'll want to expand your base as you discover and gather new resources. Leave room for expansion, as you unlock new structures, and start to build outward.

5 Build a base
You'll want to build a base that you can return to if you ever get into trouble. Make sure it's somewhere accessible and easy for you to get to, so you can rush back whenever you're in danger.

6 Learn from others
Everyone has different ideas about how to play. See what your friends have built and see what YouTubers playing the same game have tried out. Ideas and inspiration can come from anywhere, so watch others play!

Kerbal Space Program

4 Rather than putting together houses or small towns, you're building space rockets. You'll need all your brainpower to put together a rocket that will shoot for the stars rather than tumble helplessly back down to Earth.

Don't Starve

5 *Don't Starve* is a game where you build to survive. With strange, hostile creatures roaming the land around you, you need to build a shelter to stay safe. Once you have a shelter you can call home, you can then build further structures, such as Meat Effigies or Bee Boxes.

EVE Online

6 You could play *EVE Online* for years and not see everything it has to offer, because of the huge universe you play in. You can play however you want—space pirate, goods trader, rogue explorer. You'll carve out a slice of the universe as your own, as you build your faction.

Slime Rancher

7 You're a space farmer in *Slime Rancher*, a job that has you creating your own farm before heading off to round up the slime creatures. The more you catch, the bigger you'll need to build your farm. You exert your influence over the world, using the strength and might of your farm.

Stardew Valley

9 In this relaxing game about farming, you work to salvage a rundown farm that you've inherited. Once the weeds and boulders have been cleared, you can start to expand your farm, building it up. Soon, you can make it bigger and better than it ever was when you first moved into it.

THE EXPERT SAYS ...
FYNNPIRE
Popular Australian YouTuber

Slime Rancher has been a really popular game on my Youtube channel. I enjoy it because it's really easy to forget what I'm doing and I end up watching Slimes play with other Slimes, other animals or even their food, not to mention being able to feed entire chickens to Slimes by shooting them out of a gun is heaps of fun. To me, the game feels like it's somewhere between *Harvest Moon* and *Pokémon*—there is always something to do. It's laid-back gaming at it's finest. *Slime Rancher* allows me to be creative with how I build my ranch, and that is what my viewers find entertaining, when I'm able to create a world that they can comment on and contribute to.

Starbound

8 *Starbound* is a space-exploration game in which you can call any planet your own. You can beam down to new worlds and begin exploring, terraforming, and sculpting the earth to create new settlements. You can construct houses and lease them out to other villagers. It's so generous with what it allows you to do, from fighting to finding a new home, it almost feels like you can create your own game.

Crashlands

10 *Crashlands* proves that you don't need a PC or console to play through massive worlds. This mobile game has you crash landing in an alien world, fending for yourself as the strange creatures see you as a tasty snack. You start by building a base and a weapons bench, then expand its size as you gather more resources.

THOR

HULK

STRIDER HIRYU

CAPTURE THIS!

ULTIMATE MARVEL VS. CAPCOM 3

Perform a 100-hit combo or even higher

Crazy combos are the name of the game in Capcom's crossover fighting games! Can you prove that you're good enough to throw down with the best by stringing together over 100 blows? If you're struggling, try finishing your combo with several Hyper Combos that hit many times, such as Super Skrull's Inferno.

GLOSSARY

4K

Ultra high-definition resolution, supported by high-end TVs and monitors. The actual resolution is 3840x2160, boasting four times as many pixels as a 1080p display.

AI

"Artificial intelligence," the code used to make in-game characters behave as they do. *The Last Guardian* is a great example of complex AI, used to make Trico behave like a real creature, but it's also what powers enemies in nearly every game.

AR

Augmented reality; a fusion of the real world and digital assets. *Pokémon GO* uses this to great effect by superimposing wild Pokémon over a live feed from your phone's camera, and various Vita and 3DS games also embrace this new technology.

BOSS

A bigger, badder enemy commonly seen at the end of a level or guarding something particularly valuable. These larger foes tend to test all of your gaming skills and come with amazing rewards if you're able to beat them.

Beta

A game in an unfinished state, sometimes with select players (a "closed beta") or the public at large (an "open beta") invited to test key features ahead of release. Occasionally, developers will offer this access even earlier—this is known as the "alpha" phase.

Bug

An error in a game that causes something unexpected to happen. May also be referred to as a glitch, depending on the nature of the bug. Some are extremely minor—such as several objects clipping into one another—while the most harmful can completely prevent progress. Save often, just in case!

Camping

The act of hanging around in one spot in a multiplayer game, usually either near where enemies spawn into a map or in a remote area, using a long-range weapon to repeatedly pick off players. Camping is usually frowned upon.

Casting

Can be short for either "broadcasting"—using services like Twitch, Beam, and YouTube to stream live gameplay—or "shoutcasting," which is play-by-play commentary of a gaming event, much like with live sports on TV.

COSPLAY

The art of creating costumes based on video-game characters, and often wearing them to events and conventions. Cosplay isn't limited to video games—enthusiasts also cosplay as movie, comic book, and anime characters as well!

CCG

"Collectible card game," although you may also see TCG, which is "trading card game." They're effectively the same thing, though—games like *Hearthstone* where you earn new cards to make the very best deck you can.

Clutch

An unlikely comeback against all odds is known as a clutch play. An example would be using your Ultimate as the last hero standing to wipe out the enemy team, and prevent the payload from being delivered in the dying seconds of an *Overwatch* game.

Co-op

Teaming up with other players to work together toward a common goal. Co-op games usually increase the difficulty based on the number of players, so bear that in mind if you don't feel like your group is up to the challenge!

Cross-up

An attack that forces the opponent to block from the opposite direction in a fighting game, usually performed by jumping over them to clip them in the back of the head. Some characters can perform cross-ups by dashing or teleporting through opponents as well.

DLC

Downloadable content. Extra levels, maps, characters, outfits, items, and modes made available for a game after release are collectively known as DLC.

DPS

"Damage per second," which can either refer to how much damage a character or weapon is able to do, or even characters whose role is primarily to deal damage, such as Black Mages in *Final Fantasy XIV*, or Tracer in *Overwatch*.

Easter egg

A secret hidden in a game that typically serves no function other than to amuse or entertain. These can sometimes be references to other games, or even other media entirely.

eSports

Professional gaming, as played by both individuals and full teams depending on the game being played. Prize pools are often massive for the biggest events, and the standard of play is incredibly high— major events are even broadcast live, just like a real sporting event.

GLOSSARY

F2P

"Free-To-Play," referring to games that can be downloaded and played for free. These often have some kind of in-game purchases, so watch out for those, but remember: never spend anything without getting your parents' permission!

FPS

First-person shooter—a game genre where you see through the eyes of the character, like *Destiny* or *Star Wars Battlefront*.

Frame-rate

The number of individual images that make up one second of moving game visuals. 30 frames per second (30fps) is common, and offers relatively smooth performance, with higher frame rates looking even smoother.

GG

"Good game." This is used in chat after multiplayer games in order to congratulate everyone involved on their success.

Griefing

Doing something just to annoy other players in a multiplayer game. This can be anything from standing in a doorway, so people can't get through, to attacking your own teammates. Don't do this—play nice!

Grinding

Repeating the same actions over and over again, like running in circles in tall grass in *Pokémon* to raise your team's levels, or doing the same quest repeatedly in *Monster Hunter* in the hopes of getting a rare reward.

HDR

A relatively new term, HDR stands for "high dynamic range," and is something you only see in new, high-end displays and TVs. Supported games boast much brighter and more vibrant colors in HDR than on a standard set—*Rez*'s Area X is one mind-blowing example.

Indie

"Independent," used to refer to games or studios that don't have support from a major publisher. Indie studios are typically quite small, but the games that they create are often incredibly creative and original.

Kiting

The act of manipulating enemy placement to your advantage, such as a tank pulling a boss away from other players in an MMO, or Link running circles around enemies that only have close-range attacks.

Lag

A delay between player inputs and on-screen actions, usually caused by poor connections in online games. Minor lag is generally bearable, but extreme cases can make games unplayable.

Leaderboard

A high-score table. These are usually online elements, so you can see how your best results compare against the world's greatest players!

Metroidvania

A genre where exploration and back-tracking are key features, using new abilities that are unlocked to allow you to open previously inaccessible areas. *Ori and the Blind Forest* is one such example.

Mid-laner

A player who stays in the central area in MOBAs like *Dota 2*. There are also top and bottom-laners.

MMO

"Massively multiplayer online," games where many players can connect and communicate with one another. Most common are RPGs, but some—like *The Crew*—tackle other genres as well.

MOBA

"Multiplayer online battle arena" describes online games such as *League of Legends* and *Dota 2*. It's a relatively new genre, but one of the most popular in the world today!

Mod

Additional software that can alter how a game looks or plays, or even add completely new features. Though most common on PC, these are starting to be seen on consoles as well.

Noob

This is short for "newbie," a term used to describe someone who is new to playing a particular game. However, it is more commonly heard as an insult used against bad players.

NPC

NPC—or non-playable character—is the term used to refer to a non-hostile character. They might be important, like a quest-giver, or they might just be someone who exists in the game world.

Patch

A post-release update for a game that fixes bugs and/or adds new content. These are growing increasingly common.

Permadeath

Refers to games where progress is lost upon death, forcing players to start over from scratch. Titles such as *Nuclear Throne* and *Don't Starve* are good examples of this.

PVE

"Player Versus Environment," a term used to refer to modes in games (typically ones with multiplayer components) where players take on AI opponents together rather than competing against one another.

Port

A game that is adapted from one system to another, sometimes with improvements (if the new system is more powerful than the original), or cuts to get it running on a weaker platform.

Post-game

Not all games end when the credits roll—in some cases, that's when the real fun begins! Games like *Pokémon* are rich in post-game content, and there's loads you can do after the game is "over."

RPG

"Role-playing game," sometimes encountered with additional letters: JRPG refers to Japanese titles, ARPG is used for action-heavy RPGs, MMORPG means online games, while SRPG means "strategy RPG," describing games such as *Disgaea* or *Fire Emblem*.

RTS

"Real-time strategy," a genre that shot to popularity with games like *Command & Conquer* and *StarCraft*, now dominated by the likes of the *Total War* series.

PvP

The opposite of PvE, this means "player versus player," meaning competitive multiplayer modes rather than cooperative ones.

Reboot

A game that looks to reinvent a series while returning to its roots, usually reverting to a basic title rather than using numbers or subtitles.

Remaster

This is a little different from a full remake—remasters tend to be slight upgrades of older games for new systems, using the same characters and levels, often sporting enhanced graphics or new modes.

Re-spec

Being able to cancel and redo things like skill-point distribution or other stats, enabling you to deal with various situations by quickly changing a character's specializations in a matter of seconds. A very useful feature!

Rogue-like

A genre of games where procedural generation is used to make every dungeon, session, or adventure different. It's named after classic 1980 dungeon-crawler *Rogue*.

SEASON PASS

Modern games often have downloadable extras that offer the ability to pre-purchase all of it in one bundle—this kind of package is known as a season pass, but actual contents will vary from game to game.

Sandbox

Open-world games where players are free to play around and experiment however they wish—things like the Hub areas in LEGO games, or the open worlds of *Minecraft* and *Dragon Quest Builders*.

Scrub

An insult aimed at bad players, or those who rely on cheap, basic tactics, such as spamming the same moves over and over in a fighting game.

Sherpa

A player who helps others through difficult content in multiplayer games, such as Raids in *Destiny*. Sherpas are usually experts who know their way around, and often there's little in it for them outside of just being helpful.

Speedrun

The act of playing through games as quickly as possible, often using glitches and other tricks to beat games in record time. Runners often post their best efforts online, and compete with others on ranking sites to see who is the fastest at any given game.

Tank

A strong character in a game whose job is to soak up damage, and protect more fragile characters. Tanks are common in MMO games, but you'll also find them in class-based online games like *Overwatch*.

Top-deck

In a card game, top-decking is where you find yourself relying on the next card you draw, whether it's because your hand is empty or because you find yourself in a situation where there are only a couple of cards in your deck that will actually be useful.

Trolling

Misbehaving in an online game purely to annoy other players. This comes in many forms, from getting in the way of others, or hurting your own team, to intentionally doing the opposite of what you're supposed to do. Don't do it!

UGC

"User-generated content," used to describe things that players have made using in-game tools. Original *Minecraft* worlds, *Super Mario Maker* stages, and *LittleBigPlanet* creations are all perfect examples of this.

Vanilla

Used to refer to the original version of a game before patches and updates were applied. Vanilla base games are sometimes still supported (as is the case with *Destiny*), but in other cases, the only way to play the original versions is on special fan-run servers.

VR

Virtual reality, the hot new technology that is taking the gaming world by storm. Players wear headsets and are completely immersed in the action, moving as if it's really happening around them.

Whiff

To miss with an attack or move. This can either be completely accidental or done intentionally to mess with other players, or for some other purpose, like building meter in fighting games.

XP

"Experience points," used to level up in RPGs or any progress system like those of the *Forza* games. Sometimes written as EXP, but the purpose is typically the same—gain loads and level up!